The
Greatest
Treasure-Hunting Stories
Ever Told

Books by Charles Elliott

The Transplanted Gardener
The Gap in the Hedge
The Potting-Shed Papers

Books Edited by Charles Elliott

The Quotable Gardener
The Quotable Cat Lover
The Greatest Cat Stories Ever Told

The
Greatest
Treasure-Hunting Stories
Ever Told

Twenty-One Unforgettable
Tales of Discovery

EDITED AND WITH AN INTRODUCTION BY
CHARLES ELLIOTT

THE LYONS PRESS
Guilford, Connecticut
An imprint of The Globe Pequot Press

The Lyons Press is an imprint of The Globe Pequot Press.

10 9 8 7 6 5 4 3 2 1

Printed in the United States of America

ISBN 1-58574-683-5

The Library of Congress Cataloging-in-Publication data is available on file.

Contents

Introduction

Most people who read at all have one essential book lurking at the back of their consciousness, something they read in childhood and won't ever forget. It may be the Bible, it may be *Winnie-the-Pooh*, it may be (for all I know) *Forever Amber* or a treatise on quantum mechanics, but in my case, it's a book called *Coronado's Children* by J. Frank Dobie. Except in Texas, where he is remembered with some affection as a chronicler of the cowboy era, I don't suppose anyone pays much attention to Dobie anymore. But in the United States in the 1930s his tales of the Southwest frontier, especially those dealing with lost mines and buried treasure, were bestsellers. They certainly sold me—except for a certain boring (and intermittent) streak of practicality, I've been ready since 1939 to depart for West Texas to search for the Lost Bowie Mine.

Part of the charm of *Coronado's Children* for me are the little tailpiece illustrations by Ben Carlton Mead—a cluster of decaying adobe walls, a rock with some initials and a date (17-something) carved on it, a view across a bleak valley with an old-fashioned Mexican ox-cart—presumably full of Spanish gold—slowly moving away. They are almost palpably romantic, offering an intoxicating combination of topographical emptiness, historical density, and the promise of gratified desire. Looking at them, it wasn't (and still isn't) at all difficult for me to imagine what it must be like to go searching over those vast expanses of uninhabited desert and badlands with a ancient chart in your hand and a mule trailing along behind. ("It may be," says a typical Dobie passage, "that the mute finger of the old pick on the shoulder of a long, rough mountain still points to the source of the drift gold. The granite hills of the Llano guard well their secrets." Doesn't that get to you?)

I have never been to West Texas. Judging from its appearance on a modern map, with roads running all over the place and plenty of little towns cluttering up the long lonely trails where the Spanish trekked and after them the cowboys driving cattle, I'm not sure I want to. It looks to be about as wild as Peoria these days, and I'd rather hang onto the vision Dobie and Mead vouchsafed me. But that doesn't mean I've given up on lost mines and buried treasure. There are more places to look, Horatio, than the Big Bend country or the Guadalupes.

For example, there's the west side of Cleveland Mountain, just above the Connecticut line in the Berkshire Hills of Massachusetts. As mountains go, it's a pretty small mountain; in fact because of all the second-growth timber, brush, pocket swamps, and rock outcroppings, it is a bit hard to see it as a mountain at all. It tops out at 1500 feet, but that's only two or three hundred feet higher than what you might call ground level—that is, the altitude of the valley containing the small house a few miles away that I once owned.

Somewhere between Cleveland Mountain and a neighboring protuberance called Benton Hill, there was supposed to be a gold mine. I'm ashamed to say that I cannot now recall with any certainty how I knew this, but it was probably from running across the fact in a book of local history. Some time in the early nineteenth century, this mine was being worked in a modest way. There was most likely nothing mysterious or "lost" about it then. In spite of the roughness of the topography, the neighborhood was largely cleared and farmed. A number of small industries dependent on waterpower had created dams along every brook. We had the remains of a sawmill behind our house.

By the middle of the century, however, the Berkshires had changed radically. The opening of the Erie Canal meant that farmers could give up cropping stones and head for the deep soil of the Midwest; at the same time steam power began making water power obsolete, and with it the awkwardly placed industrial hamlets. As for mining, who would want to batter ledge rock for a pittance when the gold of California beckoned? The mine on Cleveland Mountain was abandoned.

When I got around to hunting for it, about 100 years later, it could legitimately be classed as lost. Given the state of the landscape, in fact, it could hardly be anything else. The plowed fields and meadows had been replaced by deep woods interspersed by impenetrable thickets of brambles and wild rose. The only signs of civilization were crumbling stone walls marked by slightly bigger trees, the occasional cellar hole, and plenty of wild apples. You could imagine bears.

If the mine was lost, so was this hunter, more than once. What had been called a mountain on the map seemed to break up into all sorts of irregular hills that had no logic or direction to them. Following a stream downhill, usually a sure way of getting your bearings in a forest, led more often than not into an impassable beaver flow spiky with dead trees. Promising tracks that I figured might have led to the gold mine workings either turned out to have been made by animals or petered out entirely, usually both.

As might be expected, I never found the mine. This may be just as well; I don't what I would have done with it if I had found it. "When it came to mining," writes Dobie of some less than competent old-timers, "not one of these men knew spilt beans from coffee." You could say the same of me. Yet perhaps my failure was fated, anyway. As more than one treasure hunter in *Coronado's Children* ruefully observes, if the treasure doesn't want you to find it, you won't. You can't argue with an excuse like that.

Still, destiny has not always been against me. On another occasion I did succeed in finding something. Not much, but something.

Stretching ten or fifteen miles out to the north and west of Bermuda, a vast expanse of reefs has for centuries trapped and wrecked ships of all sorts. Among the victims were Spanish galleons laden with treasure and trade goods from the mines and plantations of South and Central America. Having cleared the Florida Straits, their course across the Atlantic on the Gulf Stream could take them dangerously close—sometimes all too close—to the Bermuda reefs.

Dozens—perhaps hundreds—of wrecks lie scattered among the coral heads and sandy pockets of these reefs, often at depths of no more than thirty feet or so. Of the older ones, there's not as a rule much to be seen—a pile of ballast stone if you're lucky, sometimes even less than that.

The great expert on these wrecks forty years ago (as he is today) was a Bermudian salvage operator named Teddy Tucker, about whom one might have said (except for a slight change of scene) what Dobie said about an old Texas frontiersman: "He appears to have swung a wide loop and heard the owl hoot in all sorts of places." In the 1950s Teddy happened to be pals with a *Life* magazine photographer. The photographer had a girlfriend in Bermuda. Every few years Teddy would wire the photographer saying he had just found a new wreck that looked very promising. The photographer would promptly wangle an assignment to go to Bermuda to do a story about the wreck. This time I, as a novice reporter on *Life*, was assigned to go along, possibly to keep an eye on the photographer (which I failed to do).

I took it all very seriously indeed. I went to Abercrombie & Fitch and bought a pair of bright yellow swim fins, a new bathing suit, and a canvas belt with pockets in it for lead weights. I went to the library and read up on Spanish galleons. If there was treasure to be found, I'd be ready.

Aboard Teddy's boat, things started to go wrong immediately. My yellow fins wouldn't do, I was told; they would simply attract barracuda. Worse from my point of view was the fact that I was getting increasingly seasick. We had five miles to travel, rolling and pitching over what appeared to me to be a completely featureless sea, though if you looked down you could see rocks. Teddy claimed to know exactly where we were. I lay in the scuppers praying that we would arrive soon so that I could get into the water. This had suggested itself to me as a solution to my nausea—you aren't supposed to be seasick while actually swimming.

We anchored. I quickly pulled a facemask attached to an oxygen supply tube over my head, strapped on my weight belt and leaped into the sea, promptly sinking thirty feet like a stone because I had put too many weights in the belt. By the time I got the belt off, the mask—which I had failed to adjust—was filling with water. I shot back to the surface, sputtering. The nausea, thank God, was gone.

"There is something about a treasure," says Conrad in *Nostromo*, "that fastens on a man's mind." Well, to this day I don't know whether our wreck was a Spanish galleon or not, or whether it had been carrying the sort of thing that Teddy had discovered on other occasions (a gold pectoral cross set with emeralds, for example, and plenty of pieces of eight). But for those few hours in the warm sunny water, my mind was fastened securely on the possibility that it was. I certainly wanted to believe that riches were imminent. My spirits soared when I inadvertently stuck my hand into a rotted wooden crate, causing a huge blue cloud to spread out through the water. Indigo! a familiar product of the Spanish Main in the sixteenth century. It was enough to make me forget (temporarily) the circling dark shadows of barracuda.

I should have known better. Doggedly fanning sand with ping-pong paddles, we vainly tried to clear the wreckage—little of it identifiable apart from the heap of ballast rock—until it was clear that nothing short of a large commercial compressor and serious underwater excavation equipment would achieve anything. In the end we had nothing to show for our efforts. Nothing, that is, except for very blue hands, fresh respect for barracuda, and—wait for it: two tiny links of gold chain that turned up under a piece of rock!

Every few years I read *Coronado's Children* over again. There is something about the whole subject of treasure hunting that continues to fascinate. I'm obviously not alone in this. Browsing the Web not long ago, I discovered a whole netherworld of treasure-hunting magazines, metal-detector clubs and lost mine information exchanges that apparently engage the funds and spare time of thousands of hopefuls. But digging up tin cans and discarded horseshoes or crashing through the Superstitions in a "recreational vehicle" somehow goes against the romantic grain.

On the other hand, an interesting story came to my attention the other day that may bear following up. I now live in England, and we have a house near a village called Skenfrith, on the edge of Wales. Skenfrith has a ruined castle. It seems that in the year 1589 a Welshman incarcerated in the Tower of London wrote a letter to Lord Burghley, Queen Elizabeth's Lord Treasurer, to say that he had certain knowledge of the existence of "a hogshead of gold and a hogshead of silver" buried in Skenfrith Castle. If he were released, he wrote, he would undertake to dig it up "without any charge to the Queen or your lordships." You will not be surprised to hear that the prison gates failed to swing open for the enterprising Welshman. But Skenfrith Castle is just down the hill from Towerhill Cottage, and if I were to buy a metal-detector . . .

⋆   ⋆   ⋆   ⋆   ⋆

The following collection of stories (which includes, inevitably, a chapter from *Coronado's Children*) contains a few classics (Poe's "Gold Bug," for example) and a fair number of what I hope will be unfamiliar tales. Many are true—or purport to be. They encompass all the great themes—obsession, tragedy, danger, crime, frustration and terrible physical challenge, success and disappointment. They take place under the sea, in jungles, on desert islands, even in the attics of old houses. The treasure itself is not always gold and silver and diamonds—it may as well be lost documents, or the solution to a historical puzzle, or an unexpected archaeological discovery. What is common to them all is the excitement of the chase and the *possibility*—irrational, perhaps, but unavoidable—that treasure really is there for the finding.

Treasure in a Temple

BY ANDRÉ MALRAUX

Writer, connoisseur, diplomat, archaeologist, treasure hunter, thief—
André Malraux (1901–1976) combined an incredible array of talents.
His novel *La Voie Royale* (1930; translated by Stuart Gilbert under the
title *The Royal Way*, 1935), from which this extract is taken, is based
upon his own admittedly harebrained attempt to steal ancient Khmer
temple sculptures from the Cambodian jungle. In 1923, newly-wed and
in serious need of money, Malraux and his wife, Clara, set off for South-
east Asia intending, as Clara put it in her memoirs, to "take some statues
and sell them in America." They went to the remote, beautiful temple
complex of Banteai Srei, near Angkor, and managed to hack off a few
carvings. But they no sooner got back to Phnom Penh than they were
arrested by the Surete. Malraux found himself facing a three-year sentence for "archaeological theft," and would have served it had not Clara
succeeded in assembling a petition bearing the names of a number of
important French literary figures. The judge, impressed, suspended Malraux's sentence.

★   ★   ★   ★   ★

Night fell, the dawn came, another night, another dawn, and at last they reached a remote village dithering with malaria, a village lost in a world of ruin and decay under an unseen sun. Now and then they caught sight of the mountains, and each time they loomed nearer. Low-growing branches swished noisily against the hoods of the carts, but even their intermittent rustle seemed muted by the heat. The warm miasma steaming up from the earth half suffocated them, but they had a consolation—the last guide's positive assurance that there was sculpture on the temple towards which they were proceeding.

But they had grown used to such affirmations. . . . For all his doubts regarding this temple—and indeed any specific temple they might go in quest of—Claude was held to his general idea of them by a half-sceptical belief, a complex of logical assurances and doubts so deep as to have become almost physiological. It was as if his eyes and nerves protested against his hope, against the unkept promises of this phantasmal road.

At last they reached a wall.

Claude's eyes were growing familiar with the forest. When near enough to discern the centipedes scurrying across the stonework, he realized that their guide had shown more intelligence than his predecessors and had led them to a fault which obviously marked the site of the former entrance. Like all the other temples this one was ringed by a tangled palisade of cane-brake. Perken, who was beginning to know the habits of the vegetation round such sites, pointed to a spot where the green barrier was less opaque. "Flagstones," he said. There, doubtless, was the pathway leading to the sanctuary. The cartmen set to work. With a noise like crumpled paper, the canes fell slowly right and left, leaving behind them tiny specks of white, shining like stars across the gloom—the pithy stumps slashed diagonally by the wood-knives. "If we don't find any sculpture or statues in this temple," Claude reflected, "what's to be done? None of the drivers will go with the three of us— Perken, myself and the boy—as far as the Ta-Mean. Ever since we ran into that wild tribe, they've had only one desire—to do a bolt. And, if there are only three of us, how are we to shift the two-ton blocks of which the big bas-reliefs are composed? Statues . . . possibly. And, of course, luck may come our way. But it's a damned silly business—silly as a boy's treasure-hunting yarn."

He took his eyes from the flashing wood-knives and looked down at the ground. The sliced canes were already turning brown. How about taking a knife, too, and slashing—more vigorously than those wretched jungle-wallahs? Could he not mow his way through the brake, using the knife like a scythe? A gentle touch from the guide drew him from his thoughts. A clump of canes had just been hacked away, revealing some smooth blocks—the gateway, no doubt—speckled with the shadows of a few standing canes and ringed by fallen stonework.

Once again—sculptureless! The guide's lips were smiling; his forefinger still pointed to the gate. Never had Claude wanted so urgently to use his fists on a man's face. Clenching his hands, he turned to Perken—to find him smiling, too. Claude's friendship for his comrade turned suddenly to hate. Nevertheless, seeing them all staring at the same point, he followed the direction of their eyes. The main entrance had evidently been a large one and it began, not where he had expected, but on the far side of the wall. What all his companions, familiar with the forest, were looking at was one abutment of it, which stood up from the debris like a pyramid, on the apex of which was a sandstone figure, fragile but intact, crowned with a very delicately wrought diadem. And now he saw, across the leafage, a bird of stone, with a parrot's beak and wings outspread; a slanting sunbeam splintered on its claws. All his anger vanished in that brief but splendid moment. Delight possessed him; he was filled with aimless gratitude, with elation quickly yielding to a maudlin readiness to weep. Aware only of the sculpture, he moved blindly forwards till he stood just in front of the gate. The lintel had fallen, bringing down all that was above it; branches festooned the standing uprights, forming a limp but massive archway, impervious to the sun. Beyond some heaps of fallen stones whose angles stood out black against the light and all but blocked the passage, a thin veil of flimsy wall-plants and slender sprays that ramified in veins of sap was stretched across the tunnel. Perken slashed through it, bringing into view a confused splendour, a haze of broken lights facetted by spiky aloe-leaves. Claude made his way along the passage from stone to stone, steadying himself against the sides; now and again he rubbed his palms against his trousers to remove the spongy feeling the moss had given them. Suddenly he recalled the ant-infested wall. There, too, a gulf of brightness mottled with leafage had seemed to merge into an opalescent glare, the universal majesty of light brooding above its kingdom of decay.

Before him lay a chaos of fallen stones, some lying flat, but most of them upended; it looked like a mason's yard invaded by the jungle. Here were lengths of wall in slabs of purple sandstone, some carved and others plain, all plumed with pendant ferns. Some bore a red patina, the aftermath of fire. Facing him he saw some bas-reliefs of the best period, marked by Indian influences—he was now close up to them—but very beautiful work; they were grouped round an old shrine, half hidden behind a breastwork of fallen stones. It cost him an effort to take his eyes off them. Beyond the bas-reliefs were the remains of three towers razed to within six feet of the ground. Their mutilated stumps stuck out of such an overwhelming mass of rubble that all the vegetation round them was stunted; they seemed socketed in the debris like candles in their sticks. The shadows had shortened; an unseen sun was climbing up the sky. An imperceptible tremor, a continual vibration, began to stir within the leafy depths, though there was not the faintest breeze. The great heat was beginning.

A loose stone fell and sounded twice in falling, first with a muffled thud, then clearly; and Claude, in his mind's ear, caught an echo of the word: eer-ie. But it was not only the dead stones which the clumsy frogs quickened to fugitive life on this their first encounter with mankind, it was not only the utter desolation of this forsaken temple, nor was it but the veiled yet active malevolence of the vegetation that made the place seem so uncanny. Something inhuman brooded over all these ruins and the voracious plants which now seemed petrified with apprehension; a presence of numinous awe guarded with its dead hand these ancient figures holding their lonely court amongst the centipedes and vermin of the forest. Then Perken stepped past him, and in a flash the world of shimmering sea-depths died out, like a jelly-fish cast high and dry on the sea-shore; it lost its potency when faced by two white men.

"I'll fetch the tools," Perken said. His shadow swept down the tunnel between the tattered wall-plants.

It seemed that the main tower had completely collapsed only on one side, for three of its walls still stood at the end of the biggest mound of debris. At some period a deep pit had been dug within these walls; after the Siamese incendiaries, treasure-hunters had evidently visited the spot. Now, plumb in the middle of the pit, there rose an ant-hill, dun-coloured, with a pointed top; it also seemed to have been abandoned. Perken returned. He had a metal-cutting saw and a stick in his hand; from his bulging left-hand pocket a hammer-head protruded. He drew from his pocket a quarryman's sledge and impaled it on the stick.

"Svay's in the village," he said, "I ordered him to stay there."

Claude had already picked up the saw. Its nickel frame shone brightly against the sombre stonework. But, beside one of the walls which in its fall had formed a sort of staircase and on which a bas-relief was poised within his reach, he hesitated.

"What's the matter?" Perken asked.

"It's damned silly. . . . The fact is I've a feeling this isn't going to come off!"

He seemed to be seeing the stone for the first time, and could not rid himself of a sense of the disproportion between it and the saw he held. It made things seem impossible. However, he wetted the block and went at it with the saw, which bit into the sandstone with a shrill, rasping sound. At his fifth stroke it skidded; when he drew it from the fissure he found that all the teeth were gone.

They had a couple of dozen blades with them. The notch he had made was little more than half an inch deep. He threw down the saw and stared into space. Many of the stones on the ground were faced with half-obliterated traces of bas-reliefs. In his obsession with the walls he had not noticed them. Possibly, he thought, such as had fallen face-downward might have kept the carved surfaces intact.

The same idea had already occurred to Perken. Calling the drivers up, he had them cut the trunks of some young trees into levers; with these they set about turning the blocks over. Each block was heaved slowly up till it toppled over, with a dull thud. On the side which now was uppermost, across a maze of tiny furrows traced by panic-stricken wood-lice in their flight, traces of sculptured figures were apparent. Then into each successive hollow, sharply indented as a plaster mould, whence the last block had been removed, another block was tipped over, and, one by one, the surfaces which ever since the epoch of the Siamese invasions had been mouldering face downward in the soil were once again exposed to daylight. The wavering criss-cross lines made by the insects as they scurried away into the forest suggested a stampede of frenzied Lilliputians. But the more Claude examined the shattered outlines of the fallen bas-reliefs, the clearer it became that the only stones worth removing were those composing one of the still-standing sides of the main temple.

Carved on two faces, the corner-stones represented two dancing-girls. The figures extended over three stones, placed one on top of the other. It looked as if a vigorous push might bring the top one down.

"How much d'you think it's worth?" Perken asked.

"The two dancing-girls, you mean?"

"Yes."

"Hard to say. Over five hundred thousand francs anyhow."

"Sure?"

"Absolutely."

So, Perken mused, the machine-guns to buy which he had gone to raise funds in Europe had been here all the time, here in the forest he knew so well, here in these stones! Were there any temples up in his own neighbourhood? he wondered. They might, perhaps, serve him even better than machine-guns. If he could come upon a few such temples while he was "at home," he might impose his will on Bangkok, arming his men meanwhile. Each temple would mean ten machine-guns, two hundred rifles. . . . Looking at this temple, he forgot how many others had had no sculpture, forgot the Way. A picture held his eyes—his army on the march, sunlight glinting on his mitrailleuses, the target sparkling in the sun.

Meanwhile Claude had been having the ground cleared of stones, so that the bas-relief should run no risk of being chipped when it fell. While the men were moving away the fallen blocks he examined the figures more attentively. A very light grey-blue moss, like the bloom on European peaches, covered one head, which, as was usual in Khmer statues, had smiling lips. Three men put their shoulders to the stone and pushed together. It overbalanced, fell edgewise, and sank into the earth deep enough not to roll over again. In being moved it had made two grooves in the stone on which it rested and along them two armies of dull-hued ants, intent on salvaging their eggs, were hurrying in Indian file. But the second stone, the top of which was now in view, had not been laid in the same way as the first. It was wedged into the main wall between two blocks, each of which weighed several tons. It looked as if, to get it out, the whole wall would need to be demolished, and that was obviously out of the question. If the stones faced with sculpture could only be handled with much difficulty, the other enormous blocks defied human powers. They must be left intact until the passing centuries or peepul-trees sprouting in the ruins should lay them low.

How, he wondered, had the Siamese been able to wreck so many temples? There were tales of elephants harnessed in teams to the walls. . . . But he had no elephants. The only thing to do was to cut or break the stone so as to detach the sculptured face, whence the last ants were now retreating, from the part embedded in the wall.

Leaning on their improvised levers, the drivers waited. Perken produced his hammer and a chisel. The best way to set about splitting the stone was probably to chisel out a narrow groove in it. He began hammering. But, either because he handled the chisel inexpertly or because the sandstone was too hard, he only succeeded in chipping out the tiniest splinters . . . And the natives would, no doubt, be clumsier still.

Claude could not stop staring at the stone. Against the background of trembling leaves and flecks of sunlight, it seemed immensely solid, sure of itself, instinct with ponderous malevolence. The grooves, the stone-dust flickered before his eyes. The last of the ants had vanished, without forgetting a single pulpy egg. Only the stone remained, impassive, self-willed as a living creature, able to say 'No.' A rush of blind rage swept over Claude and, planting his feet firmly on the ground, he lunged against the block with all his might. In his exasperation he looked round for some object on which to vent his anger. Perken watched him, his hammer poised in mid-air, with parted lips. Yes, Perken might know the jungle well, but all his forest-lore was useless here; these stones were a sealed book to him. Ah, had he only worked as a mason for six months! He wondered what to do. Should he get the men to pull on it, all together, with a rope? As well scratch it with his nails! And how could one get a rope round it? Yet, he felt, his life hung in the balance, in peril—yes, his very life. So all his obstinacy, his tense determination, the passionate endeavour which had urged him through the jungle had served no other end than this—to bring him up against this obstacle, an immovable stone planted between himself and Siam!

The more Claude stared at the stone, the more evident it became to him that they could never push through to the Ta-Mean with the carts. And, after all, the Ta-Mean stones could only be the same as these. His ardour to succeed was like hunger or thirst, an overwhelming impulse. It clenched his fingers round the hammer he had just snatched from Perken. In his rage he lashed out at the stone with all his might. Again and again the hammer sprang back with a brittle click that sounded grotesquely futile in the silence. Then the sun glinted on the polished claw-end of the hammer. Pausing, he stared at it for a second. Then, as if afraid that his idea might somehow escape him, he hastily reversed the hammer and began striking again, with all his force, beside the gleaming notch gouged out by Perken's chisel. A stone splinter several inches long sprang out. Dropping the hammer, he rubbed his eyes. Luckily they had only been struck by flying stone-dust. As soon as his sight came back, he put on his glare-glasses. Then he fell to hammering again. The claw-head was effective. Using it directly, he could strike the stone harder and much oftener than if a chisel were interposed. Each blow dislodged a large flake. In a few hours. . . .

Meanwhile the cane-brake blocking the ways of access to the shrine had to be cleared away. Perken took a turn with the hammer. Claude went a little distance away with the cartmen to see about clearing a track. As he watched them at work he could hear the brisk clang of the hammer ringing out at rapid intervals above the soft swish of the falling reeds. It reminded him of a Morse telegraphist transmitting. In the vast silence of the forest, in the brooding heat, it had a human, an oddly trivial sound.

When he returned he found the earth around covered with flakes of stone piled round a cone of dust; the colour of the dust surprised him. It was white, notwithstanding that the sandstone from which it came was purple. When Perken turned towards him, Claude noticed that the groove, like the stone-dust, was a brilliant white, and a wide one, for it was impossible always to strike in the same place.

He took over. Perken went on with the task of getting a fairway cleared. It would be a difficult business shifting the blocks; the simplest way would be to roll them over like logs, once all the pebbles had been removed from the track. Yard by yard the trail lengthened out along a vista of straight-falling shadows. In the yellowing light, the growing heat, the ever-shorter shadows, one thing alone remained unchanged, the sound of steady hammer-blows. The heat was not merely oppressive, overpowering; it worked like a slow poison, turning their muscles to water, sapping their vitality, while the sweat poured down their faces, mingling with the stone-dust below their glasses in long, viscous streaks like blood-streams trickling from gouged-out eyes. Claude hammered away almost mechanically, as a man lost in the desert goes walking on and on. His mind had gone to pieces, fallen in ruins like the temple; all that kept it still alive was the thrill of counting each successive hammer-stroke.

That, anyhow, was one more; and that, one more again. The forest, the temple, the universe were in dissolution. He might have been struggling to bore through a prison wall, and the hammer-thuds have been so many thrusts of a file, rasping persistently against the stone.

Then suddenly there was a blank; everything fell into place, as if his world had caved in over him. He stood motionless, bewildered. Noticing that the sound of hammering had ceased, Perken stepped back a few paces. Then he saw that the two claws of the hammer-head had just broken off.

He ran up, snatched the hammer from Claude; for a moment he thought of filing the broken end into a new pair of claws, then, seeing how impossible that was, he lashed out blindly at the stone as Claude had done a little while ago. At last he sat down, and forced himself to take stock of the situation. They had several spare hammer-handles with them, but had not thought of buying an extra head.

Once he was able to shake off his feeling of catastrophe, Claude brought his mind back to the train of thoughts which had preoccupied him before he had conceived the idea of using the claw-hammer direct. That notion had come to him in a flash; might not some other happy inspiration strike him now? But now he was in danger of succumbing to sheer physical exhaustion and a mood of supine hopelessness—the inertia of a worn-out animal. Ah, how good it would be to lie down, to sleep! The very vigour of the effort he had put forth helped the forest now to reassert its prison-like dominion. He felt an impulse to let things take their course, to abrogate his will, even his body. Throb by throb, his blood seemed ebbing away. He pictured himself, his arms hugging his chest, like a man stricken by malaria, his body curled up like a sleeping animal; he would lose consciousness utterly, yielding with sublime relief to the reiterated call of heat and jungle. Then suddenly a surge of terror impelled him to renew the struggle. The stone-dust softly trickling bright and white as salt from the triangular notch cut in the stone was falling like sand in an hour-glass, emphasizing the hugeness of the block. And, as he gazed at it, suddenly the block of stone regained its semblance of a living creature, gigantic, indestructible. It held his gaze imprisoned.

His hate linked him to it as to an active enemy who barred his way and mounted guard on him, a monstrous usurper strong with the driving force which for months past had been the mainspring of his life.

He made an effort to invoke his intellect, enervated though it now was by long days in the jungle. But intellect had ceased to matter in his life; merely to live was all. The opiates of the forest had numbed his brain and it was blind instinct that launched him once more against the stone.

Gritting his teeth, he took his stand in front of it. Watching the notch out of the corner of his eye, as if it were a beast about to spring, he picked up the hammer and, giving it a full swing round his body, brought it down on the block. The stone-dust began to flow again. He stared with fascinated eyes at the bright stream. His hate grew concentrated on the dust. Keeping his eye on it, he struck ringing blows; his chest and arms seemed welded to the sledge and his whole body swayed to and fro, like a heavy pendulum. All his awareness was centered in his arms and loins. His life, the hopes that had inspired him for the past year, his present sense of failure, all were fused in rage; they existed solely in the frenzied shock which thrilled him from head to foot each time he struck, whose stunning impact freed him from the thraldom of the jungle.

He paused to take breath. Perken was bending towards a corner of the wall.

"Wait a bit!" he said. "The stone we're having all this trouble with is the only one that's set in the wall. Look at the one below. It loosely laid, like the first stone. Let's try to get it out first. Once we've done that our stone will have no direct support, and as the notch can't have improved its health . . ."

Claude called up two Cambodians and, while they pushed, tugged at the nether stone with all his might. It would not budge. The earth and the small plants surrounding it were holding it back. He remembered that Khmer temples have no foundations, and had a trench dug round and underneath the stone, to loosen it. The natives worked quickly and well while they were digging round the stone, but, for the excavation, they took their time; obviously they feared the block might crush their hands. He took their place. When the pit was deep enough he had some tree-trunks cut and put them in as props. The stench of humid soil, of rotting leaves and stones washed by the rains pervaded his soaked drill clothing more potently than ever. At last Perken and he succeeded in dragging out the stone. It toppled over, revealing its under side swarming with grey wood-lice which had taken refuge there during the excavation.

So now they possessed the dancing-girls' heads and feet; only the bodies remained on the middle stone, which projected from the wall like an overhanging turret.

Perken picked up the sledge-hammer and set to striking at the remaining stone. He expected it to give at the first blow; but it did nothing of the kind. He continued raining blows on it, mechanically, a prey once more to furious anger. He saw his men being mowed down for lack of machine-guns, flying in panic before a line of charging elephants. As he went on hammering and his thoughts grew blurred, he was gradually possessed by the sensual thrill which comes of every long-protracted struggle. Once more his blows were uniting him with his enemy, the stone.

Suddenly he noticed that the blows were sounding differently. He caught his breath, pulled off his glare-glasses. At first he had only a confused impression of a medley of blues and greens; then, as he blinked, one thing alone filled the whole field of his vision. The stone had split! Sunlight sparkled on the break; the sculptured frontage had split off clean and was lying on the ground, like a newly severed head.

He breathed again, a slow, deep breath. Claude, too, had a feeling of vast relief. Had he been weaker he would have wept. The world flowed back into him as into a man who has just escaped from drowning. The insensate gratitude he had felt on seeing the first sculptured figure welled up in him anew. Thanks to the fallen stone, he was suddenly in harmony with the forest and the temple. He pictured the three stones as they had been, one above the other; the two dancing-girls were some of the purest work he had ever seen. Well, the next thing was to load them on to the carts. . . . But he could not get his thoughts off the stones; had he been asleep he would surely have wakened, did anyone lay hands on them. The natives had begun to roll the three blocks, one after the other, along the track they had cleared. Watching his hard-won prize, and listening to the gentle thudding of the stones as they rolled over and flattened out the cane-stems, Claude caught himself counting the thuds, as a miser counts his gold.

The natives halted when they reached the great mound of debris by the gate. The oxen were not lowing, but Claude could hear them pawing the ground. Perken had two more tree-trunks cut down; then he slipped ropes round one of the stones and lashed it to the trunk. Six of the natives put their shoulders under it. But the weight proved too much for them. Claude replaced two of them by the boy and himself.

"Hoist!"

The six straightened themselves up, all together this time, slowly, in a dead silence.

Just then there was the crisp sound of a breaking twig, followed by more noises of the same kind; the noises seemed to be approaching. Claude halted and tried to plumb the depths of the forest, but, as usual, he could make out nothing. Perhaps some inquisitive native from the last village was spying on them. Or was it Svay? Claude made a sign to Perken, who came and took his place under the tree-trunk. Drawing his revolver, he went in the direction the sounds had come from. The natives who had heard the noise made by his revolver as he took it from the holster and then, more faintly, the click of the release safety-catch, looked on, puzzled and uneasy. Withdrawing his hands from the trunk, Perken propped it on his shoulder so as to be free to draw his revolver. Meenwhile Claude had gone some way into the jungle, but he could only see a maze of glimmering shadows spangled here and there by spiders' webs. Anyhow it was ridiculous to think of tracking down a native familiar with the forest. Perken had not moved. Then, a couple of yards over Claude's head, the branches dipped and swung up again, launching grey balls that shot up through the air, to land on other branches, which sagged beneath their impact. The grey balls were monkeys. Claude turned round, expecting a chorus of laughter. But the natives did not laugh. Claude walked back to them.

"It's only monkeys!"

"Not *only* monkeys," Perken replied. "Monkeys don't make branches break."

Claude put his revolver back in the holster; a futile gesture in the vast silence which had resumed its sway over all the teeming life that festered in the foul decomposition of the forest. He went back to his place amongst the natives holding up the tree-trunk. In a few minutes the mound of rubble was surmounted. He told the men to bring their carts as near as possible; they came so close that Perken had to ask them to move back a little so as to give more room for handling the stones. Intent on their little oxen, the cartmen stared at the stones lashed round with ropes, with blank indifference.

Claude was the last to move. The covered carts plunged leisurely into the leafage, pitching like boats in a rough sea. At each revolution of the wheels the axles creaked, and at regular intervals there came a bump as if each pair of wheels in turn was striking against a concealed root. Claude hardly glanced back at the open trail their passage left behind them in the jungle growth, or at the fallen canes some of which, only half crushed, were slowly swinging up again. Nor did he notice the bright scar on the wall whence they had cut the stone, lit by the ray of sunlight that had flashed on the claw-hammer at the crucial moment. He felt his muscles going limp, and to his fever and the heat was added now a sense of utter physical exhaustion. And yet, he realized, the spell of the forest, of its lianas and the spongy leaves, was weakening; against their sorcery the stones he had secured served as a counter-charm. The forest could no longer dominate his thoughts, which moved lethargically to the slow rhythm of the laden carts forging ahead. The heavy load gave a new stridency to their creaking axles as they lumbered on towards the mountains. Some red ants fell on to his sleeve; he shook them off, leapt on his pony and caught up the carts. As soon as there was room enough to do so he rode past them all, one by one. As usual, he noticed, the cartmen looked half asleep.

The Lost San Saba Mine

BY J. FRANK DOBIE

As I indicated in my introduction, J. Frank Dobie is my personal choice as the best-ever treasure-hunting writer, and this account of the Lost San Saba Mine, which comes from his book *Coronado's Children* (1930), is as evocative and romantic as anything he ever wrote. Dobie himself was deeply steeped in the folklore and legends of his native Texas, and had a professional historian's command of the background of the stories he told. Born on a ranch in Live Oak County in 1888, he worked as a reporter, a schoolteacher, and a ranch manager before becoming an English professor at the University of Texas in Austin. Dobie was a crusty and outspoken liberal, which sometimes placed him at odds with the Texas political establishment and eventually led to the loss of his teaching position. But over the years his many articles and books on cowboy life and other aspects of Southwestern culture—including lost mines and treasures—brought him a national reputation. He died in 1964.

★　★　★　★　★

O brave new world
That has such people in't!
The Tempest.

1 5

What the Golden Fleece was to the Greeks or what El Dorado—the Gilded Man—has been to South America, the lost mines on the San Saba and Llano rivers in Texas have been to all that part of the United States once owned by Spain. The story of these mines is a cycle made up of a thousand cantos. Housed mechanics, preachers, teachers, doctors, lawyers, earth-treading farmers and home-staying women, as well as roaming cowboys, rangers, outlaws and miners, have told the strange story—and believed it. It is a story of yesterday, as obsolete as the claiming of continents by priority in flag-hoisting; it is a story of today, as realistic as the salt of the earth; it is also a story of tomorrow, as fantastic and romantic as the hopes of man. Through it history walks unabashed and in it fancy sets no limit to extravagance.

Sometimes the name of the fabled source of wealth is Los Almagres; sometimes, Las Amarillas; again, La Mina de las Iguanas, or Lizard Mine, from the fact that the ore is said to have been found in chunks called *iguanas* (lizards); oftener the name is simply the Lost San Saba Mine or the Lost Bowie Mine. In seeking it, generations of men have disemboweled mountains, drained lakes, and turned rivers out of their courses. It has been found—and lost—in many places under many conditions. It is here; it is there; it is nowhere. Generally it is silver; sometimes it is gold. Sometimes it is in a cave; sometimes in water; again on top of a mountain. Now it is not a mine at all but an immense storage of bullion. It changes its place like will-o'-the-wisp and it has more shapes than Jupiter assumed in playing lover.

Only the land that hides it does not change. Except that it is brushier, groomed down in a few places by little fields, and cut across by fences, it is today essentially as the Spaniards found it. A soil that cannot be plowed under keeps its traditions—and its secrets. Wherever the mine may be, however it may appear, it has lured, it lures, and it will lure men on. It is bright Glamour and it is dark and thwarting Fate. It is the Wealth of the Indies; it is the Wealth into which Colonel Mulberry Sellers so gloriously transmuted water and turnips.

The preface to this cycle of a thousand cantos goes back to a day of the seventeenth century when a Spanish *conquistador* set out from Nueva Viscaya "to discover a rumored Silver Hill (Cerro de la Plata) somewhere to the north." At a later date La Salle's Frenchmen wandering forth from Saint Louis Bay on the Texas coast listened to Indians tell of "rivers where silver mines are found." Like most great legends, the legend of the San Saba Mine is a magnification of historical fact. The chief fact was Miranda.

Miranda's Report

In February, 1756, Don Bernardo de Miranda, lieutenant-general of the province of Texas, with sixteen soldiers, five citizens, an Indian interpreter, and several peons, rode out from the village of San Fernando (San Antonio) with orders from the governor to investigate thoroughly the mineral riches so long rumored. After traveling eight days towards the northwest, he pitched camp on the Arroyo San Miguel (now called Honey Creek), a southern tributary of the Rio de las Chanas (Llano River). Only one-fourth of a league beyond he reached the Cerro del Almagre (Almagre Hill), so called on account of its color, *almagre* meaning *red hematite,* or *red ochre.* Opening into the hill Miranda found a cave, which he commanded to be called the Cave of Saint Joseph of Alcasar. He prospected both cave and mountain—with results that brought forth the most sanguine and fulsome predictions.

"The mines which are in the Cerro del Almagre," he reported, "are so numerous that I guarantee to give to every settler of the province of Texas a full claim. . . . The principal vein is more than two *varas* in width and in its westward lead appears to be of immeasurable thickness." Pasturage for stock, wood and water for mining operations, irrigable soil—all the natural requirements for a settlement of workers—were, Miranda added, at hand. The five citizens with him denounced ten mining claims.

On the way back to San Antonio Miranda met a well-known and trusted Apache Indian, who informed him that "many more and better mines" were at "Los Dos Almagres near the source of the

Colorado River." Here the Apache people were accustomed to get silver for their own use—not ore, but solid silver, "soft like the buckles of shoes." Miranda offered the bearer of these tidings a red blanket and a butcher knife to lead him to Los Dos Almagres, but the Apache said that the Comanches out there were too numerous and hostile. However, he promised to guide the Spaniards thither later on—*mañana*.

After having been away only three weeks, Miranda reentered San Fernando. He at once dispatched to the viceroy in Mexico City a statement of his findings, together with recommendations. He declared that no mining could be carried on at El Almagre unless a presidio of "at least thirty men" were established near by as a protection against hostile Indians. And since "an abundance of silver and gold was the principal foundation upon which the kingdoms of Spain rested," Miranda urged the establishment of a presidio and the commencement of mining operations.

As evidence of his rich findings, Miranda turned over three pounds of ore to be assayed. This ran at the rate of about ten ounces of silver to the hundredweight—a good showing. But, as Manuel de Aldaco, a rich mine owner of Mexico, pointed out to the viceroy, three pounds of handpicked ore could not be relied upon to represent any extensive location. Moreover, some silver had been present in the reagent used for assaying the three pounds. Aldaco recommended that before Miranda's glowing report was acted upon "at least thirty mule loads of the ore" be carried for reduction to Camp Mazapil, seven or eight hundred miles away from the veins collectively called Los Almagres. Ten of the thirty loads were to be from the surface, ten from a depth of one fathom, and ten from a depth of at least two fathoms. "It is not prudent," concluded Aldaco, "to be exposed to the danger of deception in a matter so grave and important." Finally, to Aldaco it seemed but fair that Miranda and the citizens who had denounced mining claims should pay the cost of transporting the thirty *cargas*.

Miranda had followed his report to Mexico City, where he engaged an attorney to push his enterprise. He strongly objected that the citizens associated with him could not bear the expense of transporting so much ore, for at twenty pesos per *carga* the total cost would amount to more money than all five of the citizens together possessed. However, Miranda at length agreed to pay the cost himself on condition that he be placed in command of a presidio at Los Almagres; such an office would bring valuable perquisites. He professed to have no doubt that, once the ore was assayed, extensive mining would result and a presidio would be required to protect the miners. The haggling went on. At last, on November 23, 1757—more than twenty months after Miranda had made his "discovery"—the viceroy acceded to his proposition.

Meantime Captain Miranda had been dispatched on a mission to the eastern part of Texas. And at this point, so far as the mines are concerned, approved history stops short, drops the subject without one word of explanation. Did Miranda or anyone else ever so much as load the thirty *cargas* of ore on mules to be carried nearly a thousand miles away for assaying? Did Spanish miners then swarm out to the Almagres veins and extract fortunes from the earth? If authenticated documents cannot finish out the half-told story, other kinds of documents, as we shall see, can—and plenty of things have happened in Texas that the records say nothing about.

In the absence of positive testimony we may be sure that no presidio was established on the Llano for the protection of Almagres silver, but even while Miranda was proposing one, the Spanish government had actually planted a fort called San Luis de las Amarillas on the north bank of the San Saba River sixty miles to the northwest. At the same time a mission, for the conversion of Apaches, had been set up three miles below the fort on the south side of the river. This military establishment on the San Saba, though history may regard it as a buffer against Comanches, was according to tradition designed to protect vast mining operations. Thus hunters for the lost Spanish mine—the lost Almagres Mine, the Lost San Saba Mine, or whatever they happen to call it—look for it oftener on the San Saba than on the Llano. The mountain—of silver—went to Mahomet.

It is necessary to trace out the fate of the San Saba enterprise. Captain Diego Ortiz de Parrilla was placed in command, and on June

30, 1757—even before the stockade about his quarters was completed—
he asked the viceroy to permit him to move his garrison of one hundred
men to the Llano River. The Almagres minerals there should, he said, be
protected, for, "*if* worked," they would be "a great credit to the viceroy
and of much benefit to the royal treasury." The viceroy evidently
thought otherwise, for the move was not allowed. In March, 1758, the
mission, three miles away from military assistance, was besieged by two
thousand Comanche warriors, who so thoroughly burned and killed
that it was never reestablished.

Following this disaster, it was again officially proposed that the
presidio be moved south to Los Almagres, "for protection and defense
of the work on some rich veins of silver, which it is claimed, have been
discovered by intelligent men who know such things." Nothing came
of the proposal. The presidio, always poorly manned and almost constantly terrorized, held out for twelve years and was then (1769) abandoned forever.

The ruins of San Luis de las Amarillas and of a rock wall enclos-
ing three or four acres of ground are still visible about a mile above the
present town of Menard. Various old citizens of the region assert that in
early days they saw signs of a smelter just outside the stockade, though
these signs have been obliterated. Marvin Hunter remembers that his
father, a pioneer editor of West Texas, picked up at the smelter a piece of
slag weighing about fifteen pounds and containing silver. For years it
was used as a door prop in the office of the Menard *Record*. The Hunters
had eleven silver bullets, too, found in and around the old presidio—but
many years ago Marvin shot them at a wild goose on the Llano River.
From the smelter, so the oldest old-timers assert, a clear trail led to what
is yet called Silver Mine on Silver Creek to the northwest. Of this creek
more later.

In 1847 Doctor Ferdinand Roemer, a German geologist, traveled over Texas gathering material for a book that was printed in Ger-
many two years later. In this book he describes the San Saba ruins and
says that, although he looked for a smelter and for slag, he found no sign
of either. It is possible that Roemer overlooked the smelter as he most

certainly overlooked the old irrigation ditch, remains of which can still
be seen. It is also possible that he was too sophisticated to take burnt
rocks about an Indian kitchen midden for a smelter—a mistake often
made by ranchmen, farmers, and treasure seekers.

Two or three aged men living in Menard recall that when they
were boys swimming in the water hole below the old fort they used to
stand on a submerged cannon barrel and stick their toes in the muzzle.
In 1927 the town authorities diverted the river through an irrigation
ditch and drained the water hole in an attempt to find the cannon. No
cannon was revealed. Years before this municipal investigation, W. T.
Burnum spent fifteen hundred dollars pumping out a cave on the divide
north of the old presidio. Failing to find the mine there, he moved his
machinery to a small lake just above Menard and pumped it dry. The
Spaniards had, before evacuating the region, created the lake and diverted
the river into it, thus most effectually concealing their rich workings.

Another persistent rumor has it that a great bell to be hung in
the mission was cast within sight of it, gold and silver from near-by
mines having been molten into the metal to give it tone. On account of
the massacre, however, the bell was never hung, and so to this day certain
people versed in recondite history disturb the soil about the mission site
looking for it.

The Filibusters

The first Americans who came to Texas came for adventure:
Philip Nolan to catch mustangs, Doctor Long to set up a republic, and at
least one man in Magee's extraordinary expedition to dig a fortune out
of the ground. In 1865, more than fifty years after the remnant of
Magee's followers were dispersed, this man, whom history forgets to
mention, appeared in the Llano country. He gave his name as Harp
Perry, and he told a circumstantial story to explain his presence.

Following the last battle in which the Magee forces took part, he
said, he and a fellow adventurer, together with thirty-five Mexicans,
engaged in mining on the Little Llano River. Here they had a rich vein

of both gold and silver, a vein that bore evidence of Spanish exploitation. It was their custom to take out enough ore at one time to keep their smelter, or "furnace," as he called it, busy for a month. It was some distance from the mine, and ore was carried to it in rawhide *kiaks* loaded on burros. Always, Perry said, after taking out a supply of ore he and his associates concealed the entrance to the mine. At the smelter they had no regular moulds for running the refined metal into but poured it into hollow canes; the bars, or rods, thus moulded were buried.

The miners had to be constantly on guard against Indians. In the year 1834 a numerous band of Comanches swooped down upon their camp at the smelter, killing everybody but the two Americans and a Mexican girl. The three survivors made their way to Mexico City, where Perry's partner married the girl. Many things postponed their return to Texas—and to wealth. In 1865, however, Perry, an old man now, was back on the Little Llano. He was not looking for the mine. He was looking for twelve hundred pounds of gold and silver that he had helped mould in hollow canes and bury on a high hill a half mile due north of the smelter.

He was utterly unable to orient himself. Brush had encroached on the prairies; gullies had cut up the hillsides. A few frontiersmen were out on the Llano daring the Comanches, who still terrorized the country. Perry offered a reward of $500 to any one of them who would lead him to the old furnace, the key landmark. He said that it was near a spring and that seventy-five steps from it, in a direct line towards the storage of gold and silver, a pin oak should be found with a rock driven into a knot-hole on the east side. But no furnace or stone-marked pin oak could be found. Perry then announced that he was going to Saint Louis and attempt to find his old partner, whom he believed to be living there. He left the Llano. It was afterwards learned that he threw in with a trail outfit going north from Williamson County and that while he was mounting his horse one morning his six-shooter went off accidentally, killing him instantly.

No further attempt was made to locate the furnace until 1878, when a man by the name of Medlin, his ambition having been aroused by Harp Perry's story, engaged to herd sheep for a ranchman on the Llano. Every day while herding he prosecuted his search, and within the year he found the ruins of the old furnace, the tree with a stone fixed in the knot-hole, and the high hill half a mile due north. Medlin's excavations were as wide as the Poor Parson's parish, but the high hill, where Harp Perry had said over and over the sticks of silver and gold were buried, presented such an indefinite kind of mark that the sheep herder did most of his work about the old furnace. Beneath the ruins themselves he unearthed the skeleton of a man, by its side a "miner's spoon," which was made of burnt soapstone and which showed plainly that it had been used for stirring quicksilver into other metals. Shortly after this find, without waiting to dig up anything else, Medlin left his sheep and the Llano hills for South America.

In Galveston, where he had to wait a few days to take ship, a newspaper writer chanced to find him and took down verbatim his story of Harp Perry's unsuccessful and his own successful search for the furnace. In evidence of his veracity he showed the "miner's spoon" he had dug up. Thus, with little chance for error or exaggeration, has been preserved a record of probably the first American—Harp Perry of Magee's expedition—to be lured to Los Almagres.

Bowie's Secret

Flaming above all the other searchers is the figure of James Bowie. It is a great pity that we have no biography of him such as we have of Davy Crockett. This biography would tell—often with only legend for authority—how he rode alligators in Louisiana; how, like Plains Indians chasing the buffalo, he speared wild cattle; how, with the deadly bowie knife, he fought fearful duels in dark rooms; how he trafficked for black ivory with the pirate Laffite on Galveston Island; and then how he came to San Antonio and married the lovely Ursula de Veramendi, daughter of the vice-governor of Texas.

Bowie was a master of men and a slave to fortune. He was willing to pawn his life for a chance at a chimerical mine, and he asked no odds. Out on the Nueces and Frio rivers, far beyond the last outpost of settlement, he prospected for gold and silver. In his burning quest for the fabled Spanish mines on the San Saba he engaged in one of the most sanguinary and brilliant fights of frontier history. Four years later, at San Antonio, he mistook some bundles of hay loaded on Mexican mules for bags of silver, and led in the so-called Grass Fight. Then on March 6, 1836, leaving not one "messenger of defeat," he and one hundred eighty-odd other Texans died in the Alamo. Thousands of men have believed and yet believe that he died knowing the location of untold riches. At any rate, dying there in the Alamo he carried with him a secret as potent to keep his memory fresh in the minds of the common people as his brave part in achieving the independence of Texas. Thenceforth the mine he sought and that many believe he found took his name.

In the accounts dealing with Bowie's search history and legend freely mingle. I tell the story as frontiersmen and hunters for the Bowie Mine have handed it down.

When Bowie came to western Texas, about 1830, a band of Lipan Indians, a branch of the Apaches, were roaming the Llano region. Their chief was named Xolic, and for a long time Xolic had been in the habit of leading his people down to San Antonio once or twice a year to barter. They always brought with them some silver bullion. They did not bring much at a time, however, for their wants were simple. The Spaniards and Mexicans thought that the Lipan ore had been chipped off some rich vein; there was a touch of gold in it. Of course they tried to learn the secret of such wealth, but the Indians had a tribal under-standing that if any man of their number revealed the source of the mineral he should be tortured to death. At length the people of San Antonio grew accustomed to the silver-bearing Lipans and ceased to pry into their secret. Then came the curious Americans.

Bowie laid his plans carefully. He at once began to cultivate the friendship of the Lipans. He sent back east for a fine rifle plated with silver. When it came, he presented it to Chief Xolic. A powwow was held and at San Pedro Springs Bowie was adopted into the tribe. Now followed months of life with the savages. Bowie was expert at shooting the buffalo; he was foremost in fighting against enemies of the Lipans. He became such a good Indian and was so useful a warrior that his adopted brothers finally showed him what he had joined them to see.

He had expected much, but he had hardly expected to be dazzled by such millions as greeted his eyes. Whether it was natural veins of ore that he beheld or a great storage of smelted bullion, legend has not determined. Anyway, it was "Spanish stuff." The sight seemed to overthrow all caution and judgment. Almost immediately after learning their secret, Bowie deserted the Lipans and sped to San Antonio to raise a force for seizing the wealth.

He was between two fires. He did not want too large a body of men to share with; at the same time he must have a considerable number in order to overcome the guarding Indians. It took some time to arrange the campaign. Meanwhile old Chief Xolic died, and a young warrior named Tres Manos (Three Hands) succeeded to his position. Soon after coming to power, Tres Manos visited San Antonio. There he saw Bowie, accused him of treachery, and came near being killed for his effrontery.

The story of Bowie's adventures with the Indians thus far has no support from history. What follows is of record. On November 2, 1831, Bowie set out to find the Spanish mine. His brother, Rezin P. Bowie, was in the company and was perhaps the leading spirit. It has been claimed that he had made a previous trip of exploration into the San Saba country. Both of the brothers were remarkable men and both of them left accounts of the expedition. With them were nine other men, the name of one of whom, Cephas (or Caiaphas) K. Ham, will weave into odd patterns through the long Bowie Mine story.

If James Bowie knew exactly where he was going, he coursed in a strange manner. In fact, he took so much time in "examining the nature of the country," to use his own words, that three weeks after setting out from San Antonio he had not yet arrived at the abandoned presidio on the San Saba only a hundred and fifty miles away. Yet the San Saba fort was a chief, if not the chief, objective of the expedition, for the Bowies were certain that it had protected the Spaniards "while working the silver mines, which are a mile distant." Why then did the Bowies not go directly to the fort and the mine? Did Jim Bowie know—from a Lipan's confidence—of some other place? Where had he spent the three weeks in scouting before he was stopped? *Quien sabe?*

On the nineteenth of November a friendly Comanche warned him that hostile Indians were out. Whether Tres Manos was among them is not recorded; they were mostly Caddos, Wacos, and Tehuacanas. About daylight on the twenty-first one hundred and sixty-four hostiles—fifteen against one—swooped down upon the Bowie camp. The Texans were not unready. They had the advantage of a thicket and of being near water in a creek. The fight lasted all day. One man was killed; three others were wounded. The Indians had fifty dead and thirty-five wounded. With a comrade named Buchanan shot so in the leg that he could not ride and with most of their horses killed or crippled, the mine hunters remained in camp for eight days. They were not provided with surgical instruments or with medicines of any kind, "not even a dose of salts." They "boiled some live oak bark very strong, and thickened it with pounded charcoal and Indian meal, made a poultice of it, and tied it around Buchanan's leg." Then they sewed a piece of buffalo skin around the bandage. The wound healed rapidly.

While waiting for the disabled to recover sufficiently to travel, some of the Bowie party found a cave near camp. This is a point to remember. Ten days were required for the hobbling journey back to San Antonio.

It is generally said that the fight was on what is now known as Calf Creek in McCulloch County, twenty-five miles or so east of the San Saba fort. At any rate, the remains of a barricade called Bowie's Fort are yet visible on Calf Creek, though "the hand of the impious treasure seeker" long since scattered the stones. Rezin P. Bowie said that the fight took place six miles east of the San Saba fort, and there is good reason for accepting his word. Some six or seven miles east of the old presidio a strip of brush growing on what is known to moderns as Jackson's Creek, a tributary of the San Saba, hides a collection of rocks that looked to many frontiersmen like a hastily arranged fortification. Not a great distance from this place is a cave. Jackson's Creek is dry now, but before the country was grazed off it usually furnished water during several months of the year. Thus it affords a site corresponding to Rezin P. Bowie's description. Exact location of the battle ground would be interesting to some seekers of mine and treasure, for they say that the cave near the Bowie camp held "something."

When Doctor Roemer visited the San Saba ruins in 1847, he observed among other carvings on the stone gateposts near the northwest corner of the stockade the name of Bowie and the date 1829. Those gateposts have been shamefully mutilated, but on one of them this legend, neatly carved, is yet visible:

B O W I E
MINE
1832

Whether James Bowie carved his name with either of those discrepant dates can never be determined.

Without exception, one might say, the men of that highly individualized class who called themselves Texians knew about the Bowie Mine. Most of them who left any kind of chronicle make mention of it. The unpublished *Memoirs* of Colonel "Rip" (John S.) Ford, border ranger, journalist, and a Texian among Texians—aye, a *Texican*—contains a sequel to the Bowie expedition. This sequel came to "Old Rip" from Cephas K. Ham, who survived "the Calf Creek Fight" for many, many years and became a veritable high priest to the Bowie Mine tradition.

According to Ham's story, he (and not Bowie) was adopted by the Indians and was—*almost*—shown the mine. His warrior brothers were a band of Comanches under the leadership of Chief Incorroy. In 1831 he was wandering around with these Comanches, trading for horses and catching mustangs in order to make up a bunch to drive to Louisiana. One pint of powder, eight balls of lead, one plug of tobacco, one butcher knife, and two brass rings made the price of a good horse. "A certain fat warrior," Ham narrates, "was frequently my hunting companion. One day he pointed to a hill and said: 'There is plenty of silver on the other side. We will go out by ourselves, and I will show it to you. If the other Indians find I have done so, they will kill both of us.'" But camp was hurriedly moved next day and the fat warrior never fulfilled his promise.

Not long afterward Bowie sent a message to Ham advising him that, as the Mexicans were about to make war on the Comanches, he had better cut loose from them. He came into San Antonio, only to find that Bowie's real motive in sending a warning was to get him to join an expedition in search of the San Saba Mine.

Rezin P. Bowie, Ham's story goes on, had already visited the mine. "It was not far from the fort. The shaft was about eight feet deep." Rezin P. Bowie went down to the bottom of it "by means of steps cut in a live oak log" and hacked off some ore "with his tomahawk." He carried the ore to New Orleans and had it assayed. "It panned out rich." He came back to San Antonio. The results of his next move have already been recounted.

Here Rezin P. Bowie drops out of the story, but Jim Bowie did not give up the quest. Ham and other like authorities agree that he raised a second expedition of thirty men. This time, according to Ham, Bowie reached the San Saba but could not find the shaft, as it had been filled up either by rains or by Indians. Others say that about the time Bowie got ready to exploit the mineral riches he had located, the Texan war for independence broke out. Among many Texans the legend is persistent that Bowie's chief motive in searching for the San Saba treasure was to secure means for financing the Texas army—a view hardly tenable by anyone who knows anything about the real Bowie.

Thus Bowie's name lives on. Wes Burton, a lost mine hunter who has been very successful in telling of his hunts, says that the Lipan Indians never showed Bowie a mine but merely five hundred jack loads of pure silver stored in a cave. The Spaniards mined the silver and moulded it into bars faster than they could transport it. Consequently, when the Indians forced them to abandon their workings they left behind an immense store of bullion. Burton also knew a man who paid $500 to a Mexican in San Antonio for a document purporting to have been taken off Bowie's dead body in the Alamo by one of Santa Anna's officers. The Mexican who sold it claimed to be a descendant of the officer. It gave full and explicit directions to the Bowie Mine; yet somehow the purchaser could never follow them.

Well, James Bowie set out for the San Saba Mine. Therefore he must have known where it was. Miranda found the Almagre vein south of the Llano and powers who did not listen to him established the presidio of San Luis de las Amarillas on the north bank of the San Saba twenty leagues away. Rezin P. Bowie asserted that *the Spanish mine* was only a mile from the presidio. But the Lost San Saba, or Bowie, Mine envelops both these locations as well as many others. Sometimes it is as far east as the Colorado and sometimes it is as far west as the Nueces.

In The Burned Cedar Brake

The early settlers of the San Saba and Llano country found an old road leading south from the presidio of San Luis de las Amarillas. As it was their belief that the Spaniards had hauled bullion over it to San Antonio and Mexico, they called it Silver Trail and they traveled it themselves until the country was fenced. Like other roads laid out by men who must beware of ambuscade, it kept as much as possible to high and open ground. The land it traversed on the North Fork of the Llano came to be known as Lechuza Ranch.

In 1881 the Lechuza came into the possession of a young Scotchman, Captain George Keith Gordon, who, after having hunted slavers on the East Coast of Africa and mapped many of its harbors, had lately retired from the British Navy. Nearly fifty years have passed now since Captain Gordon became interested in the San Saba Mine; he is still interested and has a trail to hunt out. This is his story.

Twenty-five miles or so northwest of the Lechuza Ranch was Fort McKavett, occupied during the seventies for the purpose of frontier defense. After it was abandoned, the camp sutler remained in the country. He was not an uncommunicative sort of being, and he was not tardy in letting the newly arrived owner of the Lechuza know that the hillsides and valleys of his estate contained something more valuable than the eye-delighting mesquite grass.

One day while scouting out in the vicinity of a large cedar brake on the Lechuza range, the sutler, so he said, saw three Indians. He himself was hidden on a hill above them, and he watched. Presently they disappeared in a very queer manner—vanished as if into the earth—then reappeared and left. Curious to see what they had been up to, the sutler rode down to the spot. He found a hole in the ground about thirty inches in diameter. Looking down into it, he could distinguish nothing clearly and so became more curious. He dragged up a small log, tied his lariat to it, and lowered himself. Something over twenty feet down he struck bottom.

He was in a concave about fifteen feet across. Against the wall on one side, the disheveled skeleton of a man sprawled over a heap of silver bars. The bars were so heavy that the sutler could not take even one with him, for it would be all he could do to pull his own weight out of the hole. He would return to the fort, he told himself, and make immediate preparations for securing the silver bars and hauling them away. After clambering to the surface, he marked the spot carefully and left. But a man attached to the army even in the loosest way is very often not his own master. For reasons not necessary to delineate here, it was a full two years before the sutler got back to haul out the silver.

When he did get back, he found that a fire had swept the cedar brake, obliterating all surface markings. The hole thirty inches in diameter was lost.

This account reminded Captain Gordon of a cavity he himself had observed in a cedar brake in his pasture but had not investigated. He was thinking of investigating it when one morning a stranger drove up to the Lechuza headquarters and, after the usual beating about the bush, asked permission to hunt silver on the ranch. He was willing to give the owner half of whatever he should find. Telling him nothing, Captain Gordon hitched up his buggy and drove the prospector to a spot on the old Silver Trail where some irons from a burnt wagon had given rise to a tale about Spanish treasure.

"It was a hot July day," Captain Gordon narrates. "I was not feeling very well; so I sat in the shade and let the stranger have his way. He produced a divining rod and followed its pull into a dense cedar brake—directly away from the wagon irons but towards the cave I knew about. After an hour's struggle with the heat and cedar limbs, he returned, claiming that the farther he went the harder the rod pulled. 'There must be a wagon load of the stuff at least,' he said. I now told him the sutler's story.

"The next morning he, two young Englishmen who were staying with me, and I, all well provided with ropes, picks, crowbars, and shovels, got into a wagon and headed for the cave. On our arrival the rod in the stranger's hand at once told us that the silver was still in the hole. We let him down and I entered also. The rod pulled towards one side. The cave was not so deep as the sutler had described his as being and it appeared to have been filled with loose rocks. My theory was that the cedar fire had ignited bat guano in the cave and that the heat had caused rocks to crack and fall. The young Englishmen flew in to moving the debris and within three hours were down to solid rock bottom—but not to silver. The mineral rod still pointed to the spot, but we were disgusted and quit."

So much for the silver cache. The mine out of which the Spaniards took silver affords the problem that Captain Gordon has really been interested in. Some time after the experience in the cave, he was over on the Nueces River and there met General John R. Baylor, whose exploits as a mineralogist will be told of in the next chapter of this book. Baylor showed Captain Gordon an outcropping of curious sandstone from which he had assayed a showing of silver. The Captain began tracing that formation. He found that, cropping out in various places, it led in a north-northeast direction, across his own ranch, and on straight towards the old presidio at Menard. He and his brother assayed some of the rock found on the Lechuza and got a good percentage of silver.

The way to find the San Saba Mine is to trace this sandstone to the vicinity of the old Spanish fort. Captain Gordon never tracked the outcroppings to the inevitable shaft on the San Saba. Few people realize how tied down the average ranchman is, how little time he has for taking up asides. But the old captain, living now in San Antonio—his house a veritable museum of objects of art and aboriginal artifacts collected from many lands—is at last free of ranch bondage. At the very moment of this writing he is preparing to follow the sandstone trail to its end—the long-hidden Spanish silver mine on the San Saba.

Yellow Wolf: "Three Suns West"

Even if there were no "Spanish charts" to the mineral wealth on the Llano and the San Saba, no Silver Trail, no rocks pointing always *más allá*, there would yet remain as a guide to Coronado's trustful children the tales of the aboriginal red men. In the beginning it was Indians who inspired the search for the Hill of Silver. An Apache told Miranda of the Dos Almagres, where solid silver, "soft like the buckles of shoes," could be found. A Comanche pointed out, somewhere over the hill, a mine to Cephas K. Ham. A legendary Lipan gave the secret to Bowie himself. Years after Bowie's death another Lipan led, for the modest reward of $300, some Austin citizens to "the old Spanish mine" near the San Saba mission. It was out in a "bald-open prairie." According to the latest available report, in the *Telegraph and Texas Register*, Houston, June 22, 1842, the ore from this Lipan's mine "has not yet been accurately analysed."

Oftener than either Spaniards or Bowie, the Comanches appear as witnesses in tales of the great lode. A century and a quarter ago these fierce and extraordinary people boasted their nation to be the peer of the United States, whose citizens they at that time respected and treated as friends. Towards Spanish power, however, never did they express any other feelings than contempt and hatred. They learned to outride the race of horsemen who had introduced the horse to America; they ran Spaniards and Mexicans down, roped them, and dragged them to death. They were particularly jealous of the Llano-San Saba territory, from which they evicted the Apaches; they prevented the Spaniards from getting a firm foothold in the region; they fought against Anglo-American settlement of it until the very end.

Living at Liberty Hill is an old mustanger and trail driver named Andy Mather. The mountains of the West and canyons of the Plains are mapped in his grizzled features. I see him now, a great hat on his head, wearing a vest but no coat, "all booted and spurred and ready to ride," but sitting with monarchial repose in an ample rawhide-bottomed chair on his shady gallery. He was born in 1852 on the North Fork of the San Gabriel River in Williamson County, where his father owned a wheat mill and blacksmith shop. Two miles above the Mather place a band of Comanches under Chief Yellow Wolf made their headquarters. They were peaceable at the time and were friendly with the few settlers.

"In 1851," says Andy Mather, "Yellow Wolf brought some silver ore to my father to be hammered into ornaments. Of course I was not yet born, but one of my earliest and clearest recollections is of my father's telling me about the silver. He knew a good deal about metals and said that the ore was almost pure silver. Yellow Wolf told him that he got it from a place 'three suns to the west.' He described the deposit as being under a bluff near the junction of two streams. He offered to show it, but my father would not at that time think of leaving his family in order to go prospecting into the wild country beyond.

"How far 'three suns west' would be I do not know. A Comanche warrior could go a far piece in a day's time. From our place west to the old San Saba fort it was close to a hundred miles—just about three days' travel as we used to ride. Some people have figured that Yellow Wolf must have got his silver in the vicinity of the fort. I have known plenty of men to lose what little money they had in looking for silver in the hills west of here. I never hunted for the mines myself. All I know is what my father told me. I know that he was a calm man and that he told nothing but the truth. He knew Yellow Wolf well. He hammered Yellow Wolf's ore on his own anvil."

Captive Witnesses

As if to corroborate the Indians, Indian captives have added their tales to the ever-increasing cycle. Captain Jess Billingsley, who won his fame in the Texas Revolution, was the "old rock" itself. Such was his prowess that his followers as long as they lived called themselves and were proud to be called "the Billingsley men." In the speech to his men that preceded the charge at San Jacinto Billingsley used a phrase that became a nation's battle cry and that seems destined to live as long as the name of Texas lives: "Remember the Alamo! Remember Goliad!"

Along in the forties, while San Jacinto and the Alamo were yet freshly remembered, Captain Billingsley heard a Baptist preacher tell how for years he had been held captive by the Comanches and how through them he had obtained knowledge of the Bowie Mine. As proof of his knowledge of the mine he offered to lead the way to it. Billingsley organized a small expedition and with the preacher as guide set out for the San Saba. Up in the hills somewhere the Comanches attacked the party and killed their escaped captive. The survivors of the fight nearly starved to death before they got back to a country in which they were not afraid to shoot a deer—and that was the last of that search.

★　　★　　★　　★　　★

One time in the early fifties a *Comanchero* (a Mexican trader with the Comanches) while out in the hills north of San Antonio bought a Mexican woman from a band of Comanches, with whom she had been for several years. He took her to San Antonio and released her. Naturally many people questioned her as to her experiences with *los Indios broncos*. Among other things she told of how she had helped them gather silver ore up on the San Saba and beat it into ornaments.

Now, about this time a bachelor named Grumble was ranching on the San Saba below the mouth of Brady Creek—a good seventy-five miles east of the old fort. He had fought Comanches a plenty; he had seen silver on their buckskin trappings; he had even picked up spent silver bullets from their guns. When echoes of the Mexican woman's story reached his ears, he determined to visit her in San Antonio and find out more concerning the source of Comanche silver. This was a year or two after the captive's liberation, she having married in the meantime. She talked to Grumble without reservation.

"The Comanches often camped," she said, "at the old presidio, and right there they made bracelets and conchas and other ornaments out of silver. I have helped to bring the ore into camp, but I will not deceive you by telling you that I saw where it was taken out of the ground. I was a slave and had to obey others. I tell you only what I myself have seen.

"The Indians would leave their camp at the fort and cross the San Saba River. Then they would go on south for about two miles, following up Los Moros Creek. Then the men would leave the squaws and captives at a regular stopping place. Sometimes they would be gone a long time; sometimes not over an hour. I do not think the mine was over half a mile away. When the men got back to where we were waiting, they always gave us their ore to carry on in. It was well understood that the mine was kept hidden so that no stranger could find it."

After hearing this account, Grumble asked the woman if she would go with him to the San Saba and guide him as far as she could towards the Comanche mine.

"All I could do," she answered, "would be to lead you to our waiting ground on Los Moros Creek. At this place I could only point out the brush into which I saw the warriors enter empty-handed and from which I saw them return carrying silver."

All that Grumble asked was to be "put on the right track." The woman and her husband were willing to undertake the trip under his protection. Arrangements were made for immediate departure.

Grumble was a race horse man and gambler. He had formerly lived in New Braunfels, and he chose now to pass through that place and several other towns that offered chances for profitable games and races. Riding at his own convenience, he was sometimes ahead of the Mexicans and sometimes behind them. The arrangement with them was kept secret. Late one evening all three arrived in the village of San Saba, where Grumble went to the hotel while the Mexicans made camp.

As soon as he arose the next morning, the American entered a saloon to get a drink. At the bar he saw another gambler and racer named Sinnet Musset with whom he had recently had "a difficulty."

Each man "reached." Musset drew a fraction the quicker, and Grumble was a dead man. This was in 1857.

The Mexicans were naturally frightened. The woman had no desire to fall again into the hands of the Comanches. They went back to Lampasas, through which they had passed on their way up, got work there, and for five years did not tell a soul of their secret engagement with Grumble. When, finally, they did tell, no man was enterprising enough to take up the trail that Grumble had so precipitately quitted.

Perhaps there is some connection between the silver up Los Moros Creek and Mullins' chart. Mullins is a bachelor. He lives at Menard in a feed store and makes money trading real estate. He uses some of his money to keep two or three men digging for San Saba treasure. He is not particular where they dig, provided they dig the holes deep enough. Sometimes they dig above the old presidio, sometimes below it; sometimes on one side of the river, sometimes on the other. The laborers get their wages every Saturday night and are satisfied; so is Mullins.

His prize chart is drawn in blue ink on the scraped hide of a javelina. He bought it from a young man who confessed to have stolen it from an old trapper in East Texas. I doubt if Mullins would sell it for a thousand dollars. It shows the San Saba River and Los Moros Creek. A cross represents the presidio. Near it an Indian with a long scalp-lock is drawing a bow. An owl looks down from a tree. A half dozen irregular stars sprinkled conspicuously over the map indicate where silver is to be found. The largest of the stars is up Los Moros Creek. A line projected southward from the old presidio up Los Moros Creek would very nearly coincide with the line of silver-bearing sandstone that Captain George Keith Gordon traced to the Lechuza Ranch.

★ ★ ★ ★ ★

The silver ledge on the Frio River must be too many suns west for the location that Yellow Wolf alluded to, and it could not be the location on Los Moros Creek that the Mexican woman told Grumble of. Yet it belongs to the tradition of captives who ranged with their captors over the San Saba territory. A "little rancher" named Whitley out in McMullen County told me about it. Could I reproduce the starlight on his beard, as we sat in front of his house, and the far-away barking of coyotes that mingled with his tones, the story would be a thousand times more real.

"When I was a young man in Refugio County," Whitley said, "I got to knowing an old, old Mexican named Benito who had been raised by the Comanches. They had captured him down on the Rio Grande as a boy and they kept him until he was grown. Whenever the Indians came to San Antonio to trade, he said they always put him and other captives under the supervision of squaws, who stayed hid out.

"The main thing these Indians had to trade was ore. They made bullets out of it too. It was mostly silver. For a long time Benito didn't know where they got it, but finally they trusted him far enough to let him see. There was a big ledge of it up towards the head of the Frio.

"Well, Benito finally slipped away from the Indians and took in a couple of Mexican pardners to go with him for a lot of the ore. The Indians got on their trail and killed both his *compañeros*, and he barely escaped. After that he never tried to go back to the Frio.

"When I knew him he was over a hundred years old, and he would often tell me about the rich silver vein. I wanted to go in search of it, and he thought he could make the trip in spite of his feebleness if we fixed it so he could ride in a hack. He knew he could find the ledge if he ever got up the Frio Canyon, but he would not go unless a good-sized party went. He said that he would pick six Mexicans to go and I could pick six white men.

"Well, we got everything about ready, wagon, provisions, and so forth, when the man in our party who was bearing most of the fitting-out expense up and took down sick. So we naturally had to put the trip off. The man got well and a while after that we got ready to go again. But luck seemed to be against us. This time the old Mexican guide was taken down. It was out of the question for him to go. He was dying. He gave us the clearest directions he could and thought we could follow them. From what he said, the vein of silver could not be got to on horseback. It is in the south bank of one of three arroyos that run into the Frio close together. At it the arroyo makes a sharp turn, and a man would have to get down and go afoot along the bank. No doubt it was concealed, for the Indians always covered it up well after they had hacked off what they wanted. Benito said that if he could get just one sight of the lay of the land, he could tell which one of the three arroyos the vein was in. But he never got that sight; so he gave the best way-bill he could and died.

"The treasure hunting party broke up and things rocked along for years without me doing anything. Meanwhile a brother-in-law of mine had moved into the upper Frio country. I decided to pay him and my sister a visit and to find the ore at the same time. I took my dogs along, and the first thing we struck the very first morning we rode out to find those three arroyos was a bear. Well, sir, I got to hunting bear, and we never looked for that silver at all. But I know good and well if I had left my dogs at home, I'd 'a' had it.

"I say I know, because my brother-in-law found it after I left. I gave him the directions and he agreed to notify me if he made the find. Well, he made it and was leaving his place to come down the country to tell me, when he was murdered in cold blood. But that is another matter. He had confided in his wife, and of course she told me; but as he hadn't explained to her where he located the vein, that didn't do much good.

"You see, I have known two living witnesses to that silver. It wasn't hearsay with them. If I just had time, I believe I could go up there yet and find it myself."

$$\star \quad \star \quad \star \quad \star \quad \star$$

Living in Fort Worth is an old-time Texas frontiersman named W. A. McDaniel. He appears to have swung a wide loop and to have heard the owl hoot in all sorts of places. The following is one of many tales that he tells.

"Soon after the Civil War, while I was just a kid, my father went out to Coleman County to work for the Stiles and Coggin outfit. The Indians were so bad that at times only about half the cowboys worked on the range, the others keeping guard over the horses and the ranch quarters. My mother cooked on the fireplace for a couple dozen men, but the work and anxiety were so hard on her that father said he wouldn't let her stay in such a country any longer. So one day he put her and us children in a wagon and drove us to Burnet County to stay with an uncle and aunt. The Comanches were raiding there too, but not so bad, and there were more settlers to afford protection.

"Not long after we got there, two or three neighbor families came to see us. Of course, we boys must go swimming and fishing in the creek. The grown folks were afraid for us to go alone—afraid of Indians; so a kind of picnic party was made up. After we got to the creek another boy and I slipped across and ran to a hole that was hid by a bend.

"We were pulling fish out and bragging about our luck when twelve Comanche warriors rode down upon us out of the bushes. Two of them dragged the other boy and myself up on their horses behind them. As soon as they got off a little distance they stopped and blind-folded us. They did not torture us.

"It was about eleven o'clock when they captured us, and all that afternoon and into the night we rode like the devil beating tan bark. We could not see a wink, but we knew by the coolness of the air and the sounds of insects and coyotes when night came. We also knew that we were traveling over a hilly country. At last the Indians stopped, pulled us off, undid our bandages, and told us to lie down and go to sleep. We slept.

"When we awoke next morning, we found ourselves in a shallow cave. I noticed some of the Comanches picking up what looked to be gravel. They had a fire, a little iron pot, and a bullet mould. They were melting these pebbles and running them into bullets. I picked up four or five of the pebbles and put them in my pocket. We stayed in the cave all that day, all the next night, and until late the third night. Of course both of us boys were looking for a chance to escape, but we were afraid to make any move. We were not tied but we were guarded.

"On the second afternoon of our captivity, the Comanches brought in a jug of fire water—regular old tarantula juice—from somewhere and they all got as drunk as a covey of biled owls. By good dark the warrior guarding us was as drunk as the other Indians. He let the fire go out and keeled over dead to the world. We were in a kind of pen made by the cave wall on one side and the sleeping Comanches on the other. Now was our time.

"We slipped out and found a horse tied in the hollow. We both got on him and headed him southeast. He kept a general course except when we misguided him, which we frequently did; it later turned out that he had been stolen from a settler on the Lampasas. After riding the night out and then, with a few stops, until nearly sundown next day, we struck the settlement from which we had been stolen. While we were telling the story, I pulled the pebbles from my pocket. They proved, upon examination by a man who knew, to contain gold and silver as well as lead.

"I have tried many a time to ride back to the cave. It's been like looking for the white cow with a black face. I went to that cave in darkness; I left it in darkness; it is still in darkness. It can hardly be more than fifty miles from Burnet. When the Comanches saw that the white men were going to take the country for good, they doubtless filled up the entrance to the cave. Some day—perhaps it may be a hundred years from now—the cave and the mine will be found."

Whether this cave paved with pebbles of silver is the same as the one hung with icicles of silver, I cannot say. Living in Sweetwater, Texas, until recently was a blind man named Johnson, very old. Back in the fifties he was a ranger and Indian fighter. One time the band of rangers to which he belonged struck a party of Indians west of the Colorado River and, after killing two or three of them, scattered in pursuit. It was seldom that rangers bothered with Indian prisoners, but the captain of this company took his man alive. The prisoner turned out to be a Mexican.

The Indians, he said, had stolen him as a child, reared him, and shared with him a great secret. If his life were now spared, he would show his captor *mucha plata*. The ranger agreed, and the Mexican led him back into the hills for a few miles until they arrived at a very thick motte of hog, or Mexican, persimmons. Crawling into this, they came upon a broad rock slab. They lifted it back. Underneath was a slanting hole. Peering in, the ranger saw what appeared to be a myriad "icicles of silver." They hung glistening from the roof of the cavity like stalactites.

The captain now regarded himself a wealthy man, but what with chasing Comanche raiders, fighting Mexican bandits, and quelling domestic outlaws, he had no time to realize immediately on his wealth. In fact, he saw the icicles of silver but the one time. He confided the secret to Johnson, and was shortly afterwards killed. The years passed, and by the time Johnson got ready to search for the wonderful hole amid the hog persimmons he was blind. He knew the hill country, every canyon of it; he knew where he and his fellow rangers had met the Indians and in what direction his captain had followed the warrior captive who surrendered and paid such a wonderful ransom for his life; he had the captain's directions in minute detail. But a blind man cannot make his way through dense thickets and into box canyons; a blind man cannot lead the blind.

Beasley's Cavern

Beasley has been dead more than ten years now, and he was perhaps eighty-five years old when he died. As a youth he came to live in the settlement about Lampasas. Following one of the Comanche raids he went with a little band of settlers in pursuit. The trail was plain, and they rode fast towards the west. They crossed the Colorado and veered northward in the direction of the San Saba. The moonlight was too dim to reveal tracks and so at dark the trailers camped to await dawn.

When Beasley went out early next morning to get his horse, he found that a coyote had chewed the picket rope, a rawhide *reata* greased with fresh tallow, in two, and that his horse had "made tracks." It was well after sunup before he found the animal, on the side of a rocky draw. He caught him and was making a *bozal*—a nose-hitch, used in place of a bridle—preparatory to mounting bareback, when his eye caught the mouth of a cave near at hand.

There is something about a cave that draws all natural men. A cave may conceal anything. This cave faced east, and the rising sun was shining directly into it. Beasley led his horse over and peered within. For fifteen or twenty feet the hole sloped down at a steep angle and then seemed to become a horizontal tunnel. The walls of the opening were reflecting and refracting the sun's rays like a chamber of mirrors. Beasley forgot at once both murderous Indians and his impatient comrades. He made a pair of hobbles out of a bandana, thus securing his mount, and then with the free rope lowered himself into the cave. Now that he could examine the walls near at hand, he saw that they were lined, plated, cased with ore almost pure—ore that was undoubtedly silver.

However, he did not tarry. As quickly as possible he climbed out of the cavern, unhobbled his horse, mounted, and galloped to camp, where he found all hands awaiting him. He privately told the leader of the party what he had found. The leader chided him for having delayed the pursuit of the Indians and at once took up the trail. It was a long trail, a twisting trail, and at the end of it there was blood. When the frontiersmen turned back towards the Lampasas country, they left their leader behind them.

Beasley had communicated his secret to no one else. He alone now possessed it. There was only one other person in the world with whom he would share it. Almost immediately he went east to marry the girl who had been waiting for him to make a stake. He told his bride that their fortune was found, though not yet gathered. Daring the privations and hazards of the then utmost frontier, the couple settled a few miles below the mouth of the San Saba River. Beasley picked the site as being near his silver cavern. He remembered exactly, he thought, where his party had camped that night, where he had found his horse, and where he had seen the metal plating flash against the early sun. He was a good man in the ways of camp, trail, and unfenced range.

Yet after he had established a home—a base of operations—and set out to work his mine, he could not find it. He was so disturbed that for a long time he would not tell his wife of his failure. When he told her, she encouraged him by going out with him. The country settled up, and he went on looking for his cavern. In time he told neighbors of his quest—of his rich find and of his loss. The years by fives and tens shuttled by; he farmed and ran a few cattle; he worked hard; he raised a family; but he never entirely gave up the search. When death came he was still hopeful of some day recovering the fortune that one bright morning in his youth, when the land was youthful like himself, had gleamed before his eyes. To this good day, however, Beasley's cavern, like the tomb of Moses, remains an unseen monument.

Perchance the bald, old eagle
On gray Packsaddle's height
Out of his rocky eyrie
Looks on the wondrous sight;
Perchance the panther stalking
Still knows that hunted spot;
For beast and bird have seen and heard
That which man knoweth not.

The Gold Bug

BY EDGAR ALLAN POE

Possibly the best known of all treasure-hunting stories, "The Gold Bug" was first published in the *Dollar Newspaper* in Philadelphia in June of 1843. Poe (1809–1849) had already sold it to another publisher (for $52) when he learned that the *Dollar* was offering a $100 short story prize. He quickly arranged to swap "The Gold Bug" for some critical reviews, submitted it for the prize, and won. Within two months it had been dramatized and produced on stage. The setting, on Sullivan's Island off the South Carolina coast, was known to Poe first-hand; he had been stationed there during a short spell as an Army enlisted man at the end of the 1820s, when he also developed the keen interest in shells laid to Legrand in the story. Poe's skill in cryptography is similarly authentic. In 1839, he published a challenge to readers of *Alexander's Weekly Messenger* offering to solve any cryptogram submitted. A hundred came in and he solved them all, except for one that he proved to be unsolvable.

★   ★   ★   ★   ★

What ho! what ho! this fellow is dancing mad!
He hath been bitten by the Tarantula.
All in the Wrong.

45

M any years ago, I contracted an intimacy with a Mr. William Legrand. He was of an ancient Huguenot family, and had once been wealthy; but a series of misfortunes had reduced him to want. To avoid the mortification consequent upon his disasters, he left New Orleans, the city of his forefathers, and took up his residence at Sullivan's Island, near Charleston, South Carolina.

This Island is a very singular one. It consists of little else than the sea sand, and is about three miles long. Its breadth at no point exceeds a quarter of a mile. It is separated from the mainland by a scarcely perceptible creek, oozing its way through a wilderness of reeds and slime, a favorite resort of the marsh-hen. The vegetation, as might be supposed, is scant, or at least dwarfish. No trees of any magnitude are to be seen. Near the western extremity, where Fort Moultrie stands, and where are some miserable frame buildings, tenanted, during summer, by the fugitives from Charleston dust and fever, may be found, indeed, the bristly palmetto; but the whole island, with the exception of this western point, and a line of hard, white beach on the sea-coast, is covered with a dense undergrowth of the sweet myrtle so much prized by the horticulturists of England. The shrub here often attains the height of fifteen or twenty feet, and forms an almost impenetrable coppice, burdening the air with its fragrance.

In the inmost recesses of this coppice, not far from the eastern or more remote end of the island, Legrand had built himself a small hut, which he occupied when I first, by mere accident, made his acquaintance. This soon ripened into friendship—for there was much in the recluse to excite interest and esteem. I found him well educated, with unusual powers of mind, but infected with misanthropy, and subject to perverse moods of alternate enthusiasm and melancholy. He had with him many books, but rarely employed them. His chief amusements were gunning and fishing, or sauntering along the beach and through the myrtles, in quest of shells or entomological specimens;—his collection of the latter might have been envied by a Swammerdamm. In these excursions he was usually accompanied by an old negro, called Jupiter, who had been manumitted before the reverses of the family, but who could be induced, neither by threats nor by promises, to abandon what he considered his right of attendance upon the footsteps of his young "Massa Will." It is not improbable that the relatives of Legrand, conceiving him to be somewhat unsettled in intellect, had contrived to instill this obstinacy into Jupiter, with a view to the supervision and guardianship of the wanderer.

The winters in the latitude of Sullivan's Island are seldom very severe, and in the fall of the year it is a rare event indeed when a fire is considered necessary. About the middle of October, 18—, there occurred, however, a day of remarkable chilliness. Just before sunset I scrambled my way through the evergreens to the hut of my friend, whom I had not visited for several weeks—my residence being, at that time, in Charleston, a distance of nine miles from the island, while the facilities of passage and re-passage were very far behind those of the present day. Upon reaching the hut I rapped, as was my custom, and getting no reply, sought for the key where I knew it was secreted, unlocked the door, and went in. A fine fire was blazing upon the hearth. It was a novelty, and by no means an ungrateful one. I threw off an overcoat, took an arm-chair by the crackling logs, and awaited patiently the arrival of my hosts.

Soon after dark they arrived, and gave me a most cordial welcome. Jupiter, grinning from ear to ear, bustled about to prepare some marsh-hens for supper. Legrand was in one of his fits—how else shall I term them?—of enthusiasm. He had found an unknown bivalve, forming a new genus, and, more than this, he had hunted down and secured, with Jupiter's assistance a *scarabaeus* which he believed to be totally new, but in respect to which he wished to have my opinion on the morrow.

"And why not to-night?" I asked, rubbing my hands over the blaze, and wishing the whole tribe of *scarabaei* at the devil.

"Ah, if I had only known you were here!" said Legrand, "but it's so long since I saw you; and how could I foresee that you would pay me a visit this very night of all others? As I was coming home I met Lieutenant G——, from the fort, and, very foolishly, I lent him the bug; so it will be impossible for you to see it until the morning. Stay here to-night, and I will send Jup down for it at sunrise. It is the loveliest thing in creation!"

"What?—sunrise?"

"Nonsense no!—the bug. It is of a brilliant gold color—about the size of a large hickory-nut—with two jet black spots near one extremity of the back, and another, somewhat longer, at the other. The *antennae* are—"

"Dey ain't *no* tin in him, Massa Will, I keep a tellin' on you," here interrupted Jupiter; "de bug is a goole-bug, solid, ebery bit of him, inside and all, sep him wing—neber feel half so hebby a bug in my life."

"Well, suppose it is, Jup," replied Legrand, somewhat more earnestly, it seemed to me, than the case demanded; "is that any reason for your letting the birds burn? The color"—here he turned to me—"is really almost enough to warrant Jupiter's idea. You never saw a more brilliant metallic lustre that the scales emit—but of this you cannot judge till to-morrow. In the meantime I can give you some idea of the shape." Saying this, he seated himself at a small table, on which were a pen and ink, but no paper. He looked for some in a drawer, but found none.

"Never mind," he said at length, "this will answer;" and he drew from his waistcoat pocket a scrap of what I took to be very dirty foolscap, and made upon it a rough drawing with the pen. While he did this, I retained my seat by the fire, for I was still chilly. When the design was complete, he handed it to me without rising. As I received it, a loud growl was heard, succeeded by a scratching at the door. Jupiter opened it, and a large Newfoundland, belonging to Legrand, rushed in, leaped upon my shoulders, and loaded me with caresses; for I had shown him much attention during previous visits. When his gambols were over, I looked at the paper, and, to speak the truth, found myself not a little puzzled at what my friend had depicted.

"Well!" I said, after contemplating it for some minutes, "This is a strange *scarabaeus*, I must confess; new to me; never saw anything like it before—unless it was a skull, or a death's-head, which it more nearly resembles than anything else that has come under *my* observation."

"A death's-head!" echoed Legrand. "Oh—yes—well, it has something of that appearance upon paper, no doubt. The two upper black spots look like eyes, eh? and the longer one at the bottom like a mouth—and then the shape of the whole is oval."

"Perhaps so," said I; "but, Legrand, I fear you are no artist. I must wait until I see the beetle itself, if I am to form any idea of its personal appearance."

"Well, I don't know," said he, a little nettled, "I draw tolerably—*should* do it at least—have had good masters, and flatter myself that I am not quite a blockhead."

"But, my dear fellow, you are joking, then," said I, "this is a very passable *skull*—indeed, I may say that it is a very *excellent* skull, according to the vulgar notions about such specimens of physiology—and your *scarabaeus* must be the queerest *scarabaeus* in the world if it resembles it. Why, we may get up a very thrilling bit of superstition upon this hint. I presume you will call the bug *scarabaeus caput horminís*, or something of that kind—there are many similar titles in the Natural Histories. But where are the *antennae* you spoke of?"

"The *antennae!*" said Legrand, who seemed to be getting unaccountably warm upon the subject; "I am sure you must see the *antennae*. I made them as distinct as they are in the original insect, and I presume that is sufficient."

"Well, well," I said, "perhaps you have—still I don't see them;" and I handed him the paper without additional remark, not wishing to ruffle his temper; but I was much surprised at the turn affairs had taken; his ill humor puzzled me—and, as for the drawing of the beetle, there were positively *no antennae* visible, and the whole *did* bear a very close resemblance to the ordinary cuts of a death's-head.

He received the paper very peevishly, and was about to crumple it, apparently to throw it in the fire, when a casual glance at the design seemed suddenly to rivet his attention. In an instant his face grew violently red—in another excessively pale. For some minutes he continued to scrutinize the drawing minutely where he sat. At length he arose, took a candle from the table, and proceeded to seat himself upon a sea-chest in the farthest corner of the room. Here again he made an anxious examination of the paper; turning it in all directions. He said nothing however, and his conduct greatly astonished me; yet I thought it prudent not to exacerbate the growing moodiness of his temper by any comment. Presently he took from his coat-pocket a wallet, placed the paper carefully in it, and deposited both in a writing-desk, which he locked. He now grew more composed in his demeanor; but his original air of enthusiasm had quite disappeared. Yet he seemed not so much sulky as abstracted. As the evening wore away he became more and more absorbed in revery, from which no sallies of mine could arouse him. It had been my intention to pass the night at the hut, as I had frequently done before, but, seeing my host in this mood, I deemed it proper to take leave. He did not press me to remain, but, as I departed, he shook my hand with even more than his usual cordiality.

It was about a month after this (and during the interval I had seen nothing of Legrand) when I received a visit, at Charleston, from his man, Jupiter. I had never seen the good old negro look so dispirited, and I feared that some serious disaster had befallen my friend.

"Well, Jup," said I, "what is the matter now?—how is your master?"

"Why, to speak the troof, massa, him not so berry well as mought be."

"Not well! I am truly sorry to hear it. What does he complain of?"

"Dar! dat's it!—him neber plain of notin—but him berry sick for all dat."

"*Very* sick, Jupiter!—why didn't you say so at once? Is he confined to bed?"

"No, dat he aint!—he aint find nowhar—dat's just whar he shoe pinch—my mind is got to be berry hebby bout poor Massa Will."

"Jupiter, I should like to understand what it is you are talking about. You say your master is sick. Hasn't he told you what ails him?"

"Why, massa, taint worf while for to git mad about de matter— Massa Will say noffin at all aint de matter wid him—but den what make him go about looking dis here way, wid he head down and he soldiers up, and as white as a gose? And den he keep a syphon all de time—"

"Keeps a what, Jupiter?"

"Keeps a syphon wid de figgurs on de slate—de queerest figgurs I ebber did see. Ise gittin to be skeered, I tell you. Hab for to keep mighty tight eye pon him noovers. Todder day he gib me slip fore de sun up and was gone de whole ob de blessed day. I had a big stick ready cut for to gib him deuced good beating when he did come—but Ise sich a fool dat I hadn't de heart arter all—he looked so berry poorly."

"Eh?—what?—ah yes!—upon the whole I think you had better not be too severe with the poor fellow—don't flog him, Jupiter—he can't very well stand it—but can you form no idea of what has occasioned this illness, or rather this change of conduct? Has anything unpleasant happened since I saw you?"

"No, massa, dey ain't bin noffin onpleasant *since* den—'twas *fore* den I'm feared—'twas be berry day you was dare."

"How? what do you mean?"

"Why, massa, I mean de bug—dare now."

"That what?"

"De bug—I'm berry sartain dat Massa Will bin bit somewhere 'bout he head by dat goole-bug."

"And what cause have you, Jupiter, for such a supposition."

"Claws enuff, massa, and mouff, too. I never did see sich a deuced bug—he kick and he bite ebery ting what cum near him. Massa Will cotch him fuss, but had for to let him go gin mighty quick, I tell you—den was de time he must ha got de bite. I didn't like de look ob de bug mouff, myself, no how, so I wouldn't take hold ob him wid my finger, but I cotch him wid a piece of paper dat I found. I rap him up in de paper and stuff a piece of it in he mouff—dat was de way."

"And you think then, that your master was really bitten by the beetle, and that the bite made him sick?"

"I don't think noffin about it—I nose it. What make him dream bout de goole so much, if taint cause he bit by the goole-bug? Ise heered bout dem goole-bugs fore dis."

"But how do you know he dreams about gold?"

"How I know? why, cause he talk about it in he sleep—dat's how I nose."

"Well, Jup, perhaps you are right; but to what fortunate circumstance am I to attribute the honor of a visit from you to-day?"

"What de matter, massa?"

"Did you bring any message from Mr. Legrand?"

"No, massa, I bring dis here pissel;" and here Jupiter handed me a note which ran thus:

"My Dear—

"Why have I not seen you for so long a time? I hope you have not been so foolish as to take offence at any little *brusquerie* of mine; but no, that is improbable.

"Since I saw you I have had great cause for anxiety. I have something to tell you, yet scarcely know how to tell it, or whether I should tell it at all.

"I have not been quite well for some days past, and poor old Jup annoys me, almost beyond endurance, by his well-meant attentions. Would you believe it?—he had prepared a huge stick, the other day, with which to chastise me for giving him the slip, and spending the day, *solus*, among the hills on the mainland. I verily believe that my ill looks alone saved me a flogging.

"I have made no addition to my cabinet since we met.

"If you can, in any way, make it convenient, come over with Jupiter. Do come. I wish to see you *to-night*, upon business of importance. I assure you that it is of the *highest* importance.

"Ever yours,
"WILLIAM LEGRAND."

There was something in the tone of this note which gave me great uneasiness. Its whole style differed materially from that of Legrand. What could he be dreaming of? What new crotchet possessed his excitable brain? What "business of the highest importance" could *he* possibly have to transact? Jupiter's account of him boded no good. I dreaded lest the continued pressure of misfortune had, at length, fairly unsettled the reason of my friend. Without a moment's hesitation, therefore, I prepared to accompany the negro.

Upon reaching the wharf, I noticed a scythe and three spades, all apparently new, lying in the bottom of the boat in which we were to embark.

"What is the meaning of all this, Jup?" I inquired.

"Him syfe, massa, and spade."

"Very true; but what are they doing here?"

"Him de syfe and de spade what Massa Will sis pon my buying for him in de town, and de debbils own lot of money I had to gib for em."

"But what, in the name of all that is mysterious, is your 'Massa Will' going to do with scythes and spades?"

"Dat's more dan I know, and debbil take me if I don't blieve 'tis more dan he know too. But it's all cum ob de bug."

Finding that no satisfaction was to be obtained of Jupiter, whose whole intellect seemed to be absorbed by "de bug," I now stepped into the boat, and made sail. With a fair and strong breeze we soon ran into the little cove to the northward of Fort Moultrie, and a walk of some two miles brought us to the hut. It was about three in the afternoon when we arrived. Legrand had been awaiting us in eager expectation. He grasped my hand with a nervous *empressement* which alarmed me and strengthened the suspicions already entertained. His countenance was pale even to ghastliness, and his deep-set eyes glared with unnatural lustre. After some inquiries respecting his health, I asked him, not knowing what better to say, if he had yet obtained the *scarabaeus* from Lieutenant G—.

"Oh, yes," he replied, coloring violently, "I got it from him the next morning. Nothing should tempt me to part with that *scarabaeus*. Do you know that Jupiter is quite right about it?"

"In what way?" I asked, with a sad foreboding at heart.

"In supposing it to be a bug of *real gold*." He said this with an air of profound seriousness, and I felt inexpressibly shocked.

"This bug is to make my fortune," he continued, with a triumphant smile; "to reinstate me in my family possessions. Is it any wonder, then, that I prize it? Since Fortune has thought fit to bestow it upon me, I have only to use it properly, and I shall arrive at the gold of which it is the index. Jupiter, bring me that *scarabaeus!*"

"What! de bug, massa? I'd rudder not go fer trubble dat bug; you mus git him for your own self." Hereupon Legrand arose, with a grave and stately air, and brought me the beetle from a glass case in which it was enclosed. It was a beautiful *scarabaeus*, and, at that time, unknown to naturalists—of course a great prize in a scientific point of view. There were two round black spots near one extremity of the back, and a long one near the other. The scales were exceedingly hard and glossy, with all the appearance of burnished gold. The weight of the insect was very remarkable, and, taking all things into consideration, I could hardly blame Jupiter for his opinion respecting it; but what to make of Legrand's concordance with that opinion, I could not, for the life of me, tell.

"I sent for you," said he, in a grandiloquent tone, when I had completed my examination of the beetle, "I sent for you that I might have your counsel and assistance in furthering the views of Fate and of the bug—"

"My dear Legrand," I cried, interrupting him, "you are certainly unwell, and had better use some little precautions. You shall go to bed, and I will remain with you a few days, until you get over this. You are feverish and—"

"Feel my pulse," said he.

I felt it, and, to say the truth, found not the slightest indication of fever.

"But you may be ill and yet have no fever. Allow me this once to prescribe for you. In the first place go to bed. In the next—"

"You are mistaken," he interposed, "I am as well as I can expect to be under the excitement which I suffer. If you really wish me well, you will relieve this excitement."

"And how is this to be done?"

"Very easily. Jupiter and myself are going upon an expedition into the hills, upon the main land, and, in this expedition, we shall need the aid of some person in whom we can confide. You are the only one we can trust. Whether we succeed or fail, the excitement which you now perceive in me will be equally allayed."

"I am anxious to oblige you in any way," I replied; "but do you mean to say that this infernal beetle has any connection with your expedition into the hills?"

"It has."

"Then, Legrand, I can become a party to no such absurd proceeding."

"I am sorry—very sorry—for we shall have to try it by ourselves."

"Try it by yourselves! The man is surely mad!—but stay!—how long do you propose to be absent?"

"Probably all night. We shall start immediately, and be back, at all events, by sunrise."

"And will you promise me, upon your honor, that when this freak of yours is over, and the bug business (good God!) settled to your satisfaction, you will then return home and follow my advice implicitly, as that of your physician?"

"Yes; I promise; and now let us be off, for we have no time to lose."

With a heavy heart I accompanied my friend. We started about four o'clock—Legrand, Jupiter, the dog, and myself. Jupiter had with him the scythe and spades—the whole of which he insisted upon carrying—more through fear, it seemed to me, of trusting either of the implements within reach of his master, than from any excess of industry or complaisance. His demeanor was dogged in the extreme, and "dat deuced bug" were the sole words which escaped his lips during the journey. For my own part, I had charge of a couple of dark lanterns, while Legrand contented himself with the *scarabaeus,* which he carried attached to the end of a bit of whipcord: twirling it to and fro, with the air of a conjuror, as he went. When I observed this last, plain evidence of my friend's aberration of mind, I could scarcely refrain from tears. I thought it best, however, to humor his fancy, at least for the present, or until I could adopt some more energetic measures with a chance of success. In the meantime I endeavored, but all in vain, to sound him in regard to the object of the expedition. Having succeeded in inducing me to accompany him, he seemed unwilling to hold conversation upon any topic of minor importance, and to all my questions vouchsafed no other reply than "we shall see!"

We crossed the creek at the head of the island by means of a skiff, and, ascending the high grounds on the shore of the main land, proceeded in a northwesterly direction, through a tract of country excessively wild and desolate, where no trace of a human footstep was to be seen. Legrand led the way with decision; pausing only for an instant, here and there, to consult what appeared to be certain landmarks of his own contrivance upon a former occasion.

In this manner we journeyed for about two hours, and the sun was just setting when we entered a region infinitely more dreary than any yet seen. It was a species of tableland, near the summit of an almost inaccessible hill, densely wooded from base to pinnacle, and interspersed with huge crags that appeared to lie loosely upon the soil, and in many cases were prevented from precipitating themselves into the valleys below, merely by the support of the trees against which they reclined. Deep ravines, in various directions, gave an air of still sterner solemnity to the scene.

The natural platform to which we had clambered was thickly overgrown with brambles, through which we soon discovered that it would have been impossible to force our way but for the scythe; and Jupiter, by direction of his master, proceeded to clear for us a path to the foot of an enormously tall tulip-tree, which stood, with some eight or ten oaks, upon the level, and far surpassed them all, and all other trees which I had then ever seen, in the beauty of its foliage and form, in the wide spread of its branches, and in the general majesty of its appearance. When we reached this tree, Legrand turned to Jupiter, and asked him if he thought he could climb it. The old man seemed a little staggered by the question, and for some moments made no reply. At length he approached the huge trunk, walked slowly around it, and examined it with minute attention. When he had completed his scrutiny, he merely said:

"Yes, massa, Jup climb any tree he ebber see in he life."

"Then up with you as soon as possible, for it will soon be too dark to see what we are about."

"How far mus go up, massa?" inquired Jupiter.

"Get up the main trunk first, and then I will tell you which way to go—and here—stop! take this beetle with you."

"De bug, Massa Will!—de goole-bug!" cried the negro, drawing back in dismay—"What for mus tote de bug way up de tree?—d—n if I do!"

"If you are afraid, Jup, a great big negro like you, to take hold of a harmless little dead beetle, why you can carry it up by this string—but, if you do not take it up with you in some way, I shall be under the necessity of breaking your head with this shovel."

"What de matter now, massa?" said Jup, evidently shamed into compliance; "always want for to raise fuss wid old nigger. Was only funnin anyhow. *Me* feered de bug! what I keer for de bug?" Here he took cautiously hold of the extreme end of the string, and, maintaining the insect as far from his person as circumstances would permit, prepared to ascend the tree.

In youth, the tulip-tree, or *Liriodendron tulipiferum*, the most magnificent of American foresters, has a trunk peculiarly smooth, and often rises to a great height without lateral branches; but, in its riper age, the bark becomes gnarled and uneven, while many short limbs make their appearance on the stem. Thus the difficulty of ascension, in the present case, lay more in semblance than in reality. Embracing the huge cylinder, as closely as possible, with his arms and knees, seizing with his hands some projections, and resting his naked toes upon others, Jupiter, after one or two narrow escapes from falling, at length wriggled himself into the first great fork, and seemed to consider the whole business as virtually accomplished. The *risk* of the achievement was, in fact, now over, although the climber was some sixty or seventy feet from the ground.

"Which way mus go now, Massa Will?" he asked.

"Keep up the largest branch—the one on this side," said Legrand. The negro obeyed him promptly, and apparently with but little trouble; ascending higher and higher, until no glimpse of his squat figure could be obtained through the dense foliage which enveloped it. Presently his voice was heard in a sort of halloo.

"How much fudder is got for go?"

"How high up are you?" asked Legrand.

"Ebber so fur," replied the negro; "can see de sky fru de top ob de tree."

"Never mind the sky, but attend to what I say. Look down the trunk and count the limbs below you on this side. How many limbs have you passed?"

"One, two, tree, four, fibe—I done pass fibe big limb, massa, pon dis side."

"Then go one limb higher."

In a few minutes the voice was heard again, announcing that the seventh limb was attained.

"Now, Jup," cried Legrand, evidently much excited, "I want you to work your way out upon that limb as far as you can. If you see anything strange let me know."

By this time what little doubt I might have entertained of my poor friend's insanity was put finally at rest. I had no alternative but to conclude him stricken with lunacy, and I became seriously anxious about getting him home. While I was pondering upon what was best to be done, Jupiter's voice was again heard.

"Mos feered for to ventur pon dis limb berry far—'tis dead limb putty much all de way."

"Did you say it was a *dead* limb, Jupiter?" cried Legrand in a quavering voice.

"Yes, massa, him dead as de doornail—done up for sartain—done departed dis here life."

"What in the name of heaven shall I do?" asked Legrand, seemingly in the greatest distress.

"Do!" said I, glad of an opportunity to interpose a word, "why come home and go to bed. Come now!—that's a fine fellow. It's getting late, and, besides, you remember your promise."

"Jupiter," cried he, without heeding me in the least, "do you hear me?"

"Yes, Massa Will, hear you ebber so plain."

"Try the wood well, then, with your knife, and see if you think it *very* rotten."

"Him rotten, massa, sure nuff," replied the negro in a few moments, "but not so berry rotten as mought be. Mought venture out leetle way pon de limb by myself, dat's true."

"By yourself!—what do you mean?"

"Why, I mean de bug. 'Tis *berry* hebby bug. Spose I drop him down fuss, and den de limb won't break wid just de weight of one nigger."

"You infernal scoundrel!" cried Legrand, apparently much relieved, "what do you mean by telling me such nonsense as that? As sure as you drop that beetle I'll break your neck. Look here, Jupiter, do you hear me?"

"Yess, massa, needn't hollo at poor nigger dat style."

"Well! now listen!—if you will venture out on the limb as far as you think safe, and not let go the beetle, I'll make you a present of a silver dollar as soon as you get down."

"I'm gwine, Massa Will—deed I is," replied the negro very promptly—"mos out to the eend now."

"Out to the end!" here fairly screamed Legrand; "do you say you are out to the end of that limb?"

"Soon be to de eend, massa—o-o-o-o-oh! Lor-gol-a-marcy! what *is* dis here pon de tree?"

"Well!" cried Legrand, highly delighted, "what is it?"

"Why 'taint noffin but a skull—somebody bin lef him head up de tree, and de crows done gobble ebery bit ob de meat off."

"A skull, you say!—very well,—how is it fastened to the limb?—what holds it on?"

"Sure nuff, massa; mus look. Why dis berry curious sarcumstance, pon my word—dare's a great big nail in de skull, what fastens ob it on to de tree."

"Well now, Jupiter, do exactly as I tell you—do you hear?"

"Yes, massa."

"Pay attention, then—find the left eye of the skull."

"Hum! hoo! dat's good! why dare ain't no eye lef at all."

"Curst your stupidity! do you know your right hand from your left?"

"Yes, I nose dat—nose all about dat—tis my lef hand what I chops de wood wid."

"To be sure! you are left-handed; and your left eye is on the same side as your left hand. Now, I suppose, you can find the left eye of the skull, or the place where the left eye has been. Have you found it?"

Here was a long pause. At length the negro asked.

"Is de lef eye of de skull pon de same side as de lef hand of de skull too?—cause de skull aint got not a bit ob a hand at all—nebber mind! I got de lef eye now—here de lef eye! what mus do wid it?"

"Let the beetle drop through it, as far as the string will reach—but be careful and not let go your hold of the string."

"All dat done, Massa Will; mighty easy ting for to put de bug fru de hole—look out for him dare below!"

During this colloquy no portion of Jupiter's person could be seen; but the beetle, which he had suffered to descend, was now visible at the end of the string, and glistened, like a globe of burnished gold, in the last rays of the setting sun, some of which still faintly illumined the eminence upon which we stood. The *scarabaeus* hung quite clear of any branches, and, if allowed to fall, would have fallen at our feet. Legrand immediately took the scythe, and cleared with it a circular space, three or four yards in diameter, just beneath the insect, and, having accomplished this, ordered Jupiter to let go the string and come down from the tree.

Driving a peg, with great nicety, into the ground, at the precise spot where the beetle fell, my friend now produced from his pocket a tape-measure. Fastening one end of this at that point of the trunk of the tree which was nearest the peg, he unrolled it till it reached the peg, and thence farther unrolled it, in the direction already established by the two points of the tree and the peg, for the distance of fifty feet—Jupiter clearing away the brambles with the scythe. At the spot thus attained a second peg was driven, and about this, as a centre, a rude circle, about four feet in diameter, described. Taking now a spade himself, and giving one to Jupiter and one to me, Legrand begged us to set about digging as quickly as possible.

To speak the truth, I had no especial relish for such amusement at any time, and, at that particular moment, would willingly have declined it; for the night was coming on, and I felt much fatigued with the exercise already taken; but I saw no mode of escape, and was fearful of disturbing my poor friend's equanimity by a refusal. Could I have depended, indeed upon Jupiter's aid, I would have had no hesitation in attempting to get the lunatic home by force; but I was too well assured of the old negro's disposition, to hope that he would assist me, under any circumstances, in a personal contest with his master. I made no doubt that the latter had been infected with some of the innumerable Southern superstitions about money buried, and that his phantasy had received confirmation by the finding of the *scarabaeus*, or, perhaps, by Jupiter's obstinacy in maintaining it to be "a bug of real gold." A mind disposed to lunacy would readily be led away by such suggestions—especially if chiming in with favorite preconceived ideas—and then I called to mind the poor fellow's speech about the bettle's being "the index of his fortune." Upon the whole, I was sadly vexed and puzzled, but, at length, I concluded to make a virtue of necessity—to dig with a good will, and thus the sooner to convince the visionary, by ocular demonstration, of the fallacy of the opinions he entertained.

The lanterns having been lit, we all fell to work with a zeal worthy a more rational cause; and, as the glare fell upon our persons and implements, I could not help thinking how picturesque a group we composed, and how strange and suspicious our labors must have appeared to any interloper who, by chance, might have stumbled upon our whereabouts.

We dug very steadily for two hours. Little was said; and our chief embarrassment lay in the yelpings of the dog, who took exceeding interest in our proceedings. He, at length, became so obstreperous that we grew fearful of his giving the alarm to some stragglers in the vicinity,—or, rather, this was the apprehension of Legrand;—for myself, I should have rejoiced at any interruption which might have enabled me to get the wanderer home. The noise was, at length, very effectually silenced by Jupiter, who, getting out of the hole with a dogged air of deliberation, tied the brute's mouth up with one of his suspenders, and then returned, with a grave chuckle, to his task.

When the time mentioned had expired, we had reached a depth of five feet, and yet no sign of any treasure became manifest. A general pause ensued, and I began to hope that the farce was at an end. Legrand, however, although evidently much disconcerted, wiped his brow thoughtfully and recommenced. We had excavated the entire circle of four feet diameter, and now we slightly enlarged the limit, and went to the farther depth of two feet. Still nothing appeared. The gold-seeker, whom I sincerely pitied, at length clambered from the pit, with the bitterest disappointment imprinted upon every feature, and proceeded, slowly and reluctantly, to put on his coat, which he had thrown off at the beginning of his labor. In the meantime I made no remark. Jupiter, at a signal from his master, began to gather up his tools. This done, and the dog having been unmuzzled, we turned in profound silence toward home.

We had taken, perhaps, a dozen steps in this direction, when, with a loud oath, Legrand strode up to Jupiter, and seized him by the collar. The astonished negro opened his eyes and mouth to the fullest extent, let fall the spades, and fell upon his knees.

"You scoundrel!" said Legrand, hissing out the syllables from between his clenched teeth—"you infernal black villain!—speak, I tell you!—answer me this instant, without prevarication!—which—which is your left eye?"

"Oh, my golly, Massa Will! aint dis here my lef eye for sartain?" roared the terrified Jupiter, placing his hand upon his *right* organ of vision, and holding it there with a desperate pertinacity, as if in immediate dread of his master's attempt at a gouge.

"I thought so!—I knew it! hurrah!" vociferated Legrand, letting the negro go and executing a series of curvets and caracols, much to the astonishment of his valet, who, arising from his knees, looked, mutely, from his master to myself, and then from myself to his master.

"Come! we must go back," said the latter, "the game's not up yet"; and he again led the way to the tulip-tree.

"Jupiter," said he, when we reached its foot, "come here! Was the skull nailed to the limb with the face outward, or with the face to the limb?"

"De face was out, massa, so dat de crows could get at de eyes good, widout any trouble."

"Well, then, was it this eye or that through which you dropped the beetle?" here Legrand touched each of Jupiter's eyes.

"'Twas dis eye, massa—de lef eye—jis as you tell me," and here it was his right eye that the negro indicated.

"That will do—we must try it again."

Here my friend, about whose madness I now saw, or fancied that I saw, certain indications of method, removed the peg which marked the spot where the beetle fell, to a spot about three inches to the westward of its former position. Taking, now, the tape measure from the nearest point of the trunk to the peg, as before, and continuing the extension in a straight line to the distance of fifty feet, a spot was indicated, removed, by several yards, from the point at which we had been digging.

Around the new position a circle, somewhat larger than in the former instance, was now described, and we again set to work with the spades. I was dreadfully weary, but, scarcely understanding what had occasioned the change in my thoughts, I felt no longer any great aversion from the labor imposed. I had become most unaccountably interested—nay, even excited. Perhaps there was something, amid all the extravagant demeanor of Legrand—some air of forethought, or of deliberation, which impressed me. I dug eagerly, and now and then caught myself actually looking, with something that very much resembled expectation, for the fancied treasure, the vision of which had demented my unfortunate companion. At a period when such vagaries of thought most fully possessed me, and when we had been at work perhaps an hour and a half, we were again interrupted by the violent howlings of the dog. His uneasiness, in the first instance, had been, evidently, but the result of playfulness or caprice, but he now assumed a bitter and serious tone. Upon Jupiter's again attempting to muzzle him, he made furious resistance, and, leaping into the hole, tore up the mould frantically with his claws. In a few seconds he had uncovered a mass of human bones, forming two complete skeletons, intermingled with several buttons of metal, and what appeared to be the dust of decayed woolen. One or two strokes of a spade upturned the blade of a large Spanish knife, and, as we dug farther, three or four loose pieces of gold and silver coin came to light.

At sight of these the joy of Jupiter could scarcely be restrained, but the countenance of his master wore an air of extreme disappointment. He urged us, however, to continue our exertions, and the words were hardly uttered when I stumbled and fell forward, having caught the toe of my boot in a large ring of iron that lay half buried in the loose earth.

We now worked in earnest, and never did I pass ten minutes of more intense excitement. During this interval we had fairly unearthed an oblong chest of wood, which, from its perfect preservation and wonderful hardness, had plainly been subjected to some mineralizing process—perhaps that of the Bi-chloride of Mercury. This box was three feet and a half long, three feet broad, and two and a half feet deep. It was firmly secured by bands of wrought iron, riveted, and forming a kind of open trellis-work over the whole. On each side of the chest, near the top, were three rings of iron—six in all—by means of which a firm hold could be obtained by six persons. Our utmost united endeavors served only to disturb the coffer very slightly in its bed. We at once saw the impossibility of removing so great a weight. Luckily, the sole fastenings of the lid consisted of two sliding bolts. These we drew back—trembling and panting with anxiety. In an instant, a treasure of incalculable value lay gleaming before us. As the rays of the lanterns fell within the pit, there flashed upwards a glow and a glare, from a confused heap of gold and jewels, that absolutely dazzled our eyes.

I shall not pretend to describe the feelings with which I gazed. Amazement was, of course, predominant. Legrand appeared exhausted with excitement, and spoke very few words. Jupiter's countenance wore, for some minutes, as deadly a pallor as it is possible, in the nature of things, for any negro's visage to assume. He seemed stupefied—thunderstricken. Presently he fell upon his knees in the pit, and burying his naked arms up to the elbows in gold, let them there remain, as if enjoying the luxury of a bath. At length, with a deep sigh, he exclaimed, as if in a soliloquy:

"And dis all cum ob de goole-bug! de putty goole-bug! de poor little goole-bug, what I boosed in dat sabage kind ob style! Aint you shamed ob yourself, nigger?—answer me dat!"

It became necessary, at last, that I should arouse both master and valet to the expediency of removing the treasure. It was growing late, and it behooved us to make exertion, that we might get every thing housed before daylight. It was difficult to say what should be done, and much time was spent in deliberation—so confused were the ideas of all. We, finally, lightened the box by removing two-thirds of its contents, when we were enabled, with some trouble to raise it from the hole. The articles taken out were deposited among the brambles, and the dog left to guard them, with strict orders from Jupiter neither, upon any pretence, to stir from the spot, nor to open his mouth until our return. We then hurriedly made for home with the chest; reaching the hut in safety, but after excessive toil, at one o'clock in the morning. Worn out as we were, it was not in human nature to do more immediately. We rested until two, and had supper; starting for the hills immediately afterward, armed with three stout sacks, which, by good luck, were upon the premises. A little before four we arrived at the pit, divided the remainder of the booty, as equally as might be, among us, and, leaving the holes unfilled, again set out for the hut, at which, for the second time, we deposited our golden burthens, just as the first faint streaks of the dawn gleamed from over the tree-tops in the East.

We were now thoroughly broken down; but the intense excitement of the time denied us repose. After an unquiet slumber of some three or four hours' duration, we arose, as if by preconcert, to make examination of our treasure.

The chest had been full to the brim, and we spent the whole day, and the greater part of the next night, in a scrutiny of its contents. There had been nothing like order or arrangement. Everything had been heaped in promiscuously. Having assorted all with care we found ourselves possessed of even vaster wealth than we had at first supposed. In coin there was rather more than four hundred and fifty thousand dollars—estimating the value of the pieces, as accurately as we could, by the tables of the period. There was not a particle of silver. All was gold of antique date and of great variety—French, Spanish, and German money, with a few English guineas, and some counters, of which we had never seen specimens before. There were several very large and heavy coins, so worn that we could make nothing of their inscriptions. There was no American money. The value of the jewels we found more difficulty in estimating. There were diamonds—some of them exceedingly large and fine—a hundred and ten in all, and not one of them small; eighteen rubies of remarkable brilliancy;—three hundred and ten emeralds, all very beautiful; and twenty-one sapphires, with an opal. These stones had all been broken from their settings and thrown loose in the chest. The settings themselves, which we picked out from among the other gold, appeared to have been beaten up with hammers, as if to prevent identification. Besides all this, there was a vast quantity of solid gold ornaments; nearly two hundred massive finger and earrings; rich chains—thirty of these, if I remember; eighty-three very large and heavy crucifixes; five gold censers of great value; a prodigious golden punch-bowl, ornamented with richly chased vine-leaves and Bacchanalian figures; with two sword-handles exquisitely embossed, and many other smaller articles which I cannot recollect. The weight of these valuables exceeded three hundred and fifty pounds avoirdupois; and in this estimate I have not included one hundred and ninety-seven superb gold watches; three of the number being worth each five hundred dollars, if one. Many of them were very old, and as timekeepers valueless; the works having suffered, more or less, from corrosion—but all were richly jewelled and in cases of great worth. We estimated the entire contents of the chest, that night, at a million and a half of dollars; and upon the subsequent disposal of the trinkets and jewels (a few being retained for our own use), it was found that we had greatly under-valued the treasure.

When, at length, we had concluded our examination, and the intense excitement of the time had, in some measure, subsided, Legrand, who saw that I was dying with impatience for a solution of this most extraordinary riddle, entered into a full detail of all the circumstances connected with it.

"You remember," said he, "the night when I handed you the rough sketch I had made of the *scarabaeus*. You recollect also, that I became quite vexed at you for insisting that my drawing resembled a death's-head. When you first made this assertion I thought you were jesting; but afterwards I called to mind the peculiar spots on the back of the insect, and admitted to myself that your remark had some little foundation in fact. Still, the sneer at my graphic powers irritated me—for I am considered a good artist—and, therefore, when you handed me the scrap of parchment, I was about to crumple it up and throw it angrily into the fire."

"The scrap of paper, you mean," said I.

"No; it had much of the appearance of paper, and at first I supposed it to be such, but when I came to draw upon it, I discovered it at once to be a piece of very thin parchment. It was quite dirty, you remember. Well, as I was in the very act of crumpling it up, my glance fell upon the sketch at which you had been looking, and you may imagine my astonishment when I perceived, in fact, the figure of a death's-head just where, it seemed to me, I had made the drawing of the beetle. For a moment I was too much amazed to think with accuracy. I knew that my design was very different in detail from this—although there was a certain similarity in general outline. Presently I took a candle, and seating myself at the other end of the room, proceeded to scrutinize the parchment more closely. Upon turning it over, I saw my own sketch upon the reverse, just as I had made it. My first idea, now, was mere surprise at the really remarkable similarity of outline—at the singular coincidence involved in the fact that, unknown to me, there should have been a skull upon the other side of the parchment, immediately beneath my figure of the *scarabaeus*, and that this skull, not only in outline, but in size, should so closely resemble my drawing. I say the singularity of this coincidence absolutely stupefied me for a time. This is the usual effect of such coincidences. The mind struggles to establish a connexion—a sequence of cause and effect—and, being unable to do so, suffers a species of temporary paralysis. But, when I recovered from this stupor, there dawned upon me gradually a conviction which startled me even far more than the coincidence. I began distinctly, positively, to remember that there had been no drawing upon the parchment, when I made my sketch of the *scarabaeus*. I became perfectly certain of this; for I recollected turning up first one side and then the other, in search of the cleanest spot. Had the skull been then there, of course I could not have failed to notice it. Here was indeed a mystery which I felt it impossible to explain; but, even at that early moment, there seemed to glimmer, faintly, within the most remote and secret chambers of my intellect, a glow-worm-like conception of that truth which last night's adventure brought to so magnificent a demonstration. I arose at once, and putting the parchment securely away, dismissed all further reflection until I should be alone.

"When you had gone, and when Jupiter was fast asleep, I betook myself to a more methodical investigation of the affair. In the first place I considered the manner in which the parchment had come into my possession. The spot where we discovered the *scarabaeus* was on the coast of the mainland, about a mile eastward of the island, and but a short distance above high-water mark. Upon my taking hold of it, it gave me a sharp bite, which caused me to let it drop. Jupiter, with his accustomed caution, before seizing the insect, which had flown toward him, looked about him for a leaf, or something of that nature, by which to take hold of it. It was at this moment that his eyes, and mine also, fell upon the scrap of parchment, which I then supposed to be paper. It was lying half buried in the sand, a corner sticking up. Near the spot where we found it, I observed the remnants of the hull of what appeared to have been a ship's long boat. The wreck seemed to have been there for a very great while; for the resemblance to boat timbers could scarcely be traced.

"Well, Jupiter picked up the parchment, wrapped the beetle in it, and gave it to me. Soon afterward we turned to go home, and on the way met Lieutenant G——. I showed him the insect, and he begged me to let him take it to the fort. Upon my consenting, he thrust it forthwith into his waistcoat pocket, without the parchment in which it had been wrapped, and which I had continued to hold in my hand during his inspection. Perhaps he dreaded my changing my mind, and thought it best to make sure of the prize at once—you know how enthusiastic he is on all subjects connected with Natural History. At the same time, without being conscious of it, I must have deposited the parchment in my own pocket.

"You remember that when I went to the table, for the purpose of making a sketch of the beetle, I found no paper where it was usually kept. I looked in the drawer, and found none there. I searched my pockets, hoping to find an old letter, when my hand fell upon the parchment. I thus detail the precise mode in which it came into my possession; for the circumstances impressed me with a peculiar force.

"No doubt you will think me fanciful—but I had already established a kind of *connexion*. I had put together two links of a great chain. There was a boat lying upon a sea-coast, and not far from the boat was a parchment—*not a paper*—with a skull depicted upon it. You will, of course, ask 'where is the connexion?' I reply that the skull, or death's-head, is the well-known emblem of the pirate. The flag of the death's-head is hoisted in all engagements.

"I have said that the scrap was parchment, and not paper. Parchment is durable—almost imperishable. Matters of little moment are rarely consigned to parchment; since, for the mere ordinary purposes of drawing or writing, it is not nearly so well adapted as paper. This reflection suggested some meaning—some relevancy—in the death's-head. I did not fail to observe, also, the *form* of the parchment. Although one of its corners had been, by some accident, destroyed, it could be seen that the original form was oblong. It was just such a slip, indeed, as might have been chosen for a memorandum—for a record of something to be long remembered and carefully preserved."

"But," I interposed, "you say that the skull was *not* upon the parchment when you made the drawing of the beetle. How then do you trace any connexion between the boat and the skull—since this latter, according to your own admission, must have been designed (God only knows how or by whom) at some period subsequent to your sketching the *scarabaeus*?"

"Ah, hereupon turns the whole mystery; although the secret, at this point, I had comparatively little difficulty in solving. My steps were sure, and could afford but a single result. I reasoned, for example, thus: When I drew the *scarabaeus*, there was no skull apparent upon the parchment. When I had completed the drawing I gave it to you, and observed you narrowly until you returned it. You, therefore, did not design the skull, and no one else was present to do it. Then it was not done by human agency. And nevertheless it was done.

"At this stage of my reflections I endeavored to remember, and *did* remember, with entire distinctness, every incident which occurred about the period in question. The weather was chilly (oh, rare and happy accident!), and a fire was blazing upon the hearth. I was heated with exercise and sat near the table. You, however, had drawn a chair close to the chimney. Just as I placed the parchment in your hand, and as you were in the act of inspecting it, Wolf, the Newfoundland, entered, and leaped upon your shoulders. With your left hand you caressed him and kept him off, while your right, holding the parchment, was permitted to fall listlessly between your knees, and in close proximity to the fire. At one moment I thought the blaze had caught it, and was about to caution you, but, before I could speak, you had withdrawn it, and were engaged in its examination. When I considered all these particulars, I doubted not for a moment that *heat* had been the agent in bringing to light, upon the parchment, the skull which I saw designed upon it. You are well aware that chemical preparations exist, and have existed time out of mind, by means of which it is possible to write upon either paper or vellum, so that the characters shall become visible only when subjected to the action of fire. Zaffre, digested in *aqua regia*, and diluted with four times its weight of water, is sometimes employed; a green tint results. The regulus of cobalt, dissolved in spirit of nitre, gives a red. These colors disappear at longer or shorter intervals after the material written upon cools, but again become apparent upon the re-application of heat.

"I now scrutinized the death's-head with care. Its outer edges—the edges of the drawing nearest the edge of the vellum— were far more *distinct* than the others. It was clear that the action of the caloric had been imperfect or unequal. I immediately kindled a fire, and subjected every portion of the parchment to a glowing heat. At first, the only effect was the strengthening of the faint lines in the skull; but, upon persevering in the experiment, there became visible, at the corner of the slip, diagonally opposite to the spot in which the death's-head was delineated, the figure of what I at first supposed to be a goat. A closer scrutiny, however, satisfied me that it was intended for a kid."

"Ha! ha!" said I, "to be sure I have no right to laugh at you—a million and a half of money is too serious a matter for mirth—but you are not about to establish a third link in your chain—you will not find any especial connexion between your pirates and a goat—pirates, you know, have nothing to do with goats; they appertain to the farming interest."

"But I have just said that the figure was *not* that of a goat."

"Well, a kid then—pretty much the same thing."

"Pretty much, but not altogether," said Legrand. "You may have heard of one *Captain* Kidd. I at once looked upon the figure of the animal as a kind of punning or hieroglyphical signature. I say signature; because its position upon the vellum suggested this idea. The death's-head at the corner diagonally opposite, had, in the same manner, the air of a stamp, or seal. But I was sorely put out by the absence of all else— of the body to my imagined instrument—of the text for my context."

"I presume you expected to find a letter between the stamp and the signature."

"Something of that kind. The fact is, I felt irresistibly impressed with a presentiment of some vast good fortune impending. I can scarcely say why. Perhaps, after all, it was rather a desire than an actual belief;—but do you know that Jupiter's silly words, about the bug being of solid gold, had a remarkable effect upon my fancy? And then the series of accidents and coincidents—these were so *very* extraordinary. Do you observe how mere an accident it was that these events should have occurred upon the *sole* day of all the year in which it has been, or may be sufficiently cool for fire, and that without the fire, or without the intervention of the dog at the precise moment in which he appeared, I should never have become aware of the death's-head, and so never the possessor of the treasure."

"But proceed—I am all impatience."

"Well; you have heard, of course, the many stories current—the thousand vague rumors afloat about money buried, somewhere upon the Atlantic coast, by Kidd and his associates. These rumors must have had some foundation in fact. And that the rumors have existed so long and so continuous, could have resulted, it appeared to me, only from the circumstance of the buried treasures still *remaining* entombed. Had Kidd concealed his plunder for a time, and afterward reclaimed it, the rumors would scarcely have reached us in their present unvarying form. You will observe that the stories told are all about money-seekers, not about money-finders. Had the pirate recovered his money, there the affair would have dropped. It seemed to me that some accident—say the loss of a memorandum indicating its locality—had deprived him of the means of recovering it, and that this accident had become known to his followers, who otherwise might never have heard that the treasure had been concealed at all, and who, busying themselves in vain, because unguided, attempts to regain it, had given first birth, and then universal currency, to the reports which are now so common. Have you ever heard of any important treasure being unearthed along the coast?"

"Never."

"But that Kidd's accumulations were immense, is well known. I took it for granted, therefore, that the earth still held them; and you will scarcely be surprised when I tell you that I felt a hope, nearly amounting to certainty, that the parchment so strangely found involved a lost record of the place of deposit."

"But how did you proceed?"

"I held the vellum again to the fire, after increasing the heat, but nothing appeared. I now thought it possible that the coating of dirt might have something to do with the failure: so I carefully rinsed the parchment by pouring warm water over it, and, having done this, I placed it in a tin pan, with the skull downward, and put the pan upon a furnace of lighted charcoal. In a few minutes, the pan having become thoroughly heated, I removed the slip, and, to my inexpressible joy, found it spotted, in several places, with what appeared to be figures arranged in lines. Again I placed it in the pan, and suffered it to remain another minute. Upon taking it off, the whole was just as you see it now."

Here Legrand, having re-heated the parchment, submitted it to my inspection. The following characters were rudely traced, in a red tint, between the death's head and the goat:

53‡‡†305))6*;4826)4‡.)4‡);806*;48†8¶60))
85;1‡(;:‡*8†83(88)5*†;46(;88*96*?;8)*‡
(;485);5*†2:*‡(;4956*2(5*−4)8¶8*;406928
5);)6†8)4‡‡;1(‡9;48081;8:8‡1;48†85;4)485†5
28806*81(‡9;48;(88;4(‡?34;48)4‡;161;:188;
‡?;

"But," said I, returning him the slip, "I am as much in the dark as ever. Were all the jewels of Golconda awaiting me upon my solution of this enigma, I am quite sure that I should be unable to earn them."

"And yet," said Legrand, "the solution is by no means so difficult as you might be led to imagine from the first hasty inspection of the characters. These characters, as any one might readily guess, form a cipher—that is to say, they convey a meaning; but then from what is known of Kidd, I could not suppose him capable of constructing any of the more abstruse cryptographs. I made up my mind, at once, that this was a simple species—such, however, as would appear, to the crude intellect of the sailor, absolutely insoluble without the key."

"And you really solved it?"

"Readily; I have solved others of an abstruseness ten thousand times greater. Circumstances, and a certain bias of mind, have led me to take interest in such riddles, and it may well be doubted whether human ingenuity can construct an enigma of the kind which human ingenuity may not, by proper application, resolve. In fact, having once established connected and legible characters, I scarcely gave a thought to the mere difficulty of developing their import.

"In the present case—indeed in all cases of secret writing—the first question regards the *language* of the cipher; for the principles of solution, so far, especially, as the more simple ciphers are concerned, depend upon, and are varied by, the genius of the particular idiom. In general, there is no alternative but experiment (directed by probabilities) of every tongue known to him who attempts the solution, until the true one be attained. But, with the cipher now before us all difficulty was removed by the signature. The pun upon the word 'Kidd' is appreciable in no other language than the English. But for this consideration I should have begun my attempts with the Spanish and French, as the tongues in which a secret of this kind would most naturally have been written by a pirate of the Spanish main. As it was, I assumed the cryptograph to be English.

"You observe there are no divisions between the words. Had there been divisions the task would have been comparatively easy. In such cases I should have commenced with a collation and analysis of the shorter words, and, had a word of a single letter occurred, as is most likely, (*a* or *I*, for example,) I should have considered the solution as assured. But, there being no division, my first step was to ascertain the predominant letters, as well as the least frequent. Counting all, I constructed a table thus:

Of the character 8 there are 33.

;	"	26.
4	"	19.
‡)	"	16.
★	"	13.
5	"	12.
6	"	11.
† 1	"	8.
0	"	6.

Of the character 9 2 there are 5.

: 3	"	4.
?	"	3.
¶	"	2.
—.	"	1.

"Now, in English, the letter which most frequently occurs is *e*. Afterward, the succession runs thus: *a o i d h n r s t u y c f g l m w b k p q x z*. *E* predominates so remarkably, that an individual sentence of any length is rarely seen, in which it is not the prevailing character.

"Here, then, we have, in the very beginning, the groundwork for something more than a mere guess. The general use which may be made of the table is obvious—but, in this particular cipher, we shall only very partially require its aid. As our predominant character is 8, we will commence by assuming it as the *e* of the natural alphabet. To verify the supposition, let us observe if the 8 be seen often in couples—for *e* is doubled with great frequency in English—in such words, for example, as 'meet,' 'fleet,' 'speed,' 'seen,' 'been,' 'agree,' &c. In the present instance we see it doubled no less than five times, although the cryptograph is brief.

"Let us assume 8, then, as *e*. Now, of all *words* in the language, 'the' is most usual; let us see, therefore, whether there are not repetitions of any three characters, in the same order of collocation, the last of them being 8. If we discover repetitions of such letters, so arranged, they will most probably represent the word 'the.' Upon inspection, we find no less than seven such arrangements, the characters being ;48. We may, therefore, assume that; represents *t*, 4 represents *h*, and 8 represents *e*—the last being now well confirmed. Thus a great step has been taken.

"But, having established a single word, we are enabled to establish a vastly important point; that is to say, several commencements and terminations of other words. Let us refer, for example, to the last instance but one, in which the combination ;48 occurs—not far from the end of the cipher. We know that the ; immediately ensuing is the commencement of a word, and, of the six characters succeeding this 'the,' we are cognizant of no less than five. Let us set these characters down, thus, by the letters we know them to represent, leaving a space for the unknown—

t eeth

"Here we are enabled, at once, to discard the '*th*,' as forming no portion of the word commencing with the first *t*; since, by experiment of the entire alphabet for a letter adapted to the vacancy, we perceive that no word can be formed of which this *th* can be a part. We are thus narrowed into

t ee

and, going through the alphabet, if necessary, as before, we arrive at the word 'tree,' as the sole possible reading. We thus gain another letter, *r*, represented by (, with the words 'the tree' in juxtaposition.

"Looking beyond these words, for a short distance, we again see the combination ;48, and employ it by way of *termination* to what immediately precedes. We have thus this arrangement:

the tree ;4(‡?34 the,

or, substituting the natural letters, where known, it reads thus:

the tree thr‡?3h the.

"Now, if, in place of the unknown characters, we leave blank spaces, or substitute dots, we read thus:

the tree thr . . . h the,

when the word '*through*' makes itself evident at once. But this discovery gives us three new letters, *o, u,* and *g,* represented by ‡, ?, and 3.

"Looking now, narrowly, through the cipher for combinations of known characters, we find, not very far from the beginning, this arrangement,

83(88, or egree,

which plainly, is the conclusion of the word 'degree,' and gives us another letter, *d,* represented by †.

"Four letters beyond the word 'degree,' we perceive the combination

;46(;88.

"Translating the known characters, and representing the unknown by dots, as before, we read thus:

th.rtee

an arrangement immediately suggestive of the word 'thirteen,' and again furnishing us with two new characters, *i* and *n,* represented by 6 and ⋆.

"Referring, now, to the beginning of the cryptograph, we find the combination,

53‡‡†.

"Translating as before, we obtain

.good,

which assures us that the first letter is A, and that the first two words are 'A good.'

"It is now time that we arrange our key, as far as discovered, in a tabular form, to avoid confusion. It will stand thus:

5	represents	a
†	"	d
8	"	e
3	"	g
4	"	h
6	"	i
★	"	n
‡	"	o
(	"	r
;	"	t

"We have therefore, no less than ten of the most important letters represented, and it will be unnecessary to proceed with the details of the solution. I have said enough to convince you that ciphers of this nature are readily soluble, and to give you some insight into the *rationale* of their development. But be assured that the specimen before us appertains to the very simplest species of cryptograph. It now only remains to give you the full translation of the characters upon the parchment, as unriddled. Here it is:

'A good glass in the bishop's hostel in the devil's seat forty-one degrees and thirteen minutes northeast and by north main branch seventh limb east side shoot from the left eye of the death's-head a bee line from the tree through the shot fifty feet out.' "

"But," said I, "the enigma seems still in as bad condition as ever. How is it possible to extort a meaning from all this jargon about 'devil's seats,' 'death's-heads,' and 'bishop's hotels?' "

"I confess," replied Legrand, "that the matter still wears a serious aspect, when regarded with a casual glance. My first endeavor was to

divide the sentence into the natural division intended by the cryp-
tographist."

"You mean, to punctuate it?"

"Something of that kind."

"But how was it possible to effect this?"

I reflected that it had been a *point* with the writer to run his
words together without division, so as to increase the difficulty of
solution. Now, a not over-acute man, in pursuing such an object,
would be nearly certain to overdo the matter. When, in the course of
his composition, he arrived at a break in his subject which would naturally require a pause, or a point, he would be exceedingly apt to run
his characters, at this place, more than usually close together. If you
will observe the MS., in the present instance, you will easily detect five
such cases of unusual crowding. Acting upon this hint, I made the
division thus:

*"A good glass in the Bishop's hostel in the Devil's seat—forty-one degrees and
thirteen minutes—northeast and by north—main branch seventh limb east
side—shoot from the left eye of the death's-head—a bee-line from the tree
through the shot fifty feet out."*

"Even this division," said I, "leaves me still in the dark."

"It left me also in the dark," replied Legrand, "for a few days;
during which I made diligent inquiry in the neighborhood of Sullivan's
Island, for any building which went by the name of the 'Bishop's
Hotel'; for, of course, I dropped the obsolete word 'hostel.' Gaining no
information on the subject, I was on the point of extending my sphere
of search, and proceeding in a more systematic manner, when, one
morning, it entered into my head, quite suddenly, that this 'Bishop's
Hostel' might have some reference to an old family, of the name of
Bessop, which, time out of mind, had held possession of an ancient
manor-house, about four miles to the northward of the Island. I accordingly went over to the plantation, and re-instituted my inquiries among
the older negroes of the place. At length one of the most aged of the
women said that she had heard of such a place as *Bessop's Castle*, and

thought that she could guide me to it, but that it was not a castle, nor a tavern, but a high rock.

"I offered to pay her well for her trouble, and, after some demur, she consented to accompany me to the spot. We found it without much difficulty, when, dismissing her, I proceeded to examine the place. The 'castle' consisted of an irregular assemblage of cliffs and rocks—one of the latter being quite remarkable for its height as well as for its insulated and artificial appearance. I clambered to its apex, and then felt much at a loss as to what should be next done.

"While I was busied in reflection, my eyes fell upon a narrow ledge in the eastern face of the rock, perhaps a yard below the summit upon which I stood. This ledge projected about eighteen inches, and was not more than a foot wide, while a niche in the cliff just above it gave it a rude resemblance to one of the hollow-backed chairs used by our ancestors. I made no doubt that here was the 'devil's-seat' alluded to in the MS., and now I seemed to grasp the full secret of the riddle.

"The 'good glass,' I knew, could have reference to nothing but a telescope; for the word 'glass' is rarely employed in any other sense by seamen. Now here, I at once saw, was a telescope to be used, and a definite point of view, *admitting no variation*, from which to use it. Nor did I hesitate to believe that the phrases 'forty-one degrees and thirteen minutes,' and 'northeast and by north,' were intended as directions for the levelling of the glass. Greatly excited by these discoveries, I hurried home, procured a telescope, and returned to the rock.

"I let myself down to the ledge, and found that it was impossible to retain a seat upon it except in one particular position. This fact confirmed my preconceived idea. I proceeded to use the glass. Of course, the 'forty-one degrees and thirteen minutes' could allude to nothing but elevation above the visible horizon, since the horizontal direction was clearly indicated by the words, 'northeast and by north.' This latter direction I at once established by means of a pocket-compass; then, pointing the glass as nearly at an angle of forty-one degrees of elevation as I could do it by guess, I moved it cautiously up or down, until my attention was arrested by a circular rift or opening in the foliage of a large tree that overtopped its fellows in the distance. In the centre of this rift I perceived a white spot, but could not, at first, distinguish what it was. Adjusting the focus of the telescope, I again looked, and now made it out to be a human skull.

"Upon this discovery I was so sanguine as to consider the enigma solved; for the phrase 'main branch, seventh limb, east side,' could refer only to the position of the skull upon the tree, while 'shoot from the left eye of the death's-head' admitted, also, of but one interpretation, in regard to a search for buried treasure. I perceived that the design was to drop a bullet from the left eye of the skull, and that a bee-line, or, in other words, a straight line, drawn from the nearest point of the trunk through 'the shot' (or the spot where the bullet fell), and thence extended to a distance of fifty feet, would indicate a definite point—and beneath this point I thought it at least *possible* that a deposit of value lay concealed."

"All this," I said, "is exceedingly clear, and, although ingenious, still simple and explicit. When you left the Bishop's Hotel, what then?"

"Why, having carefuly taken the bearings of the tree, I turned homeward. The instant that I left 'the devil's-seat,' however, the circular rift vanished; nor could I get a glimpse of it afterward, turn as I would. What seems to me the chief ingenuity in this whole business, is the fact (for repeated experiment has convinced me it *is* a fact) that the circular opening in question is visible from no other attainable point of view than that afforded by the narrow ledge upon the face of the rock.

"In this expedition to the 'Bishop's Hotel' I had been attended by Jupiter, who had, no doubt, observed, for some weeks past, the abstraction of my demeanor, and took especial care not to leave me alone. But, on the next day, getting up very early, I contrived to give him the slip, and went into the hills in search of the tree. After much toil I found it. When I came home at night my valet proposed to give me a flogging. With the rest of the adventure I believe you are as well acquainted as myself."

"I suppose," said I, "you missed the spot, in the first attempt at digging, through Jupiter's stupidity in letting the bug fall through the right instead of through the left eye of the skull."

"Precisely. This mistake made a difference of about two inches and a half in the 'shot'—that is to say, in the position of the peg nearest the tree; and had the treasure been *beneath* the 'shot,' the error would have been of little moment; but 'the shot,' together with the nearest point of the tree, were merely two points for the establishment of a line of direction; of course the error, however trivial in the beginning, increased as we proceeded with the line, and by the time we had gone fifty feet threw us quite off the scent. But for my deep-seated impressions that treasure was here somewhere actually buried, we might have had all our labor in vain."

"But your grandiloquence, and your conduct in swinging the beetle—how excessively odd! I was sure you were mad. And why did you insist upon letting fall the bug, instead of a bullet, from the skull?"

"Why, to be frank, I felt somewhat annoyed by your evident suspicions touching my sanity, and so resolved to punish you quietly, in my own way, by a little bit of sober mystification. For this reason I swung the beetle, and for this reason I let it fall from the tree. An observation of yours about its great weight suggested the latter idea."

"Yes, I perceive; and now there is only one point which puzzles me. What are we to make of the skeletons found in the hole?"

"That is a question I am no more able to answer than yourself. There seems, however, only one plausible way of accounting for them— and yet it is dreadful to believe in such atrocity as my suggestion would imply. It is clear that Kidd—if Kidd indeed secreted this treasure, which I doubt not—it is clear that he must have had assistance in the labor. But this labor concluded, he may have thought it expedient to remove all participants in his secret. Perhaps a couple of blows with a mattock were sufficient, while his coadjutors were busy in the pit; perhaps it required a dozen—who shall tell?"

The Discovery of Nineveh

BY AUSTEN HENRY LAYARD

By modern standards, Austen Henry Layard (1818–1894) could scarcely be described as an archaeologist, since at the time he worked—the middle of nineteenth century—the science was little better than treasure hunting. Yet the fact remains that it was through his efforts that the great Assyrian capital of Nineveh was brought to light, and an important ancient culture lifted out of obscurity into history. Compared to such freebooters as Heinrich Schliemann, excavator of Troy and Mycenae, Layard was a careful and scholarly worker, and his book *Discoveries in the Ruins of Nineveh and Babylon* (1853) laid a foundation for modern Middle Eastern studies. But he was also an enthusiast, intent on unearthing the wonderful things he knew must be hidden under the ground. The following extract, taken from his popular account of his findings (*Nineveh and Its Remains*, 1867), shows him in an untypically excited—and reflective—mood.

★   ★   ★   ★   ★

n the morning following these discoveries, I had ridden to the encampment of Sheikh Abd-ur-rahman, and was returning to the mound, when I saw two Arabs of his tribe coming toward me and urging their mares to the top of their speed. On reaching me they stopped. "Hasten, O Bey," exclaimed one of them—"hasten to the diggers, for they have found Nimrod himself. Wallah! it is wonderful but it is true! we have seen him with our eyes. There is no God but God;" and both joining in this pious exclamation, they galloped off, without further words, in the direction of their tents.

On reaching the ruins I descended into the newly opened trench, and found the workmen, who had already seen me, as I approached, standing near a heap of baskets and cloaks. While Awad advanced and asked for a present to celebrate the occasion, the Arabs withdrew the screen they had hastily constructed, and disclosed an enormous human head sculptured in full out of the alabaster of the country. They had uncovered the upper part of a figure, the remainder of which was still buried in the earth. I saw at once that the head must belong to a winged lion or bull, similar to those of Khorsabad and Persepolis. It was in admirable preservation. The expression was calm, yet majestic, and the outline of the features showed a freedom and knowledge of art, scarcely to be looked for in works of so remote a period. The cap had three horns, and, unlike that of the human-headed bulls hitherto found in Assyria, was rounded and without ornament at the top.

I was not surprised that the Arabs had been amazed and terrified at this apparition. It required no stretch of imagination to conjure up the most strange fancies. This gigantic head, blanched with age, thus rising from the bowels of the earth, might well have belonged to one of those fearful beings which are described in the traditions of the country as appearing to mortals, slowly ascending from the regions below. One of the workmen, on catching the first glimpse of the monster, had thrown down his basket and had run off toward Mosul as fast as his legs could carry him. I learned this with regret, as I anticipated the consequences.

While I was superintending the removal of the earth, which still clung to the sculpture, and giving directions for the continuation of the work, the noise of horsemen was heard, and presently Abd-ur-rahman, followed by half his tribe, appeared on the edge of the trench. As soon as the two Arabs I had met had reached their tents, and published the wonders they had seen, every one mounted his mare and rode to the mound to satisfy himself of the truth of these inconceivable reports. When they beheld the head they all cried together, "There is no God but God, and Mohammed is his Prophet!" It was some time before the Sheikh could be prevailed upon to descend into the pit, and convince himself that the image he saw was of stone. "This is not the work of men's hands," exclaimed he, "but of those infidel giants of whom the Prophet, peace be with him! has said, that they were higher than the tallest date tree; this is one of the idols which Noah, peace be with him! cursed before the flood." In this opinion, the result of a careful examination, all the bystanders concurred.

I now ordered a trench to be dug due south from the head, in the expectation of finding a corresponding figure, and before night-fall reached the object of my search about twelve feet distant. Engaging two or three men to sleep near the sculptures, I returned to the village, and celebrated the day's discovery by a slaughter of sheep, of which all the Arabs near partook. As some wandering musicians chanced to be at Selamiyah, I sent for them, and dances were kept up during the greater part of the night. On the following morning Arabs from the other side of the Tigris, and the inhabitants of the surrounding villages, congregated on the mound. Even the women could not repress their curiosity, and came in crowds, with their children, from afar. My Cawass was stationed during the day in the trench, into which I would not allow the multitude to descend.

As I had expected, the report of the discovery of the gigantic head, carried by the terrified Arab to Mosul, had thrown the town into commotion. He had scarcely checked his speed before reaching the bridge. Entering breathless into the bazaars, he announced to every one he met that Nimrod had appeared. The news soon got to the ears of the Cadi, who called the Mufti and the Ulema together, to consult upon this unexpected occurrence. Their deliberations ended in a procession to the Governor, and a formal protest, on the part of the Mussulmans of the town, against proceedings so directly contrary to the laws of the

Koran. The Cadi had no distinct idea whether the very bones of the mighty hunter had been uncovered, or only his image; nor did Ismail Pasha very clearly remember whether Nimrod was a true-believing prophet, or an infidel. I consequently received a somewhat unintelligible message from his Excellency, to the effect that the remains should be treated with respect, and be by no means further disturbed; that he wished the excavations to be stopped at once, and desired to confer with me on the subject.

I rode to Mosul at once and called upon him accordingly. I had some difficulty in making him understand the nature of my discovery. At last he was persuaded that I had only discovered part of an ancient figure in stone, and that neither the remains of Nimrod nor of any other personage mentioned in the Koran had been disturbed. However, as he requested me to discontinue my operations until the excitement in the town had somewhat subsided, I returned to Nimrod and dismissed the workmen, retaining only two men to dig leisurely along the walls without giving cause for further interference. I ascertained by the end of March the existence of a second pair of winged human-headed lions, differing from those previously discovered in form, the human shape being continued to the waist, and being furnished with human arms, as well as with the legs of the lion. In one hand each figure carried a goat or stag, and in the other, which hung down by the side, a branch with three flowers. They formed a northern entrance into the hall or chamber, of which the human-headed lions previously described formed the western portal. I completely uncovered the latter, and found them to be entire. They were about twelve feet high and twelve feet long. The body and limbs were admirably portrayed; the muscles and bones, although strongly developed, to denote power and strength, showed at the same time a correct knowledge of the anatomy and form of the animal. Expanded wings sprung from the shoulders and spread over the back; a knotted girdle, ending in tassels, encircled the loins. As these sculptures were placed against walls forming a doorway or entrance, and thus only one side of the body was to be seen, they were carved partly in full and partly in relief. The head and fore-part, facing the chamber, were in full;

the rest of the figure was sculptured in high relief; and that the spectator might have both a perfect front and side view, it was furnished with five legs, four on the side forming the entrance, and an additional leg in front. The slab was covered, in all parts not occupied by the image, with inscriptions in the cuneiform character. Remains of color could still be traced in the eyes—the pupils being painted black, and the rest filled up with a white pigment; but on no other parts of the sculpture. These magnificent specimens of Assyrian art were in perfect preservation, even to the most minute and delicate details of the wings and ornaments.

I used to contemplate for hours these mysterious emblems, and muse over their intent and history. What more noble forms could have ushered the people into the temple of their gods? What more sublime images could have been borrowed from nature, by men who sought, unaided by the light of revealed religion, to embody their conception of the wisdom and power of a Supreme Being? They could find no better type of intellect and knowledge than the head of the man; of strength, than the body of the lion; of ubiquity, than the wings of the bird. These winged human-headed lions were not idle creations, the offspring of mere fancy; their meaning was written upon them. They had awed and instructed races which flourished 3000 years ago. Through the portals which they guarded, kings, priests, and warriors had borne sacrifices to their altars, long before the wisdom of the East had penetrated to Greece; and had furnished its mythology with symbols recognized of old by the Assyrian votaries. They may have been buried, and their existence may have been unknown, before the foundation of the eternal city. For twenty-five centuries they had been hidden from the eye of man, and they now stood forth once more in their ancient majesty. But how changed was the scene around them! The luxury and civilization of a mighty nation had given place to the wretchedness and ignorance of a few half-barbarous tribes. The wealth of temples, and the riches of great cities, had been succeeded by ruins and shapeless heaps of earth. Above the spacious hall in which they stood, the plow had passed and the corn now waved. Egypt has monuments no less ancient and no less wonderful; but they have stood forth for ages to testify her early power and renown; while those before me had but now appeared to bear witness, in the words of the prophet, that once "the Assyrian was a cedar in Lebanon with fair branches and with a shadowing shroud of an high stature; and his top was among the thick boughs. . . . his height was exalted above all the trees of the field, and his boughs were multiplied, and his branches became long, because of the multitude of waters when he shot forth. All the fowls of heaven made their nests in his boughs, and under his branches did all the beasts of the fields bring forth their young, and under his shadow dwelt all great nations;" for now is "Nineveh a desolation and dry like a wilderness, and flocks lie down in the midst of her: all the beasts of the nations, both the cormorant and bittern, lodge in the upper lintels of it; their voice sings in the windows; and desolation is in the thresholds."

Benedict Mol and the
Schatz of Compostella

BY GEORGE BORROW

Treasure hunting is generally a serious, even gloomy subject, so it is pleasant to be able to include something a bit more amusing. The story of Benedict Mol and the *Schatz* (treasure) of Santiago de Compostela occurs in George Borrow's *The Bible in Spain* (1842), and is in fact scattered in pieces throughout the book. Borrow (1803–1881), a fairly incredible character in his own right, was in Spain on commission from the British and Foreign Bible Society of London to distribute New Testaments, the ultimate aim being to convert Catholics to Protestantism. Traveling from one end of the country to the other, getting robbed and jailed and otherwise knocked about, Borrow was singularly unsuccessful in his stated enterprise. But he had a knack for meeting extraordinary people, and for writing brilliantly lively accounts of his—and their— doings. The adventures of Benedict Mol, here assembled into one narrative, are a case in point.

★　★　★　★　★

Upon my asking him who he was, the following conversation ensued between us,—

"I am a Swiss of Lucerne, Benedict Mol by name, once a soldier in the Walloon Guard, and now a soap-boiler, *para servir usted*."

89

"You speak the language of Spain very imperfectly," said I; "how long have you been in the country?"

"Forty-five years," replied Benedict; "but when the Guard was broken up, I went to Minorca, where I lost the Spanish language without acquiring the Catalan."

"You have been a soldier of the king of Spain," said I; "how did you like the service?"

"Not so well, but that I should have been glad to leave it forty years ago; the pay was bad, and the treatment worse. I will now speak Swiss to you, for, if I am not much mistaken, you are a German man, and understand the speech of Lucerne: I should soon have deserted from the service of Spain, as I did from that of the Pope, whose soldier I was in my early youth before I came here; but I had married a woman of Minorca, by whom I had two children; it was this that detained me in these parts so long; before, however, I left Minorca, my wife died, and as for my children, one went east, the other west, and I know not what became of them; I intend shortly to return to Lucerne, and live there like a duke."

"Have you, then, realised a large capital in Spain?" said I, glancing at his hat and the rest of his apparel.

"Not a cuart, not a cuart; these two wash-balls are all that I possess."

"Perhaps you are the son of good parents, and have lands and money in your own country wherewith to support yourself."

"Not a heller, not a heller; my father was hangman of Lucerne, and when he died, his body was seized to pay his debts."

"Then doubtless," said I, "you intend to ply your trade of soap-boiling at Lucerne: you are quite right, my friend, I know of no occupation more honourable or useful."

"I have no thoughts of plying my trade at Lucerne," replied Benedict; "and now, as I see you are a German man, Lieber Herr, and as I like your countenance and your manner of speaking, I will tell you in confidence that I know very little of my trade, and have already been turned out of several fabriques as an evil workman; the two wash-balls that I carry in my pocket are not of my own making. *In kurtzen,* I know little more of soap-boiling than I do of tailoring, horse-farriery, or shoe-making, all of which I have practised."

"Then I know not how you can hope to live like a hertzog in your native canton, unless you expect that the men of Lucerne, in consideration of your services to the Pope and to the king of Spain, will maintain you in splendour at the public expense."

"Lieber Herr," said Benedict, "the men of Lucerne are by no means fond of maintaining the soldiers of the Pope and the king of Spain at their own expense; many of the Guard who have returned thither beg their bread in the streets, but when I go, it shall be in a coach drawn by six mules with a treasure, a mighty schatz which lies in the church of St. James of Compostella, in Galicia."

"I hope you do not intend to rob the church," said I; "if you do, however, I believe you will be disappointed. Mendizabal and the liberals have been beforehand with you. I am informed that at present no other treasure is to be found in the cathedrals of Spain than a few paltry ornaments and plated utensils."

"My good German Herr," said Benedict, "it is no church schatz, and no person living, save myself, knows of its existence: nearly thirty years ago, amongst the sick soldiers who were brought to Madrid, was one of my comrades of the Walloon Guard, who had accompanied the French to Portugal; he was very sick and shortly died. Before, however, he breathed his last, he sent for me, and upon his death-bed told me that himself and two other soldiers, both of whom had since been killed, had buried in a certain church in Compostella a great booty which they had made in Portugal; it consisted of gold moidores and of a packet of huge diamonds from the Brazils; the whole was contained in a large copper kettle. I listened with greedy ears, and from that moment, I may say, I have known no rest, neither by day nor night, thinking of the schatz. It is very easy to find, for the dying man was so exact in his description of the place where it lies, that were I once at Compostella, I should have no difficulty in putting my hand upon it; several times I have been on the point of setting out on the journey, but something has always happened to stop me. When my wife died, I left Minorca with a determination to go to St. James, but on reaching Madrid, I fell into the hands of a Basque woman, who persuaded me to live with her, which I have done for several years; she is a great hax [witch], and says that if I desert her she will breathe a spell which shall cling to me for ever. *Dem Got sey dank,*—she is now in the hospital, and daily expected to die. This is my history, Lieber Herr."

★ ★ ★ ★ ★

I was walking late one night alone in the Alameda of St. James, considering in what direction I should next bend my course, for I had been already ten days in this place; the moon was shining gloriously, and illumined every object around to a considerable distance. The Alameda was quite deserted; everybody, with the exception of myself, having for some time retired. I sat down on a bench and continued my reflections, which were suddenly interrupted by a heavy stumping sound. Turning my eyes in the direction from which it proceeded, I perceived what at first appeared a shapeless bulk slowly advancing; nearer and nearer it drew, and I could now distinguish the outline of a man dressed in coarse brown garments, a kind of Andalusian hat, and using as a staff the long peeled branch of a tree. He had now arrived opposite the bench where I was seated, when, stopping, he took off his hat and demanded charity in uncouth tones and in a strange jargon, which had some resemblance to the Catalan. The moon shone on grey locks and on a ruddy weather-beaten countenance which I at once recognized. "Benedict Mol," said I, "is it possible that I see you at Compostella?"

"Och, mein Gott, es ist der Herr!" replied Benedict. "Och, what good fortune, that the Herr is the first person I meet at Compostella."

Myself.—I can scarcely believe my eyes. Do you mean to say that you have just arrived at this place?

Benedict.—Ow yes, I am this moment arrived. I have walked all the long way from Madrid.

Myself.—What motive could possibly bring you such a distance?

Benedict.—Ow, I am come for the schatz—the treasure. I told you at Madrid that I was coming; and now I have met you here, I have no doubt that I shall find it, the schatz.

Myself.—In what manner did you support yourself by the way?

Benedict.—Ow, I begged, I bettled, and so contrived to pick up some cuartos; and when I reached Toro, I worked at my trade of soap-making for a time, till the people said I knew nothing about it, and drove me out of the town. So I went on and begged and bettled till I arrived at Orense, which is in this country of Galicia. Ow, I do not like this country of Galicia at all.

Myself.—Why not?

Benedict.—Why! because here they all beg and bettle, and have scarce anything for themselves, much less for me whom they know to be a foreign man. Oh, the misery of Galicia. When I arrive at night at one of their pigsties, which they call posadas, and ask for bread to eat in the name of God, and straw to lie down in, they curse me, and say there is neither bread nor straw in Galicia; and sure enough, since I have been here I have seen neither, only something they call broa, and a kind of reedy rubbish with which they litter the horses: all my bones are sore since I entered Galicia.

Myself.—And yet you have come to this country, which you call so miserable, in search of treasure?

Benedict.—Ow yaw, but the schatz is buried; it is not above ground; there is no money above ground in Galicia. I must dig it up; and when I have dug it up I will purchase a coach with six mules, and ride out of Galicia to Lucerne; and if the Herr pleases to go with me, he shall be welcome to go with me and the schatz.

Myself.—I am afraid you have come on a desperate errand. What do you propose to do? Have you any money?

Benedict.—Not a cuart; but I do not care now I have arrived at St. James. The schatz is nigh; and I have, moreover, seen you, which is a good sign; it tells me that the schatz is still here. I shall go to the best posada in the place, and live like a duke till I have the opportunity of digging up the schatz, when I will pay all scores.

"Do nothing of the kind," I replied; "find out some place in which to sleep, and endeavour to seek some employment. In the meantime, here is a trifle with which to support yourself; but as for the treasure which you have come to seek, I believe it only exists in your own imagination." I gave him a dollar and departed.

Two or three days after this, as we [Borrow and a bookseller friend] were seated in my apartment in the posada, engaged in conversation, the door was opened by Antonio, who, with a smile on his countenance, said that there was a foreign *gentleman* below who desired to speak with me. "Show him up," I replied; whereupon almost instantly appeared Benedict Mol.

"This is a most extraordinary person," said I to the bookseller. "You Galicians, in general, leave your country in quest of money; he, on the contrary, is come hither to find some."

Rey Romero.—And he is right. Galicia is by nature the richest province in Spain, but the inhabitants are very stupid, and know not how to turn the blessings which surround them to any account; but as a proof of what may be made out of Galicia, see how rich the Catalans become who have settled down here and formed establishments. There are riches all around us, upon the earth and in the earth.

Benedict.—Ow yaw, in the earth, that is what I say. There is much more treasure below the earth than above it.

Myself.—Since I last saw you, have you discovered the place in which you say the treasure is deposited?

Benedict.—Oh yes, I know all about it now. It is buried 'neath the sacristy in the church of San Roque.

Myself.—How have you been able to make that discovery?

Benedict.—I will tell you: the day after my arrival I walked about all the city in quest of the church, but could find none which at all answered to the signs which my comrade who died in the hospital gave me. I entered several and looked about, but all in vain; I could not find the place which I had in my mind's eye. At last the people with whom I lodge, and to whom I told my business, advised me to send for a meiga.

Myself.—A meiga! What is that?

Benedict.—Ow! a haxweib, a witch; the Gallegos call them so in their jargon, of which I can scarcely understand a word. So I consented, and they sent for the meiga. Och! what a weib is that meiga! I never saw such a woman; she is as large as myself, and has a face as round and red as the sun. She asked me a great many questions in her Gallegan, and when I had told her all she wanted to know, she pulled out a pack of cards and laid them on the table in a particular manner, and then she said that the treasure was in the church of San Roque; and sure enough, when I went to that church, it answered in every respect to the signs of my comrade who died in the hospital. Oh, she is a powerful hax, that meiga; she is well known in the neighbourhood, and has done much harm to the cattle. I gave her half the dollar I had from you for her trouble.

Myself.—Then you acted like a simpleton; she has grossly deceived you. But even suppose that the treasure is really deposited in the church you mention, it is not probable that you will be permitted to remove the floor of the sacristy to search for it.

Benedict.—Ow, the matter is already well advanced. Yesterday I went to one of the canons to confess myself and to receive absolution and benediction; not that I regard these things much, but I thought this would be the best means of broaching the matter, so I confessed myself, and then I spoke of my travels to the canon, and at last I told him of the treasure, and proposed that if he assisted me we should share it between us. Ow, I wish you had seen him; he entered at once into the affair, and said that it would turn out a very profitable speculation; and he shook me by the hand, and said that I was an honest Swiss and a good Catholic. And then I proposed that he should take me into his house and keep me there till we had an opportunity of digging up the treasure together. This he refused to do.

Rey Romero.—Of that I have no doubt: trust one of our canons for not committing himself so far until he sees very good reason. These tales of treasure are at present rather too stale: we have heard of them ever since the time of the Moors.

Benedict.—He advised me to go to the Captain-General and obtain permission to make excavations, in which case he promised to assist me to the utmost of his power.

Thereupon the Swiss departed, and I neither saw nor heard anything farther of him during the time that I continued at St. James.

★ ★ ★ ★ ★

I had just breakfasted, and was about to sit down to my journal, when the door was flung open, and in bounded Antonio.

"Mon maître," said he, quite breathless, "who do you think has arrived?"

"The pretender, I suppose," said I, in some trepidation; "if so, we are prisoners."

"Bah, bah!" said Antonio, "it is not the pretender, but one worth twenty of him; it is the Swiss of St. James."

"Benedict Mol, the Swiss!" said I. "What! has he found the treasure? But how did he come? How is he dressed?"

"Mon maître," said Antonio, "he came on foot, if we may judge by his shoes, through which his toes are sticking; and as for his dress, he is in most villainous apparel."

"There must be some mystery in this," said I; "where is he at present?"

"Below, mon maître," replied Antonio; "he came in quest of us. But I no sooner saw him, than I hurried away to let you know."

In a few minutes Benedict Mol found his way upstairs; he was, as Antonio had remarked, in most villainous apparel, and nearly barefooted; his old Andalusian hat was dripping with rain.

"Och, lieber herr," said Benedict, "how rejoiced I am to see you again. Oh, the sight of your countenance almost repays me for all the miseries I have undergone since I parted with you at St. James."

Myself.—I can scarcely believe that I really see you here at Oviedo. What motive can have induced you to come to such an out-of-the-way place from such an immense distance?

Benedict.—Lieber herr, I will sit down and tell you all that has befallen me. Some few days after I saw you last, the canonigo persuaded me to go to the captain-general to apply for permission to disinter the schatz, and also to crave assistance. So I saw the captain-general, who at first received me very kindly, asked me several questions, and told me to come again. So I continued visiting him till he would see me no longer, and do what I might I could not obtain a glance of him. The canon now became impatient, more especially as he had given me a few pesetas out of the charities of the church. He frequently called me a bribon and impostor. At last, one morning I went to him, and said that I proposed to return to Madrid, in order to lay the matter before the government, and requested that he would give me a certificate to the effect that I had performed a pilgrimage to St. James, which I imagined would be of assistance to me upon the way, as it would enable me to beg with some colour of authority. He no sooner heard this request, than, without saying a word or allowing me a moment to put myself on my defence, he sprang upon me like a tiger, grasping my throat so hard that I thought he would have strangled me. I am a Swiss, however, and a man of Lucerne, and when I had recovered myself a little, I had no difficulty in flinging him off; I then threatened him with my staff and went away. He followed me to the gate with the most horrid curses, saying that if I presumed to return again, he would have me thrown at once into prison as a thief and a heretic. So I went in quest of yourself, lieber herr, but they told me that you were departed for Coruña, I then set out for Coruña after you.

Myself.—And what befel you on the road?

Benedict.—I will tell you: about halfway between St. James and Coruña, as I was walking along thinking of the schatz, I heard a loud galloping, and looking around me I saw two men on horseback coming across the field with the swiftness of the wind, and making directly for me. Lieber Gott, said I, these are thieves, these are factious; and so they were. They came up to me in a moment and bade me stand, so I flung down my staff, took off my hat, and saluted them. "Good-day, caballeros," said I to them. "Good-day, countryman," said they to me, and then we stood staring at each other for more than a minute. Lieber himmel, I never saw such robbers; so finely dressed, so well armed, and mounted so bravely on two fiery little hakkas, that looked as if they could have taken wing and flown up into the clouds! So we continued staring at each other, till at last one asked me who I was, whence I came, and where I was going. "Gentlemen," said I, "I am a Swiss, I have been to St. James to perform a religious vow, and am now returning to my own country." I said not a word about the treasure, for I was afraid that they would have shot me at once, conceiving that I carried part of it about me. "Have you any money?" they demanded. "Gentlemen," I replied, "you see how I travel on foot, with my shoes torn to pieces; I should not do so if I had money. I will not deceive you, however, I have a peseta and a few cuartos," and there-upon I took out what I had and offered it to them. "Fellow," said they, "we are caballeros of Galicia, and do not take pesetas, much less cuartos. Of what opinion are you? Are you for the queen?" "No, gentlemen," said I, "I am not for the queen, but, at the same time, allow me to tell you that I am not for the king either; I know nothing about the matter; I am a Swiss, and fight neither for nor against anybody unless I am paid." This made them laugh, and then they questioned me about St. James, and the troops there, and the captain-general; and not to disoblige them, I told them all I knew and much more. Then one of them, who looked the fiercest and most determined, took his trombone in his hand, and pointing it at me, said, "Had you been a Spaniard, we would have blown your head to shivers, for we should have thought you a spy, but we see you are a foreigner, and believe what you have said; take, therefore, this peseta and go your way, but beware that you tell nobody anything about us, for if you do, carra-cho!" He then discharged his trombone just over my head, so that for a moment I thought myself shot, and then with an awful shout they both galloped away, their horses leaping over the barrancos as if possessed with many devils.

Myself.—And what happened to you on your arrival at Coruña?

Benedict.—When I arrived at Coruña, I inquired after yourself, lieber herr, and they informed me that, only the day before my arrival, you had departed for Oviedo; and when I heard that, my heart died within me, for I was now at the far end of Galicia, without a friend to help me. For a day or two I knew not what to do; at last I determined to make for the frontier of France, passing through Oviedo in the way, where I hoped to see you and ask counsel of you. So I begged and bettled among the Germans of Coruña. I, however, got very little from them, only a few cuarts, less than the thieves had given me on the road from St. James, and with these I departed for the Asturias by the way of Mondonedo. Och, what a town is that, full of canons, priests, and pfaffen, all of them more Carlist than Carlos himself.

One day I went to the bishop's palace and spoke to him, telling him I was a pilgrim from St. James, and requesting assistance. He told me, however, that he could not relieve me, and as for my being a pilgrim from St. James, he was glad of it, and hoped that it would be of service to my soul. So I left Mondonedo, and got amongst the wild mountains, begging and bettling at the door of every choza that I passed, telling all I saw that I was a pilgrim from St. James, and showing my passport in proof that I had been there. Lieber herr, no person gave me a cuart, nor even a piece of broa, and both Gallegans and Asturians laughed at St. James, and told me that his name was no longer a passport in Spain. I should have starved if I had not sometimes plucked an ear or two out of the maize fields; I likewise gathered grapes from the parras and berries from the brambles, and in this manner I subsisted till I arrived at the bellotas, where I slaughtered a stray kid, which I met, and devoured part of the flesh raw, so great was my hunger. It made me, however, very ill, and for two days I lay in a barranco half dead and unable to help myself; it was a mercy that I was not devoured by the wolves. I then struck across the country for Oviedo; how I reached it I do not know; I was like one walking in a dream. Last night I slept in an empty hogsty about two leagues from here, and ere I left it, I fell down on my knees and prayed to God that I might find you, lieber herr, for you were my last hope.

Myself.—And what do you propose to do at present?

Benedict.—What can I say, lieber herr? I know not what to do. I will be guided in everything by your counsel.

Myself.—I shall remain at Oviedo a few days longer, during which time you can lodge at this posada, and endeavour to recover from the fatigue of your disastrous journeys; perhaps before I depart, we may hit on some plan to extricate you from your present difficulties.

"A strange man is this Benedict," said Antonio to me next

morning, as, accompanied by a guide, we sallied forth from Oviedo; "a strange man, mon maître, is this same Benedict. A strange life has he led, and a strange death he will die,—it is written on his countenance. That he will leave Spain I do not believe, or if he leave it, it will be only to return, for he is bewitched about this treasure. Last night he sent for a sorcière, whom he consulted in my presence; and she told him that he was doomed to possess it, but that first of all he must cross water. She cautioned him likewise against an enemy, which he supposes must be the canon of St. James. I have often heard people speak of the avidity of the Swiss for money, and here is a proof of it. I would not undergo what Benedict has suffered in these last journeys of his, to possess all the treasures in Spain."

★   ★   ★   ★   ★

Antonio.—Mon maître, I came not alone; there is one now waiting in the corridor anxious to speak to you.

Myself.—Who is it?

Antonio.—One whom you have met, mon maître, in various and strange places.

Myself.—But who is it?

Antonio.—One who will come to a strange end, *for so it is written*. The most extraordinary of all the Swiss, he of St. James,—*Der schatz gräber*.

Myself.—Not Benedict Mol?

"*Yaw, mein lieber herr*," said Benedict, pushing open the door which stood ajar; "it is myself. I met Herr Anton in the street, and hearing that you were in this place I came with him to visit you."

Myself.—And in the name of all that is singular, how is it that I see you in Madrid again? I thought that by this time you were returned to your own country.

Benedict.—Fear not, lieber herr, I shall return thither in good time; but not on foot, but with mules and coach. The schatz is still yonder, waiting to be dug up, and now I have better hope than ever; plenty of friends, plenty of money. See you not how I am dressed, lieber herr?"

And verily his habiliments were of a much more respectable appearance than any which he had sported on former occasions. His coat and pantaloons, which were of light green, were nearly new. On his head he still wore an Andalusian hat, but the present one was neither old nor shabby, but fresh and glossy, and of immense altitude of cone; whilst in his hand, instead of the ragged staff which I had observed at St. James and Oviedo, he now carried a huge bamboo rattan, surmounted by the grim head of either a bear or lion, curiously cut out of pewter.

"You have all the appearance of a treasure-seeker returned from a successful expedition," I exclaimed.

"Or rather," interrupted Antonio, "of one who has ceased to trade on his own bottom, and now goes seeking treasures at the cost and expense of others."

I questioned the Swiss minutely concerning his adventures since I last saw him, when I left him at Oviedo to pursue my route to Santander. From his answers I gathered that he had followed me to the latter place; he was, however, a long time in performing the journey, being weak from hunger and privation. At Santander he could hear no tidings of me, and by this time the trifle which he had received from me was completely exhausted. He now thought of making his way into France, but was afraid to venture through the disturbed provinces, lest he should fall into the hands of the Carlists, who he conceived might shoot him as a spy. No one relieving him at Santander, he departed and begged his way till he found himself in some part of Aragon, but where he scarcely knew. "My misery was so great," said Benedict, "that I nearly lost my senses. Oh, the horror of wandering about the savage hills and wide plains of Spain, without money and without hope! Sometimes I became desperate, when I found myself amongst rocks and barrancos, perhaps after having tasted no food from sunrise to sunset, and then I would raise my staff towards the sky and shake it, crying, Lieber herr Gott, ach lieber herr Gott, you must help me now or never; if you tarry, I am lost; you must help me now, now! And once when I was raving in this manner, methought I heard a voice, nay I am sure I heard it, sounding from the hollow of a rock, clear and strong; and it cried, 'Der schatz, der schatz, it is not yet dug up; to Madrid, to Madrid. The way to the schatz is through Madrid.' And then the thought of the schatz once more rushed into my mind, and I reflected how happy I might be, could I but dig up the schatz. No more begging then, no more wandering amidst horrid mountains and deserts; so I brandished my staff, and my body and my limbs became full of new and surprising strength, and I strode forward, and was not long before I reached the high road; and then I begged and bettled as I best could, until I reached Madrid."

"And what has befallen you since you reached Madrid?" I inquired. "Did you find the treasure in the streets?"

On a sudden Benedict became reserved and taciturn, which the more surprised me, as up to the present moment he had at all times been remarkably communicative with respect to his affairs and prospects. From what I could learn from his broken hints and innuendos, it appeared that, since his arrival at Madrid, he had fallen into the hands of certain people who had treated him with kindness, and provided him both with money and clothes; not from disinterested motives, however, but having an eye to the treasure. "They expect great things from me," said the Swiss; "and perhaps, after all, it would have been more profitable to have dug up the treasure without their assistance, always provided that were possible." Who his new friends were, he either knew not or would not tell me, save that they were people in power. He said something about Queen Christina and an oath which he had taken in the presence of a bishop on the crucifix and "the four Evangiles." I thought that his head was turned, and forbore questioning. Just before taking his departure, he observed: "Lieber herr, pardon me for not being quite frank towards you, to whom I owe so much, but I dare not; I am not now my own man. It is, moreover, an evil thing at all times to say a word about treasure before you have secured it. There was once a man in my own country, who dug deep into the earth until he arrived at a copper vessel which contained a schatz. Seizing it by the handle, he merely exclaimed in his transport, 'I have it!' that was enough, however: down sank the kettle, though the handle remained in his grasp. That was all he ever got for his trouble and digging. Farewell, lieber herr, I shall speedily be sent back to St. James to dig up the schatz; but I will visit you ere I go—farewell!"

*　*　*　*　*

I was not long in making preparations for my enterprise. A considerable stock of Testaments was sent forward by an arriero, I myself followed the next day. Before my departure, however, I received a visit from Benedict Mol.

"I am come to bid you farewell, lieber herr; to-morrow I return to Compostella."

"On what errand?"

"To dig up the schatz, lieber herr. For what else should I go? For what have I lived until now, but that I may dig up the schatz in the end?"

"You might have lived for something better," I exclaimed. "I wish you success, however. But on what grounds do you hope? Have you obtained permission to dig? Surely you remember your former trials in Galicia?"

"I have not forgotten them, lieber herr, nor the journey to Oviedo, nor 'the seven acorns,' nor the fight with death in the barranco. But I must accomplish my destiny. I go now to Galicia, as is becoming a Swiss, at the expense of the government, with coach and mule, I mean in the galera. I am to have all the help I require, so that I can dig down to the earth's centre if I think fit. I—but I must not tell your worship, for I am sworn on 'the four Evangiles' not to tell."

"Well, Benedict, I have nothing to say, save that I hope you will succeed in your digging."

"Thank you, lieber herr, thank you; and now farewell. Succeed! I shall succeed!" Here he stopped short, started, and looking upon me with an expression of countenance almost wild, he exclaimed, "Heiliger Gott! I forgot one thing. Suppose I should not find the treasure after all."

"Very rationally said; pity, though, that you did not think of that contingency till now. I tell you, my friend, that you have engaged in a most desperate undertaking. It is true that you may find a treasure. The chances are, however, a hundred to one that you do not, and in that event, what will be your situation? You will be looked upon as an impostor, and the consequences may be horrible to you. Remember where you are, and amongst whom you are. The Spaniards are a credulous people, but let them once suspect that they have been imposed upon, and above all laughed at, and their thirst for vengeance knows no limit. Think not that your innocence will avail you. That you are no impostor I feel convinced; but they would never believe it. It is not too late. Return your fine clothes and magic rattan to those from whom you had them. Put on your old garments, grasp your ragged staff, and come with me to the Sagra, to assist in circulating the illustrious gospel amongst the rustics on the Tagus' bank."

Benedict mused for a moment, than shaking his head, he cried, "No, no, I must accomplish my destiny. The schatz is not yet dug up. So said the voice in the barranco. To-morrow to Compostella. I shall find it—the schatz—it is still there—it *must* be there."

He went, and I never saw him more. What I heard, however, was extraordinary enough. It appeared that the government had listened to his tale, and had been so struck with Benedict's exaggerated description of the buried treasure, that they imagined that, by a little trouble and outlay, gold and diamonds might be dug up at St. James sufficient to enrich themselves and to pay off the national debt of Spain. The Swiss returned to Compostella "like a duke," to use his own words. The affair, which had at first been kept a profound secret, was speedily divulged. It was, indeed, resolved that the investigation, which involved consequences of so much importance, should take place in a manner the most public and imposing. A solemn festival was drawing nigh, and it was deemed expedient that the search should take place upon that day. The day arrived. All the bells in Compostella pealed. The whole populace thronged from their houses, a thousand troops were drawn up in the square, the expectation of all was wound up to the highest pitch. A procession directed its course to the church of San Roque; at its head was the captain-general and the Swiss, brandishing in his hand the magic rattan, close behind walked the *meiga*, the Gallegan witch-wife, by whom the treasure-seeker had been originally guided in the search; numerous masons brought up the rear, bearing implements to break up the ground. The procession enters the church, they pass through it in solemn march, they find themselves in a vaulted passage. The Swiss looks around. "Dig here," said he suddenly. "Yes, dig here," said the meiga. The masons labour, the floor is broken up,—a horrible and fetid odour arises . . .

Enough; no treasure was found, and my warning to the unfortunate Swiss turned out but too prophetic. He was forthwith seized and flung into the horrid prison of St. James, amidst the execrations of thousands, who would have gladly torn him limb from limb. . . .

Eager to learn the fate of the Swiss, I wrote to my old friend Rey Romero, at Compostella. In his answer he states: "I saw the Swiss in prison, to which place he sent for me, craving my assistance, for the sake of the friendship which I bore to you. But how could I help him? He was speedily after removed from St. James, I know not whither. It is said that he disappeared on the road."

Truth is sometimes stranger than fiction. Where in the whole cycle of romance shall we find anything more wild, grotesque, and sad than the easily authenticated history of Benedict Mol, the treasure-digger of St. James?

The Tomb of Tut-ankh-Amen

BY HOWARD CARTER

The discovery of the four-thousand-year-old tomb of the Egyptian pharaoh Tut-ankh-Amun must rank high among the most electrifying events in the history of archaeology. It was in 1922 that Howard Carter (1874–1939), backed by the funds and the intense interest in Egyptology of the hugely rich Lord Carnarvon, came upon the tomb, still with intact seals, and ventured to enter it. He and A. C. Mace wrote the story of the discovery, with appropriate grace notes, in a best-selling book published the next year. A more straightforward and detailed account can be found in Carter's own notebooks preserved in the Ashmolean Museum in Oxford, and the following extract is from this source. If less hyped than the literary version, it is nevertheless still charged with the sense of excitement and absolute wonder that everyone present must have felt.

★   ★   ★   ★   ★

Wednesday, November 1 . . .
Commenced operations in the Valley of the Kings. I began by continuing the former excavation where it had stopped at the N.E. corner of the entrance to the tomb of Ramses VI, trenching southwards. At this point there were ancient stone huts of the Necropolis workmen, built

rather less than a metre above the bed-rock, which had partly been exposed in our former work x (see plan L.M. 15 and 16). As we uncovered them they were found to continue under and in front of the entrance of Ramses VI tomb in a southerly direction and connected up with other similar huts on the opposite side of the valley bed discovered by Davis during previous work. These ancient huts were soon cleared of the rubbish covering them. I planned them, and removed them for investigation below, which undertaking took until the fourth of Nov.

Saturday, November 4 . . .
At about 10am I discovered beneath almost the first hut attacked the first traces of the entrance of the tomb (Tut-ankh-Amen) This comprised the first step of the N.E. corner (of the sunken-staircase). Quite a short time sufficed to show that it was the beginning of a steep excavation cut in the bed rock, about four metres below the entrance of Ramses VI's tomb, and a similar depth below the present level of the valley. And, that it was of the nature of a sunken staircase entrance to a tomb of the type of the XVIIIth Dyn., but further than that nothing could be told until the heavy rubbish above was cleared away.

Sunday, November 5 . . .
It took the whole of the preceding day and most of this day to free this excavation before the upper margins of the staircase could be demarcated on its four sides. As first conjectured it proved to be an opening (about 4 ms × 1.60 ms) excavated in the bed-rock, with its W. end abutting against the rock slope of the small hillock in which Ramses VI had excavated his tomb. As the work proceeded we found that the western end of the cutting receded under the slope of the rock, and thus was partly roofed over by the overhanging rock.

Towards sunset we had cleared down to the level of the 12th step, which was sufficient to expose a large part of the upper portion of a plastered and sealed doorway. Here before us was sufficient evidence to show that it really was an entrance to a tomb, and by the seals, to all outward appearances that it was intact.

I examined this exposed portion of the sealed doorway and noticed that the only decipherable impressions of the seals were those of the well-known Royal Necropolis seal, i.e., Anubis (symbolizing a king) over nine foes.

With the evidence of these seals, and the fact that the workmen's huts, which in all probabilities dated from the time of the construction of Rameses VI's tomb, were built over the mouth of the entrance of this newly discovered tomb without apparently disturbing it, it was clear that its content would be undisturbed at least since the XXth Dyn.

The seal-impressions suggested that it belonged to somebody of high standing but at that time I had not found any indications as to whom.

I noticed at the top of the doorway, where some of the cement-like plaster had fallen away, a heavy wooden lintel. To assure myself of the method in which the doorway was blocked, I made a small hole under this wooden lintel—the R. hand corner, about 35 × 15 cms in size. By this hole I was able to perceive with the aid of an electrical torch that a passage beyond was completely filled with stones and rubble up to its ceiling, which was again evidence of something that had required careful closing. It was a thrilling moment for an excavator, quite alone save his native staff of workmen, to suddenly find himself, after so many years of toilsome work, on the verge of what looked like a magnificent discovery—an untouched tomb. With certain reluctance I reclosed the small hole that I had made, and returned to another careful search among the seals to see if I could not find some indication that would point to the identity of the owner, but it was of no avail for the small space bared by my excavation did not expose any impression sufficiently clear to be made out, other than that of the Royal Necropolis seal already mentioned.

Though I was satisfied that I was on the verge of perhaps a magnificent find, probably one of the missing tombs that I had been seeking for many years, I was much puzzled by the smallness of the opening in comparison with those of other royal tombs in the valley. Its design was certainly of the XVIIIth Dyn. Could it be the tomb of a noble, buried there by royal consent? Or was it a royal cache? As far as my investigations had gone there was absolutely nothing to tell me. Had I known that by digging a few inches deeper I would have exposed seal impressions showing Tut-ankh-Amen's insignia distinctly I would have fervently worked on and set my mind at rest, but as it was, it was getting late, the night had fast set in, the full moon had risen high in the eastern heavens, I refilled the excavation for protection, and with my men selected for the occasion—they like myself delighted beyond all expectation—I returned home and cabled to Ld. C. [Lord Carnarvon] (then in England) the following message:—

> "At last have made wonderful discovery in Valley a magnificent tomb with seals intact recovered same for your arrival congratulations"

Monday, November 6 . . .
The men worked feverishly today covering and making safe the discovery until the time came for fully reopening. On the top of which great stones, that formed the sides of the ancient huts, were rolled.

Tuesday, November 7 . . .
The news of the discovery spread fast all over the country, and inquisitive enquiries mingled with congratulations from this moment became the daily programme.

We continued clearing the bed-rock of the valley towards the south where many more huts were exposed and on turning the corner towards the west we opened up, at a higher level than the huts a sort of stone enclosure for mortar—these like the others were evidently part of the camp for Ramses VI tomb. This investigation continued until the end of the working week—Monday, the 13th Nov. Here, as I found in most other cases, the excavations of former explorers, in this case Davis, had only skimmed the top surface and had not even laid bare the huts of the ancient workmen.

Wednesday, November 8 . . .
Received wireless from Lord C. ". . . possibly come soon . . ." A little later another wire from Ld. C. "purpose arrive Alexandria twentieth . . ."

. . . Thursday, November 23 . . .
Lord C. arrived Luxor, came over to Gurna and put up at my house. Callender restarted uncovering tomb.

Friday, November 24 . . .
Lady E. arrived.

Callender reached as far as the first doorway. There proved to be sixteen steps.

Now that the whole of the sealed doorway was laid bare various seal impressions bearing the cartouche of Tut-ankh-Amen were discernible, more in particular in the lower portion of the plastering of the doorway where the impressions were clearest.

In the upper part of this sealed doorway traces of two distinct reopenings and successive reclosings were apparent, and that the seal-impressions first noticed, Nov. 5, of the Royal Necropolis—i.e., 'Anubis over Nine Foes', had been used for the reclosing. Here was evidence of at least the reign of the tomb, but its true significance was still a puzzle, for in the lower rubbish that filled the stair-case entrance we found masses of broken potsherds, broken boxes, the latter bearing the names and protocol of Akhenaten, Smenkh-Ka-Ra, and Tut-ankh-Amen, and with what was even more upsetting a scarab of Tehutimes III, as well as a fragment bearing the cartouche of Amenhetep III. These conflicting data led us for a time to believe that we were about to open a royal cache of the El Amarna branch of the XVIIIth Dyn. Monarchs, and that from the evidence mentioned above it had been probably opened and used more than once.

Engelbach, the Chief Inspector Antiquities Dept., came and witnessed the freeing of rubbish from the first doorway. With him came several of his friends, among others Brunton.

Slept the night in the valley. Carpenters commenced upon making a temporary wooden grill for fixing over first doorway.

Saturday, November 25 . . .
Noted seals. Made photographic records, which were not, as they afterwards proved, very successful. Opened the first doorway; which comprised rough stones built up from the threshold to the lintel, plastered over on the outside face, and covered with numerous impressions from various seals of Tut-ankh-Amen and the Royal Necropolis seal. The removal of this blocking exposed the commencement of a completely blocked descending passage, the same width as the entrance staircase and rather more than 2 metres high. It was filled with its local stone and rubble, probably from its own excavation, but like the doorway it showed distinct traces of more than one filling; the mass of the filling being of clean white stone chips mingled with dust, while in the upper left hand corner a large irregular hole had been pierced through it which had been refilled with dark flint and chert stones. This coincided with reopenings and successive reclosings found on the sealed doorway. As we cleared the passage we found mixed with the rubble broken potsherds, jar seals, and numerous fragments of small objects; water skins lying on the floor together with alabaster jars, whole and broken, and coloured pottery vases; all pertaining to some disturbed burial, but telling us nothing to whom they belonged further than by their type which was of the late XVIIIth Dyn. These were disturbing elements as they pointed towards plundering.

Sunday, November 26 . . .
After clearing 9 metres of the descending passage, in about the middle of the afternoon, we came upon a second sealed doorway, which was almost the exact replica of the first. It bore similar seal impressions and had similar traces of successive reopenings and reclosings in the plastering. The seal impressions were of Tut-ankh-Amen and of the Royal Necropolis, but not in any way so clear as those on the first doorway. The entrance and passage both in plan and in style resembled almost to

measurement the tomb containing the cache of Akhenaten discovered by Davis in the very near vicinity; which seemed to substantiate our first conjecture that we had found a cache.

Feverishly we cleared away the remaining last scraps of rubbish on the floor of the passage before the doorway, until we had only the clean sealed doorway before us. In which, after making preliminary notes, we made a tiny breach in the top left hand corner to see what was beyond. Darkness and the iron testing rod told us that there was empty space. Perhaps another descending staircase, in accordance to the ordinary royal Theban tomb plan? Or may be a chamber? Candles were procured—the all important tell-tale for foul gases when opening an ancient subterranean excavation—I widened the breach and by means of the candle looked in, while Ld. C., Lady E, and Callender with the Reises waited in anxious expectation.

It was sometime before one could see, the hot air escaping caused the candle to flicker, but as soon as one's eyes became accustomed to the glimmer of light the interior of the chamber gradually loomed before one, with its strange and wonderful medley of extraordinary and beautiful objects heaped upon one another.

There was naturally short suspense for those present who could not see, when Lord Carnarvon said to me 'Can you see anything'. I replied to him Yes, it is wonderful. I then with precaution made the hole sufficiently large for both of us to see. With the light of an electric torch as well as an additional candle we looked in. Our sensations and astonishment are difficult to describe as the better light revealed to us the marvellous collection of treasures: two strange ebony-black effigies of a King, gold sandalled, bearing staff and mace, loomed out from the cloak of darkness; gilded couches in strange forms, lion-headed, Hathor-headed, and beast infernal; exquisitely painted, inlaid, and ornamental caskets; flowers; alabaster vases, some beautifully executed of lotus and papyrus device; strange black shrines with a gilded monster snake appearing from within; quite ordinary looking white chests; finely carved chairs; a golden inlaid throne; a heap of large curious white oviform boxes; beneath our very eyes, on the threshold, a lovely lotiform wishing-cup in translucent alabaster; stools of all shapes and design, of both common and rare materials; and, lastly a confusion of overturned parts of chariots glinting with gold, peering from amongst which was a mannikin. The first impression of which suggested the property-room of an opera of a vanished civilization. Our sensations were bewildering and full of strange emotion. We questioned one another as to the meaning of it all. Was it a tomb or merely a cache? A sealed doorway between the two sentinel statues proved there was more beyond, and with the numerous cartouches bearing the name of Tut-ankh-Amen on most of the objects before us, there was little doubt that there behind was the grave of that Pharaoh.

We closed the hole, locked the wooden-grill which had been placed upon the first doorway, we mounted our donkeys and return home contemplating what we had seen.

Advised the Chief Inspector of the Antiquities Department, who was with us at the commencement of the opening of the first doorway, and asked him to come as soon as possible, preferably the following afternoon to enable us to prepare an electrical installation for careful inspection of this extraordinary and pleasing discovery.

Monday, November 27 . . .
Callender prepared the electrical installation for lighting the tomb. This was ready by noon, when Lord C., Lady E., Callender and self entered and made a careful inspection of this first chamber (afterwards called the Ante-chamber).

In the course of the afternoon the local Inspector Ibrahim Effendi, of the Department of Antiquities at Luxor, came in the place of the Chief Inspector—he being absent on a visit to Kena.

It soon became obvious that we were but on the threshold of the discovery. The sight that met us was beyond anything one could conceive. The heterogeneous mass of material crowded into the chamber without particular order, so crowded that you were obliged to move with anxious caution, for time had wrought certain havoc with many of the objects, was very bewildering. Everywhere we found traces of dis-

order caused by some early intruder, objects over-turned, broken fragments lying upon the floor, all added to the confusion, and the unfamiliar plan of tomb repeatedly caused us to ask ourselves in our perplexity
whether it was really a tomb or a Royal Cache? As the better light fell
upon the objects we endeavoured to take them in. It was impossible.
They were so many. Beneath one of the couches, the Thoueris couch in
the S.W. corner, we perceived an aperture in the rock-wall which
proved to be nothing less than another sealed-doorway broken open as
by some predatory hand. With care Ld. C. and I crept under this strange
gilded couch, and we peered into the opening. There we saw that it led
into yet another chamber (afterwards called the Annexe) of smaller
dimensions than the Ante-chamber and of a lower level. Even greater
confusion prevailed here, the very stones that blocked the entrance,
forced in when the breach was made, were lying helter-skelter upon the
objects on the floor crushed by their weight. It was full of one mass of
furniture. An utter confusion of beds, chairs, boxes, alabaster and faience
vases, statuettes, cases of peculiar form, and every sort of thing over-
turned and searched for valuables. The remaining portions of the plaster
covering the blocking of this doorway bore similar seal-impressions as
on the other doorways.

In neither of these two chambers could we see any traces of a
mummy or mummies—the one pious reason for making a cache. With
such evidence, as well as the sealed doorway between the two guardian
statues of the King, the mystery gradually dawned upon us. We were
but in the anterior portion of a tomb. Behind that closed doorway was
the tomb-chamber, and that Tut-ankh-Amen probably lay there in all
his magnificent panoply of death—we had found that monarch's burial
place intact save certain metal-robbing, and not his cache.

We then examined the plaster and seal-impressions upon the
closed doorway. They were of many types of seals, all bearing the insignia of the King. We also discovered that in the bottom part of the
blocking a small breach had once been made, large enough to allow of a
small man to pass through, but it had been carefully reclosed, plastered
and sealed. Evidently the tomb beyond had been entered—by thieves!

Who knows? But sufficient evidence to tell that someone had made ingress.

The results of our investigations were, (1) it was clear the place was Pharaoh's tomb and not a mere cache; (2) that we had only entered the anterior chambers of the tomb, filled with magnificent equipment equal only to the wealth and splendour of the New Empire; (3) that we had found a royal burial little disturbed save hurried plundering at the hands of ancient tomb robbers.

It was a sight surpassing all precedent, and one we never dreamed of seeing. We were astonished by the beauty and refinement of the art displayed by the objects surpassing all we could have imagined— the impression was overwhelming.

A Search in the Tower

BY SAMUEL PEPYS

Between 1660 and 1669, Samuel Pepys kept—in shorthand for reasons of secrecy—a diary that since decipherment and publication has become known as the finest in the English language. This acclaim is less for its literary elegance than for the fact that Pepys is unfailingly frank, lively, and forthright, as much about his own doings (and misdoings) as about the colorful era he lived through. Born in modest circumstances in London in 1633, by the time of his death in 1703 Pepys had achieved financial comfort and social standing as an important civil servant, the father of the British Navy. In 1662, however, when he wrote the following account of a frustrating treasure hunt in the cellars of the Tower of London, he was in only the early stages of his ascent, still dependent on the backing of his kinsman Lord Sandwich. The treasure that Sandwich told Pepys to find was supposed to have been hidden by John Barkstead, one of the men who sentenced King Charles I to death, just before the Restoration of Charles II in 1660. Pepys seems not to have taken the matter very seriously, which makes his account of the search even more delightful to read.

★   ★   ★   ★   ★

3 0th October, 1662, To my Lord Sandwich, who was up in his chamber and all alone, and did acquaint me with his business: which was, that our old acquaintance, Mr. Wade, in Axe Yard, hath discovered [revealed] to him £7000 hid in the Tower; of which he was to have two for discovery, my Lord himself two, and the King the other three, when it was found: and that the King's warrant runs for me on my Lord's part, and one Mr. Lee for Sir Harry Bennet, to demand leave of the Lieutenant of the Tower for to make search. After he had told me the whole business I took leave, and at noon comes Mr. Wade with my Lord's letter. So we consulted for me to go first to Sir H. Bennet, who is now with many of the Privy Councillors at the Tower examining of their late prisoners, to advise with him to begin. So I went; and the guard at the Tower Gate making me leave my sword at the gate, I was forced to stay so long in the alehouse hard by, till my boy run home for my cloak, that my Lord Mayor that now is, Sir John Robinson, Lieutenant of the Tower, with all his company, was gone with their coaches to his house in Mincing Lane. So my cloak being come, I walked thither: and there, by Sir G. Carteret's means, did presently speak with Sir H. Bennet, who did give me the King's warrant for the paying of £2000 to my Lord and other two to the discoverers. After a little discourse dinner came in; and I dined with them. There was my Lord Mayor, my Lord Lauderdale, Mr. Secretary Morris (to whom Sir H. Bennet would give the upper hand), Sir William Compton, Sir G. Carteret, and myself, and some other company; and a brave dinner. After dinner Sir H. Bennet did call aside the Lord Mayor and me, and did break the business to him, who did not, nor durst, appear the least averse to it, but did promise all assistance forthwith to set upon it. So Mr. Lee and I to our office, and there walked till Mr. Wade and one Evett, his guide, did come, and W. Griffin, and a porter with his pick-axes, &c.: and so they walked along with us to the Tower, and Sir H. Bennet and my Lord Mayor did give us full power to fall to work. So our guide demands a candle, and down into the cellars he goes, enquiring whether they were the same that Barkstead[1] always had. We went

---

[1] John Barkstead, one of the regicides, Lieutenant of the Tower under Cromwell.

into several little cellars, and then went out a-doors to view, and to the Cold Harbour; but none did answer so well to the marks which was given him to find it by as one arched vault, where, after a great deal of counsel whether to set upon it now or delay for better and more full advice, to digging we went till almost eight o'clock at night, but could find nothing. But, however, our guides did not at all seem discouraged; for that they being confident that the money is there they look for, but having never been in the cellars, they could not be positive to the place, and therefore will inform themselves more fully, now they have been there, of the party that do advise them. So locking the door after us, we left work to-night, and up to the Deputy Governor, my Lord Mayor and Sir H. Bennet, with the rest of the company, being gone an hour before; and he do undertake to keep the key of the cellars, that none shall go down without his privity. But, Lord! to see what a young simple fantastic coxcomb is made Deputy Governor, would make one mad; and how he called out for his night-gown of silk, only to make a show to us: and yet for half an hour I did not think he was the Deputy Governor, and so spoke not to him about the business, but waited for another man; but at last I broke our business to him; and he promising his care, we parted. And Mr. Lee and I by coach to White Hall, where I did give my Lord Sandwich a full account of our proceedings, and some encouragement to hope for something hereafter. . . .

31st. Thus ends this month, I and my family in good health, but weary heartily of dirt, but now in hopes within two or three weeks to be out of it . . .

November 1st. . . . To my office, to meet Mr. Lee again, from Sir H. Bennet. And he and I, with Wade and his intelligencer and labourers, to the Tower cellars, to make one trial more; where we stayed two or three hours, and dug a great deal all under the arches, as it was now most confidently directed, and so seriously, and upon pretended good grounds, that I myself did truly expect to speed; but we missed of all: and so we went away the second time like fools. And to our office; and I, by appointment, to the Dolphin tavern, to meet Wade and the other, Captain Evett, who now do tell me plainly, that he that do put him upon this is one that had it from Barkstead's own mouth, and was advised with by him, just before the King's coming in, how to get it out, and had all the signs told him how and where it lay, and had always been the great confidant of Barkstead, even to the trusting him with his life and all he had. So that he did much convince me that there is good ground for what we go about. But I fear it may be that Barkstead did find conveyance of it away, without the help of this man, before he died; but he is resolved to go to the party once more, and then to determine what we shall do further. . . .

3rd . . . At night to my office and did business; and there came to me Mr. Wade and Evett, who have been again with their prime intelligencer, a woman, I perceive: and though we have missed twice, yet they bring such an account of the probability of the truth of the thing, though we are not certain of the place, that we shall set upon it once more; and I am willing and hopeful in it. So we resolved to set upon it again on Wednesday morning; and the woman herself will be there in a disguise, and confirm us in the place. . . .

7th. Being by appointment called upon by Mr. Lee, he and I to the Tower to make our third attempt upon the cellar. And now privately the woman, Barkstead's great confidant, is brought, who do positively say that this is the place which he did say the money was hid in, and where he and she did put up the £50,000 in butter-firkins; and the very day that he went out of England did say that neither he nor his would be the better for that money, and therefore wishing that she and hers might. And so left us, and we full of hope did resolve to dig all over the cellar, which by seven o'clock at night we performed. At noon we sent for a dinner, and upon the head of a barrel dined very merrily, and to work again. But at last we saw we were mistaken; and, after digging the cellar quite through and removing the barrels from one side to the other, we were forced to pay our porters and give over our expectations, though I do believe there must be money hid somewhere by him, or else he did delude this woman in hopes to oblige her to further serving him, which I am apt to believe.

Captain Phips and the Spanish Wreck

BY COTTON MATHER

One of the earliest attempts at underwater treasure salvage took place towards the end of the 17th century off the coast of what is now the Dominican Republic. It was conducted with some success by an extraordinary man named William Phips (or Phipps). Phips was an American, a New Englander, an ambitious go-getter determined to make himself a fortune, which he did, going on to become royal governor of New England and a highly-respected Colonial potentate. Modern research has established many more detailed (and correct) facts about Phips' exploits in the Caribbean than are given in the following passage from a biography of him by Cotton Mather (1663–1728), the famous American Puritan churchman and writer, published in 1702 in *Magnalia Christi Americana*. Even so, Mather's antique prose has its own charm, and he was clearly very fond of Phips—or at least happy to flatter him, a possibly wise move under the circumstances.

★   ★   ★   ★   ★

eing thus of the *True Temper*, for the doing of *Great Things*, he [William Phips] betakes himself to the *Sea*, the Right *Scene* for such Things; and upon Advice of a *Spanish Wreck* about the *Bahama*'s, he took a Voyage thither; but with little more success, than what just served to furnish him for a Voyage to *England;* whither he went in a Vessel, not much unlike that which the *Dutchmen* stamped upon their *First Coin,* with these Words about it, *Incertum quo Fata ferant.* Having first informed himself that there was another *Spanish Wreck,* wherein was lost a mighty Treasure, hitherto undiscovered, he had a strong Impressions upon his Mind that *He* must be the Discoverer; and he made such Representations of his Design at *White-Hall,* that by the Year 1683 he became the Captain of a *King's Ship,* and arrived at *New-England* Commander of the *Algier-Rose,* a Frigot of Eighteen Guns, and Ninety-Five Men.

To Relate all the *Dangers* through which he passed, both by Sea and Land, and all the Tiresome Trials of his *Patience,* as well as of his *Courage* while Year after Year the most vexing Accidents imaginable delay'd the Success of his Design, it would even Tire the patience of the Reader; For very great was the Experiment that Captain *Phips* made of the *Italian* Observation, *He that cann't suffer both Good and Evil, will never come to any great Preferment . . .*

Now with a small Company of other Men he sailed from [Jamaica] to *Hispaniola,* where by the Policy of his Address he fished out of a very old *Spaniard* (or *Portuguese*) a little Advice about the true Spot where lay the *Wreck* which he had been hitherto seeking, as unprosperously, as the *Chymists* have their *Aurifick Stone;* That it was upon a *Reef of Shoals,* a few miles to the Northward of *Port de la Plata,* upon *Hispaniola,* a Port so call'd, it seems, from the Landing of some of the Shipwreck'd Company, with a boat full of Plate, save out of their Sinking Frigot; Nevertheless, when he had searched very narrowly the Spot, whereof the old *Spaniard* had advised him, he had not hitherto exactly lit upon it. Such *Thorns* did vex his Affairs while he was in the *Rose-Frigot;* but none of these things could retund [weaken, deflect] the Edge of his Expectations to find the *Wreck;* with such Expectations he return'd then into *England,* that he might better furnish himself to Prosecute a *New Discovery;* for though he judged he might, by proceeding a little further, have come at the right *Spot,* yet he found his present Company too ill a Crew to be confided in.

So *proper* was his Behaviour, that the best Noble Men in the Kingdom now admitted him into their Conversation; but yet he was opposed by powerful Enemies, that Clogg'd his Affairs with such Demurrages, and such *Disappointments*, as would have wholly discouraged his Designs, if his Patience had not been *Invincible He who can wait, hath what he desireth*. This his Indefatigable *Patience*, with a proportionable *Diligence*, at length overcame the Difficulties that had been thrown in his way; and prevailing with the Duke of *Albemarle*, and some other Persons of Quality, to fit him out, he set Sail for the *Fishing-Ground*, which had been so well *baited* half a Hundred Years before; And as he had already discovered his *Capacity for Business* in many considerable Actions, he now added unto those Discoveries, by not only *providing* all, but also by *inventing* many of the Instruments necessary to the prosecution of his intended *Fishery*. Captain *Phips* arriving with a Ship and a *Tender* at *Port de la Plata*, made a stout *Canoo* of a stately *Cotton-Tree*, so large as to carry Eight or Ten Oars, for the making of which *Periaga* (as they call it) he did, with the same industry that he did every thing else, employ his own *Hand* and *Adse*, and endure no little hardship lying abroad in the Woods many Nights together. This *Periaga*, with the *Tender*, being Anchored at a place Convenient, the *Periaga* kept Busking to and again, but could only discover a *Reef of Rising Shoals* thereabouts, called, *The Boilers*, which Rising to be within Two or Three Foot of the Surface of the Sea, were yet so steep, that a Ship striking on them would immediately sink down, who could say *how many fathom* into the Ocean? Here they could get no other Pay for their long *peeping* among the *Boilers*, but only such as caused them to think upon returning to their Captain with the *bad News* of their total Disappointment. Nevertheless, as they were looking upon the Return, one of the Men looking over the side of the *Periaga*, into the calm Water. he spied a *Sea Feather* growing, as he judged, out of a Rock; whereupon they had one of their *Indians* to Dive and fetch this *Feather*, that they might however carry home *something* with them, and make, at least, as fair a Triumph as *Caligula's*. The *Diver* bringing up the *Feather* brought therewithal a surprizing Story, That he perceived a Number of *Great Guns* in the *Watry World* where he had found his *Feather;* the *Report* of which *Great Guns* exceedingly astonished the whole Company; and at once turned their *Despondencies* for their ill success into *Assurances,* that they had now lit upon the *true Spot* of Ground which they had been looking for; and they were further confirmed in their *Assurances,* when upon further Diving, the *Indian* fetcht up a *Sow,* as they stil'd it, or a Lump of Silver worth perhaps Two or Three Hundred Pounds. Upon this they prudently *Buoy'd* the place, that they might readily find it again, and they went back unto their Captain whom for some while they distressed with nothing but such *Bad News,* as they formerly thought they must have carried him: Nvertheless, they so slipt the Sow of Silver on one side under the Table, where they were now sitting with the Captain, and hearing him express his Resolutions to wait still patiently upon the Providence of God under these Disappointments, that when he should look on one side, he might see that *Odd Thing* before him. At last he *saw* it; seeing it, he cried out with some Agony, *Why? What is this? Whence comes this?* And then, with changed Countenances, they told him *how* and where they got it: *Then,* said he, *Thanks be to God! We are made*; and so away they went, all hands to Work; wherein they had this one further piece of Remarkable Prosperity, that whereas they had first fallen in thet part of the *Spanish Wreck,* where Pieces of Eight had been stowed in Bags among the Ballast, they had seen a more laborious, and less enriching time of it: Now, most happily, they first fell upon that Room in the *Wreck* where the *Bullion* had been stored up; and they so prospered in this *New Fishery,* that in a little while they had, without the loss of any Man's Life, brought up *Thirty Two Tuns* of Silver; for it was now come measuring of Silver by *Tuns.* Besides which, one *Adderly of Providence,* who had formerly been very helpful to Captain *Phips* in the Search of this *Wreck,* did upon former Agreement meet him now with a little Vessel here; and *he,* with his few hands, took up about *Six Tuns* of silver; whereof nevertheless he made so little use, that in a Year or Two he Died at *Bermuda,* and as I have heard, he ran *Distracted* some while before he Died. Thus did there once again come into the Light of the Sun, a Treasure which had been half an Hundred Years *groaning under the Waters:* and in this time there was grown upon the Plate a Crust like *Limestone*, to the thickness of several Inches; which Crust being broken opened by Irons contrived for that purpose, they knockt out whole Bushels of rusty Pieces of Eight which were grown thereinto. Besides that incredible Treasure of Plate in various Forms, thuis fetch'd up, from Seven or Eight Fathom under Water, there were vast Riches of *Gold*, and *Pearls*, and *Jewels*, which they also lit upon; and indeed, for a more Comprehensive *Invoice*, I must but summarily say, *All that a Spanish Frigat uses to be enricht withal.* Thus did they continue *Fishing* till their Provisions failing them, 'twas time to be gone; but before they went, Captain *Phips* caused *Adderly* and his Folk to swear, That they would none of them Discover the Place of the *Wreck*, or come to the Place any more till the next Year, when he expected again to be there himself. And it was also Remarkable, that though the Sows came up still so fast, that on the very last Day of their being there, they took up *Twenty*, yet it was afterwards found, that they had in a manner wholly cleared that Room of the Ship where those *Massy things* were Stowed.

But there was one extraordinary Distress which Captain *Phips* now found himself plunged into: For his Men were come out with him upon Seamens wages, at so much *per* month; and when they saw such vast Litters of Silver *Sows* and *Pigs*, as they call them, come on Board them at the Captain's Call, they knew not how to bear it, that they should not *share* all among themselves, and be gone to lead *a short Life and a merry*, in a Climate where the Arrest of those that had hired them should not reach them. In this terrible Distress he mad his vows unto Almighty God that if the Lord would carry him safe home to *England* with what *he* had now given him, *to suck of the Abundance of the Seas, and of the Treasures hid in the Sands*, he would for ever Devote himself unto the Interests of the Lord *Jesus Christ*, and of his People, especially in the *Country* which he did himself Originally belong unto. And then he used all the obliging *Arts* imaginable to make his Men true unto him, especially by assuring them, that besides their *Wages*, they should have ample *Requitals* made unto them; which if the rest of his Employers would not agree to, he would himself distribute his *own share* among them. Relying on the Word of One whom they had ever found worthy of their *Love*, and of their *Trust*, they declared themselves *Content*: But still keeping a most careful Eye upon them, he hastned back for *England* with as much *Money* as he thought he could then safely *Trust* his vessel withal; not counting it safe to supply himself with necessary Provisions at any nearer Port, and so return unto the *Wreck*, by which delays he wisely feared lest all might be lost, more ways than one. Though he left so much behind him, that many from divers Parts made very considerable Voyages of *Gleaning* after his *Harvest:* which came to pass by certain *Bermudians*, compelling of *Adderly*'s Boy, whom they *spirited* away with them, to tell them the exact place where the *Wreck* was to be found. Captain *Phips* now coming up to *London* in the year 1687, with near *Three Hundred Thousand Pounds Sterling* aboard him, did acquit himself with such an Exemplary Honesty, that partly by his fulfilling his Assurances to the Seamen, and partly by his exact and punctual Care to have his Employers defrauded of nothing that might conscientiously belong unto them, he had less that *Sixteen Thousand Pounds* left unto himself: As an acknowledgement of which *Honesty* in him, the Duke of *Albemarle* made unto his Wife, whom he never saw, a Present of a *Golden Cup*, near a Thousand Pound in value. The Character of an *Honest Man* he had so merited in the whole Course of his Life, and especially in this last act of it, that this Conjunction with his other serviceable Qualities, procured him the Favours of the Greatest Persons in the Nation; and *he that had been so diligent in his Business, must now stand before Kings, and not stand before mean Men.* There were indeed certain mean Men, if base little, dirty Tricks, will entitle Men to Meanness, who urged the King to seize his *whole Cargo*, instead of the Tenths, upon his first Arrival; on this pretence, that he had not been rightly inform'd of the *True state of the Case*, when he Granted the *Patent*, under the Protection whereof these *Particular Men* had made themselves Masters of all this Mighty Treasure; but the King replied, That he had been *rightly informed* by Captain *Phips* of the whole Matter, as it now proved; and that it was the Slanders of one then present, which had, unto his Damnage, hindered him from hearkning to the Information: Wherefore he would give them, he said, no Disturbance; they might keep what they had got; but Captain *Phips*, he saw, was a person of that Honesty, Fidelity and Ability, that he should not want his Countenance. Accordingly the King, in Consideration of the Service done by him, in bringing such a Treasure into the Nation, conferred upon him the Honour of *Knighthood*; and if we now reckon him, *A Knight of the Golden Fleece*, the Stile might pretend unto some Circumstances that would justifie it. Or call him, if you please, *The Knight of Honesty*; for it was *Honesty* with *Industry* that raised him; and he became a Mighty River, without the running in of Muddy Water to make him so. Reader, now make a Pause, and behold *One Raised by God!*

The Tun-Huang Treasure

BY M. AUREL STEIN

Finding a treasure is one thing, getting your hands on it quite another. Sir Aurel Stein's experience in Chinese Turkestan in 1907 is a case in point. Stein (1862–1943) was one of the greatest of all archaeological explorers, making a series of bitterly difficult journeys though the mountains and deserts of Central Asia to trace ancient routes and discover the remains of the civilizations that had once flourished there. In the course of one trip he heard rumors of a cache of manuscripts supposed to exist in a sealed room in a sacred site called the Caves of the Thousand Buddhas near Tun-huang (now spelled Dunhuang), on China's western frontier. The collection—hundreds of scrolls, paintings, artifacts and other written materials—had been walled up for more than 900 years. Yet the extremely dry climate, as Stein was to discover, had preserved them perfectly from decay. The following passage from *Ruins of Desert Cathay*, the book he published in 1912, describes how—with the invaluable help of his Chinese secretary Chiang—he managed to convince the monk guarding the hoard to let him carry away a large portion of the treasure, in part by playing on their joint admiration for the 8th century Buddhist missionary Hsüan Tsang. You can't help but admire Stein's deviousness—but it should be said that in recent years his actions have been protested with increasing vehemence in China. Like the Greeks and the Elgin Marbles, they want the treasure back.

*   *   *   *   *

Yet it was useless to disguise the fact from myself: what had kept my heart buoyant for months, and was now drawing me back with the strength of a hidden magnet, were hopes of another and more substantial kind. Their goal was that great hidden deposit of ancient manuscripts which a Taoist monk had accidentally discovered about two years earlier while restoring one of the temples. I knew that the deposit was still jealously guarded in the walled-up side chapel where it had been originally discovered, and that there were good reasons for caution in the first endeavors to secure access to it. What my sagacious secretary had gathered of the character and ways of its guardian was a warning to me to feel my way with prudence and studied slowness. It was enough that Chiang had induced Wang Tao-shih, the priest, who had come upon the hidden deposit, to await my arrival instead of starting on one of his usual tours in the district to sell blessings and charms, and to collect outstanding temple subscriptions. . . .

Next morning I started what was to be ostensibly the main object of my stay at the site, the survey of the principal grottoes, and the photographing of the more notable frescoes. Purposely I avoided any long interview with the Tao-shih, who had come to offer me welcome at what for the most of the year he might well regard his domain. He looked a very queer person, extremely shy and nervous, with an occasional expression of cunning which was far from encouraging. It was clear from the first that he would be a difficult person to handle.

But when later on I had been photographing in one of the ruined temple grottoes near the great shrine restored by him, where the manuscripts had been discovered, I could not forgo a glance at the entrance passage from which their place of deposit was approached. On my former visit I had found the narrow opening of the recess, locked with a rough wooden door; but now to my dismay it was completely walled up with brickwork. Was this a precaution to prevent the inquisitive barbarian from gaining even a glimpse of the manuscript treasures hidden within? I thought of the similar device by which the Jain monks of Jesalmir, in their temple vault, had once attempted to keep Professor Bühler from access to their storehouse of ancient texts, and mentally prepared myself for a long and arduous siege.

The first task was to assure that I should be allowed to see the whole of the manuscripts, and in their original place of deposit. Only thus could I hope to ascertain the true character and approximate date of the collection which had lain hidden behind the passage wall. In order to effect this Chiang had been dispatched in the morning to another restored cave-temple where the priest had his quarters, and proceeded to sound him in confidential fashion about the facilities which were to be given. It proved a very protracted affair. Backed up by the promise of a liberal donation for the main shrine, the Ssŭ-yeh's tactful diplomacy seemed at first to make better headway than I had ventured to hope for. The saintly guardian of the reputed treasure explained that the walling up of the door was intended for a precaution against the curiosity of the pilgrims who had recently flocked to the site in their thousands. But evidently wary and of a suspicious mind, he would not yet allow himself to be coaxed into any promise about showing the collection to us as a whole. All that he would agree to, with various meticulous reservations, was to let me see eventually such specimens of the collection as he might conveniently lay his hands on. When Chiang, in his zeal momentarily forgetting the dictates of diplomatic reticence, was cautiously hinting at the possibility of my wishing, perhaps, to acquire "for future study" one or other of those specimens, the Tao-shih showed such perturbation, prompted equally, it seemed, by scruples of a religious sort and fear of popular resentment, that my sharp-witted secretary thought it best to drop the subject for a time.

But after hours of such diplomatic wrangling he did not leave the priest's smoke-filled chapel and kitchen combined without having elicited an important piece of information. Statements heard at Tunhuang seemed to indicate that the great find of manuscripts had been reported at the time to the Tao-t'ai at Su-chou and thence to the Viceroy of Kan-su. Expression had been given also to a belief, of which we had no means of testing the foundation, that the latter had given orders for the transmission of specimens and for the safe keeping of the whole collection. If such injunctions had really been issued and, perhaps, an official inventory taken, things would necessarily, from our point of view, become far more complicated.

Fortunately Chiang's apprehensions on this score were dispelled by what the priest, turning talkative at times like many nervous people, let drop in conversation. A few rolls of Chinese texts, apparently Buddhist, had, indeed, been sent to the Viceregal Ya-mên at Lan-chou. But their contents had not been made out there, or else they had failed to attract any interest. Hence officialdom had rested satisfied with the rough statement that the whole of the manuscripts would make up about seven cartloads, and evidently dismayed at the cost of transport, or even of close examination, had left the whole undisturbed in charge of the Tao-shih as guardian of the temple.

But apart from this piece of information, the gist of Chiang-ssŭ-yeh's long report seemed far from justifying great hopes. In spite of the optimistic tinge which Chiang's ever-cheerful disposition was apt to impart to his observations, there was much reason to fear that the priest's peculiar frame of mind would prove a serious obstacle. To rely on the temptation of money alone as a means of overcoming his scruples was manifestly useless. So I thought it best to study his case in personal contact. Accompanied by Chiang I proceeded in the afternoon to pay my formal call to the Tao-shih, and asked to be shown over his restored cave-temple. It was the pride and the mainstay of his Tun-huang existence, and my request was fulfilled with alacrity. As he took me through the lofty antechapel with its substantial woodwork, all new and lavishly gilt and painted, and through the high passage or porch giving access and light to the main cella, I could not help glancing to the right where an ugly patch of unplastered brickwork then still masked the door of the hidden chapel. This was not the time to ask questions of my pious guide as to what was being guarded in that mysterious recess, but rather to display my interest in what his zeal had accomplished in the clearing of the cella and its sacred adornment.

The restoration had been only too thorough. In the middle of the large cella, some forty-six feet square, there rose on a horseshoe-shaped dais, ancient but replastered, a collection of brand-new clay images of colossal size, more hideous, I thought, than any I had seen in these caves. The seated Buddha in the center, and the disciples, saints, and Guardians of the Regions symmetrically grouped on his sides, showed only too plainly how low sculptural art had sunk in Tun-huang. But neither for this nor for the painful contrast these statues presented to the tasteful and remarkably well preserved fresco decoration on the walls and ceiling of the cella could the worthy Tao-shih reasonably be held responsible. His devotion to this shrine and to the task of religious merit which he had set himself in restoring it, was unmistakably genuine. As a poor, shiftless mendicant he had come from his native province of Shan-hsi some eight years before my visit, settled down at the ruined temple caves, and then set about restoring this one to what he conceived to have been its original glory.

The mouth of the passage was then blocked by drift sand from the silt deposits of the stream, and the original antechapel had completely decayed. When I thought of all the efforts, the perseverance, and the enthusiasm it must have cost this humble priest from afar to beg the money needed for the clearing out of the sand and the substantial reconstructions,—besides the antechapel there were several stories of temple halls built above in solid hard brick and timber, right to the top of the cliff,—I could not help feeling something akin to respect for the queer little figure by my side. It was clear from the way in which he lived with his two humble acolytes, and from all that Chiang had heard about him at Tun-huang, that he spent next to nothing on his person or private interests. Yet his list of charitable subscriptions and his accounts, proudly produced later on to Chiang-ssŭ-yeh, showed quite a respectable total, laboriously collected in the course of these years and spent upon these labors of piety.

It had not taken Chiang long to fathom Wang Tao-shih's profound ignorance of all that constitutes Chinese learning, and the very limited extent of his knowledge in general. So I knew that it would be futile to talk to him about my archaeological interests, about the need of first-hand materials for Chinese historical and antiquarian studies, and the like, as I was accustomed to do on meeting educated Chinese officials, ever ready to be interested in such topics. But the presence of this quaint priest, with his curious mixture of pious zeal, naïve ignorance, and astute tenacity of purpose, forcibly called to my mind those early Buddhist pilgrims from China who, simple in mind but strong in faith and—superstition, once made their way to India in the face of formidable difficulties.

More than once before, my well-known attachment to the memory of Hsüan-tsang, the greatest of those pilgrims, had been helpful in securing me a sympathetic hearing both among the learned and the simple. Wang Tao-shih, too, had probably heard about it. So surrounded by these tokens of lingering Buddhist worship, genuine though distorted, I thought it appropriate to tell Wang Tao-shih, as well as my poor Chinese would permit, of my devotion to the saintly traveler; how I had followed his footsteps from India for over ten thousand Li across inhospitable mountains and deserts; how in the course of this pilgrimage I had traced to its present ruins, however inaccessible, many a sanctuary he had piously visited and described; and so on.

I confess, it never cost me any effort to grow eloquent on the subject of my "Chinese patron saint," whose guidance had so often proved fruitful for my own work. But now it was made doubly easy by the gleam of lively interest which I caught in the Tao-shih's eyes, otherwise so shy and fitful. As Chiang, in reply to interjected questions, elaborated details and made the most of my familiarity with Hsüan-tsang's authentic records and the distant scenes of his travels, I could read the impression made in the Taoist priest's generally puzzling countenance. Very soon I felt sure that the Tao-shih, though poorly versed in and indifferent to things Buddhist, was quite as ardent an admirer in his own way of "T'ang-sêng," the great "monk of the T'ang period," as I am in another.

I had ocular proof of this when he took us outside into the spacious newly built loggia in front of the temple, and showed us with pride how he had caused all its walls to be decorated by a local Tun-huang artist with a series of quaint but spirited frescoes representing characteristic scenes from the great pilgrim's adventures (Figs. 189, 190). They were those fantastic legends which have transformed Hsüan-tsang in popular belief throughout China into a sort of saintly Munchausen. It is true they are not to be found in the genuine memoirs and biography. But what did that little difference in our respective conceptions of the hero matter? Gladly I let my delightfully credulous cicerone expound in voluble talk the wonderful stories of travel which each fresco panel depicted. Here the holy pilgrim was seen snatched up to the clouds by a wicked demon and then restored again to his pious companions through the force of his prayer or magic. Two queer-looking figures—one horse-, one bull-headed—were represented as his constant attendants. Elsewhere he was shown forcing a ferocious dragon which had swallowed his horse to restore it again, and so on.

But the picture in which I displayed particular interest showed a theme curiously adapted to our own case, though it was not till later that I appealed again and again to the moral it pointed. There was T'ang-sêng standing on the bank of a violent torrent, and beside him his faithful steed laden with big bundles of manuscripts. To help in ferrying across such a precious burden a large turtle was seen swimming toward the pilgrim. Here was clearly a reference to the twenty pony-loads of sacred books and relics which the historical traveler managed to carry away safely from India. But would the pious guardian read this obvious lesson aright, and be willing to acquire spiritual merit by letting me take back to the old home of Buddhism some of the ancient manuscripts which chance had placed in his keeping? For the time being it seemed safer not to tackle that question. Yet when I took my leave of the Tao-shih I instinctively felt that a new and more reliable link was being established between us.

★　★　★　★　★

I left the Ssŭ-yeh behind to make the most of the favorable impression produced, and to urge an early loan of the promised manuscript specimens. But the priest had again become nervous and postponed their delivery in a vague way "until later." There was nothing for me but to wait.

All doubt, however, disappeared in the end. Late at night Chiang groped his way to my tent in silent elation with a bundle of Chinese rolls which Wang Tao-shih had just brought him in secret, carefully hidden under his flowing black robe, as the first of the promised "specimens." The rolls looked unmistakably old as regards writing and paper, and probably contained Buddhist canonical texts; but Chiang needed time to make sure of their character. Next morning he turned up by daybreak, and with a face expressing both triumph and amazement, reported that these fine rolls of paper contained Chinese versions of certain "Sutras" from the Buddhist canon which the colophons declared to have been brought from India and translated by Hsüan-tsang himself. The strange chance which thus caused us to be met at the very outset by the name of my Chinese patron saint, and by what undoubtedly were early copies of his labors as a sacred translator, struck both of us as a most auspicious omen. Was it not "T'ang-sêng" himself, so Chiang declared, who at the opportune moment had revealed the hiding-place of that manuscript hoard to an ignorant priest in order to prepare for me, his admirer and disciple from distant India, a fitting antiquarian reward on the westernmost confines of China proper?

Of Hsüan-tsang's authorship, Wang Tao-shih in his ignorance could not possibly have had any inkling when he picked up that packet of "specimens." Chiang-ssŭ-yeh realized at once that this discovery was bound to impress the credulous priest as a special interposition on my behalf of the great traveler of sacred memory. So he hastened away to carry the news to the Tao-shih, and, backed up by this visible evidence of support from the latter's own cherished saint, to renew his pleading for free access to the hidden manuscript store. The effect was most striking. Before long Chiang returned to report that the portent could be trusted to work its spell. Some hours later he found the wall blocking the entrance to the recess of the temple removed, and on its door being opened by the priest, caught a glimpse of a room crammed full to the roof with manuscript bundles. I had purposely kept away from the Tao-shih's temple all the forenoon, but on getting this news I could no longer restrain my impatience to see the great hoard myself. The day was cloudless and hot, and the "soldiers" who had followed me about during the morning with my cameras, were now taking their siesta in sound sleep soothed by a good smoke of opium. So accompanied only by Chiang I went to the temple.

I found the priest there evidently still combating his scruples and nervous apprehensions. But under the influence of that quasi-divine hint he now summoned up courage to open before me the rough door closing the narrow entrance which led from the side of the broad front passage into the rock-carved recess, on a level of about four feet above the floor of the former. The sight of the small room disclosed was one to make my eyes open wide. Heaped up in layers, but without any order, there appeared in the dim light of the priest's little lamp a solid mass of manuscript bundles rising to a height of nearly ten feet, and filling, as subsequent measurement showed, close on 500 cubic feet. The area left clear within the room was just sufficient for two people to stand in. It was manifest that in this "black hole" no examination of the manuscripts would be possible, and also that the digging out of all its contents would cost a good deal of physical labor.

A suggestion to clear out all the bundles into the large cella of the cave-temple, where they might have been examined at ease, would have been premature; so much oppressed at the time was Wang Tao-shih by fears of losing his position—and patrons—by the rumors which any casual observers might spread against him in the oasis. So for the present I had to rest content with his offer to take out a bundle or two at a time, and to let us look rapidly through their contents in a less cramped part of the precincts. Fortunately the restorations carried out by him, besides the fine loggia already mentioned, included a kind of large antechapel, having on either side a small room provided with a door and paper-covered windows. So here a convenient "reading-room" was at hand for this strange old library, where we were screened from any inquisitive eyes, even if an occasional worshipper dropped in to "kotow" before the huge and ugly Buddha statue now set up in the temple.

While the Tao-shih was engaged in digging out a few bundles, I closely examined the passage wall behind which this great deposit of manuscripts had been hidden. The priest had told us that, when he first settled at the "Thousand Buddhas" some eight years before, he found the entrance to this cave-temple almost completely blocked by drift sand. Judging from the condition of other caves near by and the relatively low level of this particular temple, it is probable that this accumulation of drift sand rose to ten feet or more at the entrance. Keeping only a few laborers at work from the proceeds of pious donations, at first coming driblet-like with lamentable slowness, our Tao-shih had taken two or three years to lay bare the whole of the broad passage, some forty feet deep. When this task had been accomplished, and while engaged in setting up new statues in place of the decayed old stucco images occupying the dais of the cella, he had noticed a small crack in the frescoed wall to the right of the passage. There appeared to be a recess behind the plastered surface instead of the solid conglomerate from which the cella and its approach are hewn; and on widening the opening he discovered the small room with its deposit such as I now saw it.

Walled into the west face of the room had been found a large slab of black marble covered with a long and neatly engraved Chinese inscription. It had subsequently been removed and set up in a more accessible place on the left-hand wall of the passage. This inscription records imperial eulogies of a Chinese pilgrim named Hung-pien, who had visited India, and after returning with relics and sacred texts had apparently settled at these shrines to devote his remaining years to translating and other pious labors. As it is dated in the year corresponding to A.D. 851, it was clear to me from the first that the deposit of the manuscripts must have taken place some time after the middle of the ninth century.

But until we could find dated records among the manuscripts themselves there was no other indication of the lower date limit than the style of the frescoes which covered the passage walls. According to the Tao-shih's explicit assurance, borne out by the actual condition of the wall surface around the opening, mural painting had also covered the plaster in front of the latter. These frescoes, representing over-life-size Bodhisattvas marching in procession with offerings, were very well painted in a style met with again in numerous caves, the mural decorations of which had undergone no modern restoration, and appeared to me decidedly old. On various grounds it seemed improbable that they could be later than the period of the Sung dynasty, which immediately preceded the great Mongol conquest of the thirteenth century.

So there was evidence from the first to encourage my hopes that a search through this big hoard would reveal manuscripts of importance and interest. But the very hugeness of the deposit was bound to give rise to misgivings. Should we have time to eat our way through this mountain of ancient paper with any thoroughness? Would not the timorous priest, swayed by his worldly fears and possible spiritual scruples, be moved to close down his shell before I had been able to extract any of the pearls? There were reasons urging us to work with all possible energy and speed, and others rendering it advisable to display studied *insouciance* and calm assurance. Somehow we managed to meet the conflicting requirements of the situation. But, I confess, the strain and anxieties of the busy days which followed were great. . . .

All the manuscripts seemed to be preserved exactly in the same condition they were in when deposited. Some of the bundles were carelessly fastened with only rough cords and without an outer cloth wrapper; but even this had failed to injure the paper. Nowhere could I trace the slightest effect of moisture. And, in fact, what better place for preserving such relics could be imagined than a chamber carved in the live rock of these terribly barren hills, and hermetically shut off from what moisture, if any, the atmosphere of this desert valley ever contained? Not in the driest soil could relics of a ruined site have so completely escaped injury as they had here in a carefully selected rock chamber where, hidden behind a brick wall and protected by accumulated drift sand, these masses of manuscripts had lain undisturbed for centuries.

How grateful I felt for the special protection thus afforded when, on opening a large packet wrapped in a sheet of stout colored canvas, I found it full of paintings on fine gauze-like silk and on linen, ex-votos in all kinds of silk and brocade, with a mass of miscellaneous fragments of painted papers and cloth materials. Most of the paintings first found were narrow pieces from two to three feet in length, and proved by their floating streamers and the triangular tops provided with strings for fastening to have served as temple banners. These mountings made them look much more imposing when hung up. Many of them were in excellent condition, and all exactly as they had been deposited, after longer or shorter use. . . .

Nor was there time for any closer study, such as I should have loved to give there and then to these delicate, graceful paintings. My main care was how many of them I might hope to rescue from their dismal imprisonment and the risks attending their present guardian's careless handling. To my surprise and relief he evidently attached little value to these beautiful relics of pictorial art in the T'ang times. So I made bold to put aside rapidly "for further inspection," the best of the pictures on silk, linen, or paper I could lay my hands on, more than a dozen from the first bundle alone. I longed to carry away all its contents; for even among the fragments there were beautiful pieces, and every bit of silk would have its antiquarian and artistic value. But it would not have been wise to display too much *empressement*. So I restrained myself as well as I could, and put the rest away, with the firm resolve to return to the charge as soon as the ground was prepared for more extensive acquisitions.

To remains of this kind the priest seemed indifferent. The secret hope of diverting by their sacrifice my attention from the precious rolls of Chinese canonical texts or "Ching" made him now more assiduously grope for and hand out bundles of what he evidently classed under the head of miscellaneous rubbish. I had every reason to be pleased with this benevolent intention; for in the very first large packet of this kind I discovered, mixed up with Chinese and Tibetan texts, a great heap of oblong paper leaves in the variety of Indian script known as Central-Asian Brahmi. . . .

Flushed as I was with delight at these unhoped-for discoveries, I could not lose sight of the chief practical task, all-important for the time being. It was to keep our priest in a pliable mood, and to prevent his mind being overcome by the trepidations with which the chance of any intrusion and of consequent hostile rumors among his patrons would fill him. With the help of Chiang-ssŭ-yeh's genial persuasion, and what reassuring display I could make of my devotion to Buddhist lore in general and the memory of my patron saint in particular, we succeeded better than I had ventured to hope. I could see our honest Tao-shih's timorous look changing gradually to one of contentment at our appreciation of all this, to him valueless, lore. Though he visibly grew tired climbing over manuscript heaps and dragging out heavy bundles, it seemed as if he were becoming resigned to his fate, at least for a time.

When the growing darkness in the cave compelled us to stop further efforts for the day, a big bundle of properly packed manuscripts and painted fabrics lay on one side of our "reading-room" awaiting removal for what our diplomatic convention styled "closer examination." The great question was whether Wang Tao-shih would be willing to brave the risks of this removal, and subsequently to fall in with the true interpretation of our proceeding. It would not have done to breathe to him unholy words of sale and purchase; it was equally clear that any removal would have to be effected in strictest secrecy. So when we stepped outside the temple there was nothing in our hands or about our persons to arouse the slightest suspicion.

Then, tired as we all were, I took the occasion to engage the priest in another long talk about our common hero and patron saint, the great Hsüan-tsang. What better proof of his guidance and favor could I claim than that I should have been allowed to behold such a wonderful hidden store of sacred relics belonging to his own times and partly derived, perhaps, from his Indian wanderings, within a cave-temple which so ardent an admirer of "T'ang-sêng" had restored and was now guarding? Again I let the Tao-shih enlarge, as we stood in the loggia, upon the extraordinary adventures of his great saint as depicted in those cherished frescoes on its walls. The panel which showed Hsüan-tsang returning with his animal heavily laden with sacred manuscripts from India, was the most effective apologue I could advance for my eager interest in the relics the Tao-shih had discovered and was yet keeping from daylight.

The priest in his more susceptible moods could not help acknowledging that this fate of continued confinement in a dark hole was not the purpose for which the great scholar-saint had let him light upon these precious remains of Buddhist lore, and that he himself was quite incompetent to do justice to them by study or otherwise. Was it not evident, so Chiang pleaded with all the force of his soft reasoning, that by allowing me, a faithful disciple of Hsüan-tsang, to render accessible to Western students the literary and other relics which a providential discovery had placed so abundantly in his keeping, he would do an act of real religious merit? That this pious concession would also be rewarded by an ample donation for the benefit of the shrine he had labored to restore to its old glory, was a secondary consideration merely to be hinted at.

Whatever impression such and similar talks produced on the mind of the good Tao-shih, constantly vacillating between fears about his saintly reputation and a business-like grasp of the advantages to be attained by accommodating me in the matter of useless old things, the day closed with a gratifying achievement. In accordance with his own advice, I had left the Ssŭ-yeh alone to tackle the question of how to secure quietly the manuscripts and paintings selected. It was late at night when I heard cautious footsteps. It was Chiang who had come to make sure that nobody was stirring about my tent. A little later he returned with a big bundle over his shoulders. It contained everything I had picked out during the day's work.

The Tao-shih had summoned up courage to fall in with my wishes, on the solemn condition that nobody besides us three was to get the slightest inkling of what was being transacted, and that as long as I kept on Chinese soil the origin of these "finds" was not to be revealed to any living being. He himself was afraid of being seen at night outside his temple precincts. So the Ssŭ-yeh, zealous and energetic as always, took it upon himself to be the sole carrier. For seven nights more he thus came to my tent, when everybody had gone to sleep, with the same precautions, his slight figure panting under loads which grew each time heavier, and ultimately required carriage by instalments. For hands accustomed only to wield pen and paper it was a trying task, and never shall I forget the good-natured ease and cheerful devotion with which it was performed by that most willing of helpmates.

★   ★   ★   ★   ★

It would serve no useful purpose if I were to attempt to describe in detail how the search was continued day after day without remission, or to indicate in quasi-chronological order all the interesting finds with which this curious "digging" was rewarded. From the first it was certain that the contents of the hidden chapel must have been deposited in great confusion, and that any indications the original position of the bundles might have afforded at the time of discovery, had been completely effaced when the recess was cleared out, as the Tao-shih admitted, to search for valuables, and again later on for the purpose of removing the big inscribed slab from its west wall into the passage outside. It was mere chance, too, what bundles the Tao-shih would hand us out. . . .

As I worked my way in great haste through the contents of the "mixed" bundles,—we never knew how long we might rely on the Tao-shih's indulgence—I felt elated and at the same time oppressed by the constant flow of fresh materials pouring down upon us. Even in the case of art relics and manuscripts which were neither Chinese nor Tibetan, and of which I was able to estimate the full interest, there was no chance of closer examination. All I could do was to make sure of their being put apart "for further study," as our polite convention called removal. But what obsessed me most at the time was my total want of Sinologist training. How gladly would I then have exchanged one-half of my Indian knowledge for a tenth of its value in Chinese! Even with Chiang's zealous help I could never be sure of not leaving behind documents and texts of historical or literary interest amidst the smothering mass of Buddhist canonical literature and the like.

Nevertheless in this tantalizing *embarras des richesses* I was able to catch a few encouraging glimpses. It was thus that, in a series of monastic records apparently issued under the seal of the abbot of the chief establishment, I lighted upon the old name of the Ch'ien-fo-tung site, which here figured as San-chieh-ssŭ, the "Temples of the Three Regions." Subsequently I found out that even now three divisions are distinguished among the cave-temples, though the old designation of the site seems quite forgotten. Then again I found complete rolls stamped with the die of the "Temples of the Three Regions," and thus clearly marked as having formed part of a general monastic library.

Greatly delighted was I when I found that an excellently preserved roll with a well-designed block-printed picture as frontispiece, had its text printed throughout, showing a date of production corresponding to 860 A.D. Here was conclusive evidence that the art of printing books from wooden blocks was practiced long before the conventionally assumed time of its invention, during the Sung period, and that already in the ninth century the technical level had been raised practically as high as the process permitted. Then again there were spirited drawings and woodcuts to be found in the midst of the Chinese text rolls, needing no specialist experience to recognize their artistic merit.

Five days of strenuous work resulted in the extraction and rapid search of all "miscellaneous" bundles likely to contain manuscripts of special interest, paintings, and other relics which I was eager to rescue first of all. Fortunately when the Tao-shih had last stuffed back his treasures into their "black hole," these had been put mostly on the top or in other more or less accessible places, being, of course, less convenient building material than the tight uniform packets of Chinese and Tibetan rolls. But my task was not ended while there still rose against the walls of the chamber that solid rampart of manuscript bundles. They would have to be cleared out, too, and rapidly looked through. It was bound to prove a troublesome undertaking in more than one sense, though discreet treatment and judiciously administered doses of silver had so far succeeded in counteracting the Tao-shih's relapses into timorous contrariness. The labor of clearing out the whole chapel might by itself have dismayed a stouter heart than that of our priestly "librarian"; and what with this and the increased risk of exposure involved, Wang Tao-shih became now altogether refractory. However, he had already been gradually led from one concession to another, and we took care not to leave him much time for reflection.

So at last with many a sigh and plaintive remonstrance, and behind the outer temple gates carefully locked, he set to this great toil, helped now by a sort of priestly famulus whose discretion could be relied on. Previously I had sometimes feared that the little Tao-shih might get smothered under a tumbling wall of manuscript. Now I wondered whether the toil of pulling them out would not cause his slender physique to collapse. But it held out all the same, and by the evening of May 28th the regular bundles of Chinese rolls, more than 1050 in all, and those containing Tibetan texts had been transferred to neat rows in the spacious main cella of the temple.

The bundles were almost all sewn up tightly in coarse covers of linen. But the ends were generally left open, and as Wang handed out bundle after bundle through the chapel door, Chiang and myself were just able to see hastily whether, amidst the usual rolls with Chinese texts, there were embedded any Pothi leaves from Brahmi manuscripts, folded-up pictures, or other relics of special attraction. Such we picked out and put aside rapidly. But there was no time even to glance at individual rolls and to see whether they bore anywhere within or without Indian or Central-Asian writing.

Perfunctory as the operation had to be in view of the Tao-shih's visibly growing reluctance, I had a gratifying reward for my insistence on this clearing in the discovery of several miscellaneous bundles at the very bottom. They had been used there by the Tao-shih to turn a low clay platform into a level foundation for the manuscript wall above. In spite of the crushing these bundles had undergone, I recovered from them a large number of exquisite silk paintings of all sizes, and some beautiful embroidered pieces. One of the latter was a magnificent embroidery picture, remarkable for design, colors, and fineness of material, and showing a Buddha between Bodhisattvas in life size, which I shall have occasion to discuss hereafter.

Perhaps it was a lively sensation of the toil he had undergone and now longed to see ended, or else the fear that we were now touching those precious Chinese Sutra texts to which alone he seemed to attach any real value. At any rate the Tao-shih at this stage came to business, so to speak, by asking for a substantial "subscription" (*pushin*) to his temple. At the same time he protested that any cession of sacred texts or "Chings" was impossible. I myself was glad to take up the theme; for I had recognized long before that it was my duty toward research to try my utmost to rescue, if possible, the whole of the collection from the risk of slow dispersion and loss with which it was threatened in such keeping. . . .

The removal of so many cart-loads of manuscripts would inevitably give publicity to the whole transaction, and the religious resentment this was likely to arouse in Tun-huang, even if it did not lead to more serious immediate consequences, would certainly compromise my chance of further work in Kan-su.

Nevertheless, I was prepared to face these risks rather than forgo the endeavor to rescue the whole hoard. Chiang-ssǔ-yeh, in spite of misgivings justified by his knowledge of the local conditions, loyally did his best to persuade the Tao-shih that removal of the collection to a "temple of learning in Ta-Ying-kuo," or England, would in truth be an act which Buddha and his Arhats might approve as pious. He also urged that the big sum I was prepared to pay (I hinted at 40 horse-shoes, about Rs.5000, and was resolved to give twice as much, if need be, whatever the excess over my sanctioned grant) would enable Wang to return to a life of peace in his native province, distant Shan-hsi, if Tun-huang should become too hot for him. Or else he could allay any scruples by using the whole sum for the benefit of the temple, which by his restoration he could claim to have annexed as his own with all its contents known or unknown.

But all in vain. The prospect of losing his precious "Chings" as a whole or in part profoundly frightened the good priest, who had before resignedly closed his eyes to my gathering whatever I thought of special artistic or antiquarian value. For the first time our relations became somewhat strained, and it required very careful handling and our suavest manners to obviate anything like a breach. What the Tao-shih urged with all signs of sincere anxiety was that any deficiency in those piles of sacred texts would certainly be noticed by his patrons, who had helped him with their publicly recorded subscriptions to clear and restore the temple; that in consequence the position he had built up for himself in the district by the pious labors of eight years would be lost for good, and his life-task destroyed. He even vaguely reproached himself for having given up sacred things over which his lay patrons ought to have as much right of control as he himself, and doggedly asserted the need of consulting them before moving a step further. And in the depth of my heart I could bear him no grudge for these scruples and recriminations, or even gainsay them.

For two long days these discussions had to be carried on inter-mittently with a view to gain time while my examination of the miscel-laneous bundles was proceeding. I managed to complete this by the second evening. But on returning early next day to the temple in order to start the close search of the regular Chinese bundles for Central-Asian and other foreign text materials, I found to my dismay that the Tao-shih in a sudden fit of perturbation had shifted back overnight almost the whole of them to their gloomy prison of centuries. His sullen temper gave us further cause of anxiety. But the advantage we possessed by already holding loads of valuable manuscripts and antiques, and the Tao-shih's unmistakable wish to secure a substantial sum of money, led at last to what I had reason to claim as a substantial success in this diplomatic struggle.

He agreed to let me have fifty well-preserved bundles of Chi-nese text rolls and five of Tibetan ones, besides all my previous selections from the miscellaneous bundles. For all these acquisitions four horse-shoes of silver, equal to about Rs.500, passed into the priest's hands; and when I surveyed the archaeological value of all I could carry away for this sum, I had good reason to claim it a bargain. Of course, after so severe a struggle I lost no time in removing the heavy loads of Chinese and Tibetan rolls. Until now my devoted Ssŭ-yeh had struggled to my tent night by night with the loads of daily "selections"; but to this task his physical strength would not have been equal. So help had to be sought on this occasion from Ibrahim Beg and Tila, my trusted followers; and after two midnight trips to the temple, under the screening shadow of the steep river bank, the huge sackfuls were safely transferred to my storeroom without any one, even of my own men, having received an inkling.

The Tao-shih's nervousness had been increased by prolonged absence from his clients in the oasis; and now he hastened to resume his seasonal begging tour in the Tun-huang district. But a week later he returned, reassured that the secret had not been discovered and that his spiritual influence, such as it was, had suffered no diminution. So we succeeded in making him stretch a point further, and allow me to add some twenty more bundles of manuscripts to my previous selections, against an appropriate donation for the temple. When later on it came to the packing, the manuscript acquisitions needed seven cases, while the paintings, embroideries, and other miscellaneous relics filled five more. The packing of these was a very delicate task and kept me busy on the days when photographic work was impossible in the caves. There was some little trouble about getting enough boxes without exciting suspicion at Tun-huang. Luckily I had foreseen the chance and provided some "empties" beforehand. The rest were secured in disguise and by discreet installments. So everything passed off without a hitch.

The good Tao-shih now seemed to breathe freely again, and almost ready to recognize that I was performing a pious act in rescuing for Western scholarship those relics of ancient Buddhist literature and art which local ignorance would allow to lie here neglected or to be lost in the end. When I finally said good-bye to the "Thousand Buddhas," his jovial sharp-cut face had resumed once more its look of shy but self-contented serenity. We parted in fullest amity. I may anticipate here that I received gratifying proof of the peaceful state of his mind when, on my return to An-hsi four months later, he agreed to let depart for that "temple of learning" in the distant West another share of the Chinese and Tibetan manuscripts in the shape of over two hundred compact bundles. But my time for feeling true relief came when all the twenty-four cases, heavy with manuscript treasures rescued from that strange place of hiding, and the five more filled with paintings and other art relics from the same cave, had been deposited safely in the British Museum.

Under Vigo Bay

BY JULES VERNE

In *Twenty Thousand Leagues Under the Sea*, from which this extract is taken, the French novelist Jules Verne (1828–1905) made underwater treasure hunting sound simple. Captain Nemo, skipper of the submarine *Nautilus*, had only to pick up what he wanted from the ocean floor. In fact, the Vigo Bay treasure in particular has defied discovery for three hundred years, although the possibility exists that most of it was salvaged at the time the ships were scuttled. Of course Verne was hardly interested in factual accuracy anyway, but in producing his wonderfully distinctive mixture of popular science, futuristic plausibility, and sheer romance. That's why *Twenty Thousand Leagues*, along with *Voyage to the Center of the Earth* and *Around the World in Eighty Days* are still being read today, in spite of the dazzling advance in sophistication of science fiction.

★　★　★　★　★

At this moment the door of the large saloon opened, and Captain Nemo appeared. He saw me, and, without further preamble, began in an amiable tone of voice—

"Ah, sir! I have been looking for you. Do you know the history of Spain?"

Now, one might know the history of one's own country by

heart; but in the condition I was at the time, with troubled mind and head quite lost, I could not have said a word of it.

"Well," continued Captain Nemo, "you heard my question? Do you know the history of Spain?"

"Very slightly," I answered.

"Well, here are learned men having to learn," said the captain. "Come, sit down, and I will tell you a curious episode in this history.— Sir, listen well," said he; "this history will interest you on one side, for it will answer a question which doubtless you have not been able to solve."

"I listen, Captain," said I, not knowing what my interlocutor was driving at, and asking myself if this incident was bearing on our projected flight.

"Sir, if you have no objection, we will go back to 1702. You cannot be ignorant that your king, Louis XIV., thinking that the gesture of a potentate was sufficient to bring the Pyrenees under his yoke, had imposed the Duke of Anjou, his grandson, on the Spaniards. This prince reigned more or less badly under the name of Philip V., and had a strong party against him abroad. Indeed, the preceding year, the royal houses of Holland, Austria, and England, had concluded a treaty of alliance at the Hague, with the intention of plucking the crown of Spain from the head of Philip V., and placing it on that of an archduke to whom they prematurely gave the title of Charles III.

"Spain must resist this coalition; but she was almost entirely unprovided with either soldiers or sailors. However, money would not fail them, provided that their galleons, laden with gold and silver from America, once entered their ports. And about the end of 1702 they expected a rich convoy which France was escorting with a fleet of twenty-three vessels, commanded by Admiral Château-Renaud, for the ships of the coalition were already beating the Atlantic. This convoy was to go to Cadiz, but the Admiral, hearing that an English fleet was cruising in those waters, resolved to make for a French port.

"The Spanish commanders of the convoy objected to this decision. They wanted to be taken to a Spanish port, and if not to Cadiz, into Vigo Bay, situated on the north-west coast of Spain, and which was not blocked.

"Admiral Château-Renaud had the rashness to obey this injunction, and the galleons entered Vigo Bay.

"Unfortunately, it formed an open road which could not be defended in any way. They must therefore hasten to unload the galleons before the arrival of the combined fleet; and time would not have failed them had not a miserable question of rivalry suddenly arisen.

"You are following the chain of events?" asked Captain Nemo.

"Perfectly," said I, not knowing the end proposed by this historical lesson.

"I will continue. This is what passed. The merchants of Cadiz had a privilege by which they had the right of receiving all merchandise coming from the West Indies. Now, to disembark these ingots at the port of Vigo, was depriving them of their rights. They complained at Madrid, and obtained the consent of the weak-minded Philip that the convoy, without discharging its cargo, should remain sequestered in the roads of Vigo until the enemy had disappeared.

"But whilst coming to this decision, on the 22d of October 1702, the English vessels arrived in Vigo Bay, when Admiral Château-Renaud, in spite of inferior forces, fought bravely. But seeing that the treasure must fall into the enemy's hands, he burnt and scuttled every galleon, which went to the bottom with their immense riches."

Captain Nemo stopped. I admit I could not yet see why this history should interest me.

"Well?" I asked.

"Well, M. Aronnax," replied Captain Nemo, "we are in that Vigo Bay; and it rests with yourself whether you will penetrate its mysteries."

The captain rose, telling me to follow him. I had time to recover. I obeyed. The saloon was dark, but through the transparent glass the waves were sparkling. I looked.

For half a mile around the *Nautilus*, the waters seemed bathed in electric light. The sandy bottom was clean and bright. Some of the ship's crew in their diving dresses were clearing away half rotten barrels and empty cases from the midst of the blackened wrecks. From these cases and from these barrels escaped ingots of gold and silver, cascades of piastres and jewels. The sand was heaped up with them. Laden with their precious booty the men returned to the *Nautilus*, disposed of their burden, and went back to this inexhaustible fishery of gold and silver.

I understood now. This was the scene of the battle of the 22nd of October 1702. Here on this very spot the galleons laden for the Spanish Government had sunk. Here Captain Nemo came, according to his wants, to pack up those millions with which he burdened the *Nautilus*. It was for him and him alone America had given up her precious metals. He was heir direct, without any one to share, in those treasures torn from the Incas and from the conquered of Ferdinand Cortez.

"Did you know, sir," he asked, smiling, "that the sea contained such riches?"

"I knew," I answered, "that they value the money held in suspension in these waters at two millions."

"Doubtless; but to extract this money the expense would be greater than the profit. Here, on the contrary, I have but to pick up what man has lost,—and not only in Vigo Bay, but in a thousand other spots where shipwrecks have happened, and which are marked on my submarine map. Can you understand now the source of the millions I am worth?"

"I understand, Captain. But allow me to tell you that in exploring Vigo Bay you have only been beforehand with a rival society."

"And which?"

"A society which has received from the Spanish Government the privilege of seeking these buried galleons. The shareholders are led on by the allurement of an enormous bounty, for they value these rich shipwrecks at five hundred millions."

"Five hundred millions they were," answered Captain Nemo, "but they are so no longer."

"Just so," said I; "and a warning to those shareholders would be an act of charity. But who knows if it would be well received? What gamblers usually regret above all is less the loss of their money, than of their foolish hopes. After all, I pity them less than the thousands of unfortunates to whom so much riches well-distributed would have been profitable, whilst for them they will be for ever barren."

I had no sooner expressed this regret, than I felt that it must have wounded Captain Nemo.

"Barren!" he exclaimed, with animation. "Do you think then, sir, that these riches are lost because I gather them? Is it for myself alone, according to your idea, that I take the trouble to collect these treasures? Who told you that I did not make a good use of it? Do you think I am ignorant that there are suffering beings and oppressed races on this earth, miserable creatures to console, victims to avenge? Do you not understand?"

Captain Nemo stopped at these last words, regretting perhaps that he had spoken so much. But I had guessed that whatever the motive which had forced him to seek independence under the sea, it had left him still a man, that his heart still beat for the sufferings of humanity, and that his immense charity was for oppressed races as well as individuals. And I then understood for whom those millions were destined, which were forwarded by Captain Nemo when the *Nautilus* was cruising in the waters of Crete.

Treasure Island

BY ROBERT LOUIS STEVENSON

Robert Louis Stevenson (1850–1994) wrote *Treasure Island* as a boy's book, but it has had plenty of grown-up readers, and its publication in book form in 1883 brought him serious fame for the first time. A full-length tale of a hunt for pirate treasure, replete with sword-play, black-hearted villains, bloodcurdling oaths (alluded to, not spelled out), and even a parrot singing 'Yo ho ho and a bottle of rum,' it might be dismissed as so much fustian. But Stevenson was too good a writer to miss creating a classic, in spite of everything. For those unfamiliar with the book, it should be explained that in this extract two Captain Flints are mentioned: one is the late pirate chief who buried the treasure being sought, while the other is Long John Silver's parrot, named in honor of the thoroughly reprehensible original.

★   ★   ★   ★   ★

It was no wonder the men were in a good humor now. For my part, I was horribly cast down. Should the scheme he had now sketched prove feasible, Silver, already doubly a traitor, would not hesitate to adopt it. He had still a foot in either camp, and there was no doubt he would prefer wealth and freedom with the pirates to a bare escape from hanging, which was the best he had to hope on our side.

157

Nay, and even if things so fell out that he was forced to keep his faith with Dr. Livesey, even then what danger lay before us! What a moment that would be when the suspicions of his followers turned to certainty, and he and I should have to fight for dear life—he, a cripple, and I, a boy—against five strong and active seamen!

Add to this double apprehension, the mystery that still hung over the behavior of my friends; their unexplained desertion of the stockade; their inexplicable cession of the chart; or, harder still to understand, the doctor's last warning to Silver, "Look out for squalls when you find it;" and you will readily believe how little taste I found in my breakfast, and with how uneasy a heart I set forth behind my captors on the quest for treasure.

We made a curious figure, had anyone been there to see us; all in soiled sailor clothes, and all but me armed to the teeth. Silver had two guns slung about him—one before and one behind—besides the great cutlass at his waist, and a pistol in each pocket of his square-tailed coat. To complete his strange appearance, Captain Flint sat perched upon his shoulder and gabbling odds and ends of purposeless sea-talk. I had a line about my waist, and followed obediently after the sea cook, who held the loose end of the rope, now in his free hand, now between his powerful teeth. For all the world, I was led like a dancing bear.

The other men were variously burthened; some carrying picks and shovels—for that had been the very first necessary they brought ashore from the *Hispaniola*—others laden with pork, bread, and brandy for the midday meal. All the stores, I observed, came from our stock; and I could see the truth of Silver's words the night before. Had he not struck a bargain with the doctor, he and his mutineers, deserted by the ship, must have been driven to subsist on clear water and the proceeds of their hunting. Water would have been little to their taste; a sailor is not usually a good shot; and besides all that, when they were so short of eatables, it was not likely they would be very flush of powder.

Well, thus equipped, we all set out—even the fellow with the broken head, who should certainly have kept in shadow—and straggled, one after another, to the beach, where the two gigs awaited us. Even these bore trace of the drunken folly of the pirates, one in a broken thwart, and both in their muddied and unbaled condition. Both were to be carried along with us, for the sake of safety; and so, with our numbers divided between them, we set forth upon the bosom of the anchorage.

As we pulled over, there was some discussion on the chart. The red cross was, of course, far too large to be a guide; and the terms of the note on the back, as you will hear, admitted of some ambiguity. They ran, the reader may remember, thus:

"Tall tree, Spy-glass Shoulder, bearing a point to the N. of N.N.E.
"Skeleton Island E.S.E. and by E.
"Ten feet."

A tall tree was thus the principal mark. Now, right before us, the anchorage was bounded by a plateau from two to three hundred feet high, adjoining on the north the sloping southern shoulder of the Spy-glass, and rising again toward the south into the rough cliffy eminence called the Mizzenmast Hill. The top of the plateau was dotted thickly with pine trees of varying height. Every here and there, one of a different species rose forty or fifty feet clear above its neighbors, and which of these was the particular "tall tree" of Captain Flint could only be decided on the spot, and by the readings of the compass.

Yet, although that was the case, every man on board the boats had picked a favorite of his own ere we were halfway over, Long John alone shrugging his shoulders and bidding them wait till they were there.

We pulled easily, by Silver's directions, not to weary the hands prematurely; and, after quite a long passage, landed at the mouth of the second river—that which runs down a woody cleft of the Spy-glass. Thence, bending to our left, we began to ascend the slope toward the plateau.

At the first outset, heavy, miry ground and a matted, marish vegetation, greatly delayed our progress; but by little and little the hill began to steepen and become stony under foot, and the wood to change its character and to grow in a more open order. It was, indeed, a most pleasant portion of the island that we were now approaching. A heavy-scented broom and many flowering shrubs had almost taken the place of grass. Thickets of green nutmeg trees were dotted here and there with the red columns and the broad shadow of the pines; and the first mingled their spice with the aroma of the others. The air, besides, was fresh and stirring, and this, under the sheer sunbeams, was a wonderful refreshment to our senses.

The party spread itself abroad, in a fan shape, shouting and leaping to and fro. About the center, and a good way behind the rest, Silver and I followed—I tethered by my rope, he plowing, with deep pants, among the sliding gravel. From time to time, indeed, I had to lend him a hand, or he must have missed his footing and fallen backward down the hill.

We had thus proceeded for about half a mile, and were approaching the brow of the plateau, when the man upon the farthest left began to cry aloud, as if in terror. Shout after shout came from him, and the others began to run in his direction.

"He can't 'a' found the treasure," said old Morgan, hurrying past us from the right, "for that's clean a-top."

Indeed, as we found when we also reached the spot, it was something very different. At the foot of a pretty big pine, and involved in a green creeper, which had even partly lifted some of the smaller bones, a human skeleton lay, with a few shreds of clothing, on the ground. I believe a chill struck for a moment to every heart.

"He was a seaman," said George Merry, who, bolder than the rest, had gone up close, and was examining the rags of clothing. "Leastways, this is good sea-cloth."

"Ah, ay," said Silver, "like enough: you wouldn't look to find a bishop here, I reckon. But what sort of a way is that for bones to lie? 'Tain't in natur'."

Indeed, on a second glance, it seemed impossible to fancy that the body was in a natural position. But for some disarray (the work, perhaps, of the birds that had fed upon him, or of the slow growing creeper that had gradually enveloped his remains) the man lay perfectly straight—his feet pointing in one direction, his hands, raised above his head like a diver's, pointing directly in the opposite.

"I've taken a notion into my old numskull," observed Silver. "Here's the compass; there's the tip-top p'int o' Skeleton Island, stickin' out like a tooth. Just take a bearing, will you, along the line of them bones."

It was done. The body pointed straight in the direction of the island, and the compass read duly E.S.E. and by E.

"I thought so," cried the cook; "this here is a p'inter. Right up there is our line for the Pole Star and the jolly dollars. But, by thunder! if it don't make me cold inside to think of Flint. This is one of *his* jokes, and no mistake. Him and these six was alone here; he killed 'em, every man; and this one he hauled here and laid down by compass, shiver my timbers! They're long bones, and the hair's been yellow. Ay, that would be Allardyce. You mind Allardyce, Tom Morgan?"

"Ay, ay," returned Morgan, "I mind him; he owed me money, he did, and took my knife ashore with him."

"Speaking of knives," said another, "why don't we find his'n lying round? Flint warn't the man to pick a seaman's pocket, and the birds, I guess, would leave it be."

"By the powers, and that's true!" cried Silver.

"There ain't a thing left here," said Merry, still feeling round among the bones, "not a copper doit nor a baccy box. It don't look nat'ral to me."

"No, by gum, it don't," agreed Silver; "not nat'ral, nor not nice, says you. Great guns! messmates, but if Flint was living, this would be a hot spot for you and me. Six they were, and six are we; and bones is what they are now."

"I saw him dead with these here dead-lights," said Morgan. "Billy took me in. There he laid, with penny-pieces on his eyes."

"Dead—ay, sure enough he's dead and gone below," said the fellow with the bandage; "but if ever sperrit walked, it would be Flint's. Dear heart, but he died bad, did Flint!"

"Ay, that he did," observed another; "now he raged, and now he hollered for the rum, and now he sang. 'Fifteen Men' were his only song, mates; and I tell you true, I never rightly liked to hear it since. It was main hot, and the windy was open, and I hear that old song comin' out as clear as clear—and the death-haul on the man a'ready."

"Come, come," said Silver, "stow this talk. He's dead, and he don't walk, that I know; leastways, he won't walk by day, and you may lay to that. Care killed a cat. Fetch ahead for the doubloons."

We started, certainly; but in spite of the hot sun and the staring daylight, the pirates no longer ran separate and shouting through the wood, but kept side by side and spoke with bated breath. The terror of the dead buccaneer had fallen on their spirits.

★   ★   ★   ★   ★

Partly from the damping influence of this alarm, partly to rest Silver and the sick folk, the whole party sat down as soon as they had gained the brow of the ascent.

The plateau being somewhat tilted toward the west, this spot on which we had paused commanded a wide prospect on either hand. Before us, over the tree-tops, we beheld the Cape of the Woods fringed with surf; behind, we not only looked down upon the anchorage and Skeleton Island, but saw—clear across the spit and the eastern lowlands— a great field of open sea upon the east. Sheer above us rose the Spy-glass, here dotted with single pines, there black with precipices. There was no sound but that of the distant breakers, mounting from all round, and the chirp of countless insects in the brush. Not a man, not a sail upon the sea; the very largeness of the view increased the sense of solitude.

Silver, as he sat, took certain bearings with his compass.

"There are three 'tall trees,'" said he, "about in the right line from Skeleton Island. 'Spy-glass Shoulder,' I take it, means that lower p'int there. It's child's play to find the stuff now. I've half a mind to dine first."

"I don't feel sharp," growled Morgan. "Thinkin' o' Flint—I think it were—as done me."

"Ah, well, my son, you praise your stars he's dead," said Silver.

"He were an ugly devil," cried a third pirate with a shudder; "that blue in the face, too!"

"That was how the rum took him," added Merry. "Blue! well, I reckon he was blue. That's a true word."

Ever since they had found the skeleton and got upon this train of thought, they had spoken lower and lower, and they had almost got to whispering by now, so that the sound of their talk hardly interrupted the silence of the wood. All of a sudden, out of the middle of the trees in front of us, a thin, high, trembling voice struck up the well-known air and words:

"Fifteen men on The Dead Man's Chest—
Yo-ho-ho, and a bottle of rum!"

I never have seen men more dreadfully affected than the pirates. The color went from their six faces like enchantment; some leaped to their feet, some clawed hold of others; Morgan groveled on the ground.

"It's Flint, by . . . !" cried Merry.

The song had stopped as suddenly as it began—broken off, you would have said, in the middle of a note, as though someone had laid his hand upon the singer's mouth. Coming so far through the clear, sunny atmosphere among the green tree-tops, I thought it had sounded airily and sweetly; and the effect on my companions was the stranger.

"Come," said Silver, struggling with his ashen lips to get the word out, "this won't do. Stand by to go about. This is a rum start, and I can't name the voice: but it's someone skylarking—someone that's flesh and blood, and you may lay to that."

His courage had come back as he spoke, and some of the color to his face along with it. Already the others had begun to lend an ear to this encouragement, and were coming a little to themselves, when the same voice broke out again—not this time singing, but in a faint distant hail, that echoed yet fainter among the clefts of the Spy-glass.

"Darby M'Graw," it wailed—for that is the word that best

describes the sound—"Darby M'Graw! Darby McGraw!" again and again and again; and then rising a little higher, and with an oath that I leave out, "Fetch aft the rum, Darby!"

The buccaneers remained rooted to the ground, their eyes starting from their heads. Long after the voice had died away they still stared in silence, dreadfully, before them.

"That fixes it!" gasped one. "Let's go."

"They was his last words," moaned Morgan, "his last words above board."

Dick had his Bible out, and was praying volubly. He had been well brought up, had Dick, before he came to sea and fell among bad companions.

Still, Silver was unconquered. I could hear his teeth rattle in his head; but he had not yet surrendered.

"Nobody in this here island ever heard of Darby," he muttered; "not one but us that's here." And then, making a great effort, "Shipmates," he cried, "I'm here to get that stuff, and I'll not be beat by man nor devil. I never was feared of Flint in his life, and, by the powers, I'll face him dead. There's seven hundred thousand pound not a quarter of a mile from here. When did ever a gentleman o' fortune show his stern to that much dollars, for a boosy old seaman with a blue mug—and him dead, too?"

But there was no sign of re-awakening courage in his followers; rather, indeed, of growing terror at the irreverence of his words.

"Belay there, John!" said Merry. "Don't you cross a sperrit."

And the rest were all too terrified to reply. They would have run away severally had they dared; but fear kept them together, and kept them close by John, as if his daring helped them. He, on his part, had pretty well fought his weakness down.

"Sperrit? Well, maybe," he said. "But there's one thing not clear to me. There was an echo. Now, no man ever seen a sperrit with a shadow; well, then, what's he doing with an echo to him, I should like to know? That ain't in natur,' surely?"

This argument seemed weak enough to me. But you can never

tell what will affect the superstitious, and, to my wonder, George Merry was greatly relieved.

"Well, that's so," he said. "You've a head upon your shoulders, John, and no mistake. 'Bout ship, mates! this here crew is on a wrong tack, I do believe. And come to think on it, it was like Flint's voice, I grant you, but not just so clear-away like it, after all. It was liker somebody else's voice now—it was liker . . ."

"By the powers, Ben Gunn!" roared Silver.

"Ay, and so it were," cried Morgan, springing on his knees. "Ben Gunn it were!"

"It don't make much odds, do it, now?" asked Dick. "Ben Gunn's not here in the body, anymore'n Flint."

But the older hands greeted this remark with scorn.

"Why, nobody minds Ben Gunn," cried Merry; "dead or alive, nobody minds him."

It was extraordinary how their spirits had returned, and how the natural color had revived in their faces. Soon they were chatting together, with intervals of listening; and not long after, hearing no further sound, they shouldered the tools and set forth again, Merry walking first with Silver's compass to keep them on the right line with Skeleton Island. He had said the truth: dead or alive, nobody minded Ben Gunn.

Dick alone still held his Bible, and looked around him as he went, with fearful glances; but he found no sympathy, and Silver even joked him on his precautions.

"I told you," said he—"I told you, you had sp'iled your Bible. If it ain't no good to swear by, what do you suppose a sperrit would give for it? Not that!" and he snapped his big fingers, halting a moment on his crutch.

But Dick was not to be comforted; indeed it was soon plain to me that the lad was falling sick; hastened by heat, exhaustion, and the shock of his alarm, the fever predicted by Doctor Livesey was evidently growing swiftly higher.

It was fine open walking here, upon the summit; our way lay a little downhill, for, as I have said, the plateau tilted toward the west. The pines, great and small, grew wide apart: and even between the clumps of nutmeg and azalea, wide open spaces baked in the hot sunshine. Striking, as we did, pretty near northwest across the island, we drew, on the one hand, ever nearer under the shoulders of the Spy-glass, and on the other, looked ever wider over that western bay where I had once tossed and trembled in the coracle.

The first of the tall trees was reached, and by the bearing, proved the wrong one. So with the second. The third rose nearly two hundred feet in the air above a clump of underwood; a giant of a vegetable, with a red column as big as a cottage, and a wide shadow around in which a company could have manœuvred. It was conspicuous far to sea both on the east and west, and might have been entered as a sailing mark upon the chart.

But it was not its size that now impressed my companions; it was the knowledge that seven hundred thousand pounds in gold lay somewhere buried beneath its spreading shadow. The thought of the money, as they drew nearer, swallowed up their previous terrors. Their eyes burned in their heads; their feet grew speedier and lighter; their whole soul was bound up in that fortune, that whole lifetime of extravagance and pleasure, that lay waiting there for each of them.

Silver hobbled, grunting, on his crutch; his nostrils stood out and quivered; he cursed like a madman when the flies settled on his hot and shiny countenance; he plucked furiously at the line that held me to him, and, from time to time, turned his eyes upon me with a deadly look. Certainly he took no pains to hide his thoughts; and certainly I read them like print. In the immediate nearness of the gold, all else had been forgotten; his promise and the doctor's warning were both things of the past; and I could not doubt that he hoped to seize upon the treasure, find and board the *Hispaniola* under cover of night, cut every honest throat about that island, and sail away as he had at first intended, laden with crimes and riches.

Shaken as I was with these alarms, it was hard for me to keep up with the rapid pace of the treasure-hunters. Now and again I stumbled; and it was then that Silver plucked so roughly at the rope and launched at me his murderous glances. Dick, who had dropped behind us, and now brought up the rear, was babbling to himself both prayers and curses, as his fever kept rising. This also added to my wretchedness, and, to crown all, I was haunted by the thought of the tragedy that had once been acted on that plateau, when that ungodly buccaneer with the blue face—he who died at Savannah, singing and shouting for drink—had there, with his own hand, cut down his six accomplices. This grove, that was now so peaceful, must then have rung with cries, I thought; and even with the thought I could believe I heard it ringing still.

We were now at the margin of the thicket.

"Huzza, mates, altogether!" shouted Merry; and the foremost broke into a run.

And suddenly, not ten yards further, we beheld them stop. A low cry arose. Silver doubled his pace, digging away with the foot of his crutch like one possessed; and next moment he and I had come also to a dead halt.

Before us was a great excavation, not very recent, for the sides had fallen in and grass had sprouted on the bottom. In this were the shaft of a pick broken in two and the boards of several packing-cases strewn around. On one of these boards I saw, branded with a hot iron, the name *Walrus*—the name of Flint's ship.

All was clear to probation. The *cache* had been found and rifled; the seven hundred thousand pounds were gone.

Exploration Fawcett

BY P. H. FAWCETT

One treasure that would be really worth having is Col. Percy Fawcett's own report on what happened to him. There are plenty of reasons, however, to doubt that it exists. No one has seen him since he disappeared, somewhere in the depths of the Brazilian jungle, in 1925, searching for (and perhaps finding?) a lost city he was absolutely convinced simply waited for discovery. Expeditions have gone out hunting for him, without success, the latest in 1996. Fawcett just vanished. What we do have, thanks to the editorial enterprise of his son Brian Fawcett, is the Colonel's manuscript, written before his departure, explaining what had convinced him to undertake his doomed expedition. This is a chapter from it. While the evidence may seem a bit shaky to the cynical among us, Fawcett puts the case brilliantly.

* * * * *

When Diego Alvarez struggled landwards through the Atlantic swell in a welter of wreckage from the disintegrating caravel, it was to land, exhausted, on a shore absolutely unknown to this sixteenth-century Portuguese. Only twenty-four years previously Columbus had discovered the New World and fired the imaginations of Iberian adventurers. The dawn of knowledge was only just breaking after the dark night of the Middle Ages; the world in its entirety was yet a mystery, and each venture to probe it disclosed new wonders. The border between myth and reality was not fixed, and the adventurer saw strange sights with an eye distorted by superstition.

Here, on the coast of Brazil where Bahía now stands, anything might exist. Behind the forest's edge on top of those cliffs were surely to be found wonderful things, and he—Diego Alvarez—would be the first of his race to set eyes on them. There might be dangers from the natives of the country—perhaps even those weird people, half human, half monster, who, tradition had it, lived in this land—but they had to be faced if he was to find food and water. The spirit of the pioneer had driven him to join the ill-fated voyage; it spurred him on, and nothing short of death could stop him.

The place where he came ashore, sole survivor from the wreck, was in the territory of the cannibal Tupinambas. Perhaps he escaped being eaten by reason of his strangeness; perhaps his captors considered it a triumph over neighbouring tribes to display their captive alive. For his salvation the Portuguese had principally to thank an Indian girl named Paraguassu, the Pocahontas of South America, who took a fancy to him and became his wife—ultimately the favourite among several.

For many years the Portuguese mariner lived with the Indians. A number of his countrymen came to Brazil, and he was able to establish friendly relations between them and the savages. Finally he managed to bring Paraguassu into the fold of the Church, and a sister of hers married another Portuguese adventurer. The child of her sister's marriage; Melchior Dias Moreyra, spent most of his life with the Indians, and was known by them as Muribeca. He discovered many mines, and accumulated vast quantities of silver, gold and precious stones, which were worked by the skilful Tapuya tribes into so wonderful a treasure that the early European colonists were filled with envy.

Muribeca had a son called Roberio Dias, who as a lad was familiar with the mines where his father's vast wealth originated. About 1610 Roberio Dias approached the Portuguese King, Dom Pedro II, with an offer to hand over the mines in exchange for the title of Marquis das Minas. He showed a rich specimen of silver-bearing ore and temptingly promised more silver than there was iron at Bilbao. He was only partly believed, but the royal greed for treasure was strong enough to cause a patent to be drawn up for the marquisate.

If Roberio Dias thought he would leave the court a marquis he was mistaken. Old Dom Pedro II was too cunning for that. The patent was sealed and delivered to a commission entrusted to hand it over only after the mines had been disclosed. But Dias in his turn had suspicions. He was not one to trust blindly to the King's faith. While the expedition was some distance from Bahía he managed to persuade the officer in command of the Commission to open the envelope and allow him to see the patent. He found that he was down for a military commission as captain, and no more—not a word about the marquisate! That settled it. Dias refused to hand over the mines, so the enraged officer took him back by force to Bahía, where he was flung into prison. Here he remained for two years, and then he was allowed to buy his freedom for 9,000 crowns. In 1622 he died, and the secret of the mines was never disclosed. Diego Alvarez had been dead for a long time; Muribeca himself had gone, no Indian would talk even under the most frightful tortures, so Dom Pedro was left to curse his ill-judged deceit and read over again and again the official reports of the assays made of Roberio Dias's specimens.

The secret of the mines was lost, but for years expeditions scoured the country in an effort to locate them. As failure succeeded failure, belief in their existence died away to survive only as myth, yet there were always some hardy souls ready to brave hostile savages and slow starvation for the chance of discovering a New Potosi.

The region beyond the São Francisco River was as unknown to the Portuguese colonists of those times as the forests of the Gongugy are to the Brazilians of today. Exploration was too difficult. Not only was it too much to contend with hordes of wild Indians shooting poisoned arrows from impenetrable cover, but food was not available to provide for an expedition large enough to protect itself from attack: Yet one after another ventured it, and more often than not was never heard of again. They called these expeditions *Bandeiras*, or Flags, for they were officially sponsored, accompanied by Government troops, and usually by a contingent of missionaries. Occasionally civilians banded together for the purpose, armed a number of negro slaves, enlisted tame Indians as guides, and disappeared into the *Sertão* (bush) for years at a time, if not for ever.

If you are romantically minded—and most of us are, I think—you have in the foregoing the background for a story so fascinating that I know none to compare. I myself came upon it in an old document still preserved at Rio de Janeiro, and, in the light of evidence gleaned from many quarters, believe it implicitly. I am not going to offer a literal translation of the strange account given in the document—the crabbed Portuguese script is broken in several places—but the story begins in 1743, when a native of Minas Gerais, whose name has not been preserved, decided to make a search for the Lost Mines of Muribeca.

Francisco Raposo—I must identify him by some name—was not to be deterred by wild beasts, venomous snakes, savages and insects from attempting to enrich himself and his followers as the Spaniards in Peru and Mexico had done only two centuries before. They were a hardy lot, those old pioneers—superstitious, perhaps, but when gold called all obstacles were forgotten.

It was always difficult to take cargo animals through the trackless hinterland. There were numerous rivers and bogs everywhere; pasture was coarse, and the continuous attacks of vampire bats soon finished the animals off. Climate ranged from very cold to extreme heat, and total drought would be followed by days of sheer deluge, so that a fair amount of equipment had to be carried. Yet Raposo and his band gave little consideration to such drawbacks, and set out hopefully into the wilds.

Exactly where they went I have only lately discovered. It was roughly northwards. There were no maps of the country in those days, and no member of the party knew anything about land navigation, so the clues in the record they left are entirely unreliable. Indians accompanied them from point to point and suggested the routes taken, otherwise they merely wandered into the unknown and left it to fortune to bring them to the coveted objective. In the manner of all pioneers, they lived on what fish and game they could secure, and on fruit and vegetables pilfered from Indian plantations or begged from friendly tribes. It was thin living, for game is timid in the South American wilderness, but men lived more simply in those days and consequently their endurance was greater. Raposo, his compatriots, and their black slaves survived to continue their wanderings for ten years. Not counting the Indians who joined them from time to time and who would vanish when it suited them, the party was about eighteen strong. Perhaps that was the secret of their survival, for the usual *Bandeiras* numbered at least five hundred, and there is a record of one 1,400 strong, not a single member of which ever returned! Few might live where many would starve.

The time came when the party was travelling eastward again, towards the coast settlements, tired of this seemingly endless wandering, and disheartened by their failure to locate the lost mines. Raposo was almost ready to believe them a myth, and his companions had long ago decided that no such mines existed. They had come through swamps and bush country when jagged mountains showed up ahead, beyond a grassy plain broken by thin belts of green forest. Raposo in his narrative describes them poetically, "They seemed to reach the ethereal regions and to serve as a throne for the wind and the stars themselves." Anyone who has passed months on end in the monotonous flatness of the plains will appreciate his rhapsody.

These were no ordinary mountains. As the party came nearer, the sides lit up in flame, for it had been raining and the setting sun was reflected from wet rocks rich in crystals and that slightly opaque quartz which is so common in this part of Brazil. To the eager explorers they seemed to be studded with gems. Streams leaped from rock to rock, and over the crest of the ridge a rainbow formed, as though to hint that treasure was to be found at its feet.

"An omen!" cried Raposo. "See! We have found the treasure house of the great Muribeca!"

Night came down and forced them to camp before reaching the foot of those wonderful mountains; and next morning, when the sun came up from behind them, the crags appeared black and menacing. Enthusiasm waned; but there is always something fascinating about mountains for the explorer. Who knows what may be seen from the topmost ridge?

To the eyes of Raposo and his comrades their height was vast, and when they reached them it was to find sheer, unscalable precipices. All day they struggled over boulders and crevices, seeking a way up those glassy sides. Rattlesnakes abounded—and there is no remedy for the bite of the Brazilian species. Wearied by the hard going and constant vigilance to avoid these snakes, Raposo called a halt.

"Three leagues we have come and still no way up," he said. "It would be better to return to our old trail and find a way northwards. What do you say?"

"Camp!" was the reply. "Let's camp. We've had enough for one day. Tomorrow we can return."

"Very well," answered the leader; and then to two of the men, "You, José and Manoel—off you go to find wood for the fire!"

Camp was pitched and the party was resting when confused shouting and a crashing in the bush brought them to their feet, guns in hand. José and Manoel burst into view.

"*Patrão, Patrão!*" they cried. "We've found it—the way up!"

Searching for firewood in the low scrub they had seen a dead tree at the edge of a small wooded creek. This was the best fuel to be had, and they were making their way towards it when a deer sprang up on the other side of the creek and disappeared beyond a corner of the cliff. Unslinging their guns the two men followed as quickly as they could, for here was meat enough to last them several days.

The animal had vanished, but beyond the outcropping of rock they came on a deep cleft in the face of the precipice, and saw that it was possible to climb up through it to the summit. Deer and firewood were forgotten in the excitement.

They broke camp at once, shouldered their packs, and set off with Manoel leading. With ejaculations of wonder they entered the crevice in single file, to find that it widened somewhat inside. It was rough going, but here and there were traces of what looked like old paving, and in places the sheer walls of the cleft seemed to bear the almost obliterated marks of tools. Clusters of rock crystals and frothy masses of quartz gave them the feeling of having entered a fairyland, and in the dim light filtering down through the tangled mass of creepers overhead all the magic of their first impressions returned.

The climb was so difficult that three hours passed before they emerged torn and breathless on a ledge high above the surrounding plain. From here to the ridge was clear ground, and soon they were standing shoulder to shoulder at the top, gazing, dumb with amazement, at the view spread out below them.

There at their feet, about four miles away, was a huge city.

Immediately they flung themselves down and edged back behind the cover of the rocks, hoping that the inhabitants had not seen their distant figures against the sky, for this might be a colony of the hated Spaniards. Then again, it might be such a city as Cuzco, the ancient capital of the Incas in Peru, inhabited by a race of highly civilized people still holding out against the encroachments of the European invaders. Was it perhaps a Portuguese colony? It might be a stronghold of the Orizes Procazes, remnant of the mysterious Tapuyas, who showed unmistakable signs of having once been a highly civilized people.

Raposo wriggled up to the crest once more and, still lying flat; looked around him. The ridge stretched as far as he could see from south-east to north-west, and away over to the north, hazy with distance, was unbroken forest. In the immediate foreground was an extensive plain patched with green and brown, broken in places by shining pools of water. He could see where a continuation of the rocky trail they had ascended dropped down the side of the mountain to vanish below the range of vision, appearing again and winding over the plain to lose itself in the vegetation surrounding the city walls. No sign of life could he see. No smoke arose in the still air; no sound broke the utter silence.

He gave a quick sign to his followers, and one by one they crawled over the ridge and dropped down beyond the skyline to the shelter of scrub and rock. Then they made their way cautiously down the mountaim side to the valley floor, and left the trail for a camp site near a small stream of clear water.

No fires were lit that night, and the men talked in whispers. They were awed by the sight of civilization after those long years in the wilds, and by no means confident of their safety. Two hours before nightfall Raposo had sent off two Portuguese and four negroes to reconnoitre and find out what sort of people lived in this mysterious place. Nervously the rest of the party awaited their return, and every forest noise—every insect song and whisper of the foliage—was sinister. But the scouts had nothing to tell when they came back. Lack of cover had kept them from venturing too near the city, but no sign of occupation had they seen. The Indians of the party were as mystified as Raposo and his followers. By nature superstitious, certain parts of the country to them were 'taboo', and they were filled with alarm.

Raposo, however, was able to prevail on one of the Indians to scout forward singlehanded after sunrise next morning. No one had slept much during the night, and their curiosity about the Indian's fate kept them from resting in the more comfortable light of day. At midday he crept back into camp, obviously terrified, and insisting that the city was uninhabited. It was too late to push forward that day, so they spent another restless night listening to the strange forest sounds around them, ready to face some unknown danger at any moment.

Early next morning Raposo sent ahead an advance guard of four Indians and followed towards the city with the rest of the party. As they came near the overgrown walls the Indians met them with the same story—the place was deserted—and so with less caution they followed the trail to an entrance under three arches formed of huge stone slabs. So impressive was this cyclopean structure—similar, probably, to much that can yet be seen at Sacsahuaman in Peru—that no man dared speak, but slipped by the blackened stones as stealthily as a cat.

High above the central arch characters of some sort were graven deeply into the weatherworn stone. Raposo, uneducated though he was, could see that this was no modern writing. A feeling of vast age brooded over everything, and it took a distinct effort for him to issue in a hoarse, unnatural voice the orders to advance.

The arches were still in a fair state of preservation, but one or two of the colossal uprights had twisted slightly on their bases. The men passed through and entered what had once been a wide street, but littered now with broken pillars and blocks of masonry rank with the parasitic vegetation of the tropics. On either side were two-storeyed houses built of great blocks fitting together with mortarless joins of almost incredible accuracy, the porticos, narrow above and wide below, decorated with elaborate carvings of what they took to be demons.

The description, coming from men who had never seen Cuzco and Sacsahuaman, or the other wonder cities of old Peru—which were incredibly ancient when the Incas first came upon them—cannot be lightly dismissed. What they saw and related tallies closely with much that we can still see today. Uneducated adventurers could hardly invent an account so closely corroborated by the cyclopean remains now familiar to so many.

There was ruin everywhere, but many buildings were roofed with great stone slabs still in position. Those of the party who dared to enter the dark interiors and raise their voices ran out at the echoes flung back at them from walls and vaulted ceilings. It was impossible to say if any remnants of furnishings remained, for in most cases inner walls had collapsed, covering the floors with debris, and the bat droppings of centuries formed a thick carpet underfoot. So old was this place that perishables such as furniture and textiles must have disintegrated long ago.

Huddled together like a flock of frightened sheep, the men proceeded down the street and came to a vast square. Here in the centre was a huge column of black stone, and upon it the effigy, in perfect preservation, of a man with one hand on his hip and the other pointing towards the north. The majesty of this statue struck deep into the hearts of the Portuguese and they crossed themselves reverently. Carved obelisks of the same black stone, partially ruined, stood at each corner of the square, while running the length of one side was a building so magnificent in design and decoration that it must have been a palace. The walls and roof had collapsed in many places, but its great square columns were still intact. A broad flight of ruined stone steps led up and into a wide hall, where traces of colour still clung to the frescoes and carvings. Bats in countless thousands winged in circles through the dim chambers and the acrid reek of their droppings was suffocating.

The explorers were glad to get out into the clean air. The figure of a youth was carved over what seemed to be the principal doorway. It portrayed a beardless figure, naked from the waist up, with shield in hand and a band across one shoulder. The head was crowned with what looked to them like a wreath of laurel, judging by Grecian statuary they had seen in Portugal. Below were inscribed characters remarkably like those of ancient Greece. Raposo copied them on a tablet and reproduced them in his narrative.

Opposite the palace was the ruin of another huge building, evidently a temple. Eroded carvings of figures, animals and birds covered the walls that remained, and over the portal were more characters which again were copied as faithfully as Raposo or one of his followers was capable of doing.

Beyond the square and the main street the city lay in complete ruin, in some places actually buried under mounds of earth on which not a blade of grass or other vegetation grew. Here and there were gaping chasms, and when the explorers dropped rocks into these not a sound came up to indicate bottom. There was little doubt now what had devastated the place. The Portuguese knew what earthquakes were and what destruction they could do. Here whole buildings had been swallowed, leaving perhaps only a few carved blocks to show where they had stood. It was not difficult to imagine something of the awful cataclysm that had laid waste this glorious place, tumbled columns and blocks weighing perhaps fifty tons and more, and that had destroyed in a matter of minutes the painstaking labour of a thousand years!

The far side of the square terminated in a river about thirty yards wide, flowing straight and easily from the north-west and vanishing in distant forest. At one time a fine promenade had bordered on the river, but the masonry was now broken up and much had subsided into the water. On the other side of the river were fields that once were cultivated, still covered with abundant coarse grass and a carpet of flowers. Rice had propagated and thrived in the shallow swamps all about, and here the waters were alive with duck.

Raposo and his party forded the river and crossed the swamps towards an isolated building about a quarter of a mile away, and the ducks scarcely troubled to move from their path. The building was approached by a flight of steps in stone of many colours, for it stood on a rise and its frontage extended for 250 paces. The imposing entrance, behind a square monolith with deeply engraved characters, opened into a vast hall where carvings and decorations had resisted the depreciations of time in an amazing manner. They found fifteen chambers opening off the great hall, and in each was a carved serpent's head with a thin stream of water still flowing from it into the open mouth or another stone serpent beneath. The place could have been the college of a priesthood.

Deserted and ruined the city was, but its environs of rich fields provided far more food for the explorers than they could find in the virgin forest. It is therefore not surprising that in spite of their awe of the place none of the men was anxious to leave it. Their fear gave way to a lust for treasure, and this increased when Jão Antonio—the only member of the party to be mentioned by name in the document—found a small gold coin in the rubble. On one face it bore the effigy of a youth on his knees, and on the other a bow, a crown and a musical instrument of some sort. The place must be full of gold, they told themselves; when the inhabitants fled they would have taken only the things most necessary for their survival.

The document hints at the finding of treasure, but no details are given. It may well be that the heavy aura of calamity hanging over the place was in the long run too much for the nerves of these superstitious pioneers. Perhaps the millions of bats deterred them. At any rate, it is unlikely that they brought any quantity of it out with them, for they still had a formidable journey ahead if they were ever to see civilization again, and none of them would have been anxious to burden himself with more equipment than he already had.

Gathering rice from the swamps and hunting duck—if hunting it could be called—were perilous. Anacondas big enough to kill a man were common; and poisonous snakes, attracted by the game, swarmed everywhere, feeding not only on the birds but also on jerboas—'rats jumping like fleas', as the narrator describes them. Wild dogs, large grey brutes as big as wolves, haunted the plains, yet not a man would sleep within the city. Camp was pitched just beyond the gate where they first entered, and from here they watched at sunset the legions of bats emerging from the great buildings to disperse in the gloaming with a dry rustling of wings like the first breath of an approaching storm. By day the sky was black with swallows, greedy for the prolific insect life.

Francisco Raposo had no idea where they were, but at last decided to follow the river through the forest, hoping that his Indians would remember the landmarks when he returned with a properly equipped expedition to comb the wealth out of these ruins. Fifty miles down they came to a mighty waterfall, and in an adjoining cliff face were found distinct signs of mine workings. Here they tarried longer. Game was plentiful, several of the men were down with fever and the Indians were nervous about the possibility of hostile tribes in the vicinity. Below the fall the river broadened out into a series of swampy lagoons, as these South American rivers have a way of doing.

Investigation proved the suspected mineshafts to be holes they had no means of exploring, but at their mouths lay scattered about a quantity of rich silver ore. Here and there were caves hewn out of the cliff by hand, some of them sealed off by great stone slabs engraved with strange glyphs. The cave might have been the tombs of the city's monarchs and high priests. The men tried in vain to move the stone slabs.

At the time of writing these words, I am awaiting with what patience I can muster the culmination of plans for the next expedition to search for the city discovered by Raposo and his party. I now have what I believe to be the correct bearings, and given normal luck we'll reach it. Bearing in mind the very hard conditions of the journey, no risk will be taken in selecting the rest of the party. I have been prevented from reaching my objective before by lack of stamina in my companions, and I have often regretted that it is not within my power to do it alone. It will be no pampered exploration party, with an army of bearers, guides and cargo animals. Such top-heavy expeditions get nowhere; they linger on the fringe of civilization and bask in publicity. Where the real wilds start, bearers are not to be had anyway, for fear of the savages. Animals cannot be taken because of lack of pasture and the attacks of insects and bats. There are no guides, for no one knows the country. It is a matter of cutting equipment to the absolute minimum, carrying it all oneself, and trusting that one will be able to exist by making friends with the various tribes one meets. Game may or may not be obtainable; the chance that it will makes a .22-calibre rifle desirable, but even this is a burden one grudges. Certainly, the weight of express rifles, revolvers and the ammunition for them is out of the question. It is far more dangerous to shoot a large beast than to leave it alone, and as for savages— well, the savage who is intent on killing you is invisible; and a rifle cannot compete with poisoned darts or arrows in a forest ambush!

The Treasure

BY SHOLEM ALEICHEM

Treasures are sometimes—indeed often—imaginary, which makes them of peculiar value to con artists. Manipulating the gullible is only part of the game; the gullible must have more or less reasonable hopes of getting the riches they yearn for. In this classic tale by Sholem Aleichem, set like so many of his stories in a Jewish *shtetl* in Eastern Europe, no one seems to have any trouble believing in the treasure's existence. The only problem is making sure that they'll get their share.

Aleichem, born Sholem Rabinowitz in Odessa in 1859, began first writing in Hebrew (this story, in Hebrew, dates to 1889). But he soon gave up Hebrew in favor of Yiddish, the *lingua franca* of ordinary Jews in Eastern Europe, becoming a highly popular playwright, journalist, and author of novels and short stories. After living and working in various European countries, he finally settled during the last few years of his life in New York, where he died in 1916.

★　★　★　★　★

1

Mazepevkites are like no others on earth. They scatter money as though strewing ashes, to right and to left. In their eyes, rubles are like

183

ants. It's all for charity. Their generous souls care for the well-being of all in their midst, the pauper or stranger.

A Mazepevkite prays:

"Look here, merciful Father. Money and silver are Yours, are they not? You don't mind then, do You, if I, being among the needy, am chosen to become one of the rich? Am I not worthy? Merciful God! Show me Your wondrous deeds: let me win the lottery. Just this once. And You will profit. I will do in fear that which is dear to You: unstinting donations. For the synagogue that much, and for the bathhouse (pardon for mentioning both in the same breath) this much; a fine gift for the Talmud Torah; twice as much for the sick-house; alms for the poor and for benevolent societies such as 'Heal the Sick', 'Support the Fallen', 'Free the Captive', and so on and on."

Mazepevkites sprinkle money about, but still the poor go hungry, and the boys of the Talmud Torah wear tattered clothes, bare bottoms showing, and the synagogue is a fright with teetering walls about to collapse, and the bathhouse. . . .

But nobody's surprised. No Mazepevkite has ever won the lottery. Still they spread money around in full faith that "Good Fortune" himself (though he tarries) will soon be at their side on their "Great Day." Even in sleep, they speak only of riches that await them. Wealth will come, not from business and trade, or slowly and surely from labor, but all at once. It will be cast down to them from heaven. O, Sing Psalms of Joy! Thousands, tens of thousands, a hundred thousand. . . . Do you think that's impossible for God?

How did this boundless money hunger grow in such a place? Moneyed moguls do not sprout like mushrooms in Mazepevke. On the contrary, poverty rules and struts proudly about town; the numbers of destitute swell day by day; all doors to a living are barred. Jews bemoan their fate, roam about like ghosts, not knowing how to feed their families. But Mazepevkites are unequaled in faith and belief. In this dark valley, they hope all year for miracles. Roast fowl will fly straight to their mouths.

Berko, the collector, supports their faith. He sells lottery tickets by the hundreds and thousands. No house in Mazepevke is without its ticket. As yet they've won nothing, but still they hope. They patiently wait for the day, their day of destiny, but that day is dragging its feet. Legends tell of such prospects.

"Once there was a pious man, with no food nor means of support. . . ." Remember that story? Remember how he went to sleep poor, and arose rich? Now I'll tell you a story not of one pious man but of a town full of faithful folks without food or support; and of a Jewish woman, virtuous and wise. And honest! She had a treasure of two hundred million rubles, gold beyond measure.

2

It happened in the 5649th year since creation, or 1889 as Europe and other civilized lands count. On the eleventh day of the month of Iyar, the Jewish streets of Mazepevke buzzed and rocked with a rumor that the woman with the key to the locked treasure had arrived.

Everyone heard how this woman had been going from town to town near and far shedding abundance upon the poor wherever she went. How fortunate, they! "You lucky people! Come! Reach out and grab your share. Fill your knapsacks and your boxes. You think 200,000,000 pieces of gold is nothing?"

Nobody knows where that treasure is now, nor how the woman acquired custody, but at last she was in Mazepevke for only a few days. In two or three weeks, she would divulge the secret, unearth the riches.

The treasure's first sacred burial place was in the village of Khrudovka near Mazepevke between two hills where a gentile nobleman fell dead as he dug for the treasure before its time.

Some say:

Many long years ago, the commander of all the Cossack armies, the hetman Mazepa, buried it several yards deep in the earth. It held two hundred million gold rubles as well as many pieces of silver and gold, with pearls and diamonds in iron and copper pitchers and pots. The treasure was covered by a copper door secured by a golden lock which could be opened only by a key fashioned of fine spun gold. That key was now held by the Jewish woman.

But how did the key reach her hands? Some say that Mazepa lost it and a Jew, Moyshe Groys, found it and bequeathed it to his children bidding them to pass it from generation to generation. It finally reached the woman who now resides among us. Moyshe's will decreed that the treasure be unearthed on the day before Shvues, 5649. This year! The will warned that whoever touched it before its time would die. That fate befell the gentile nobleman who had tried to snatch the legacy meant for Jewish heirs.

But others say:

It was not Mazepa who buried the treasure but Gonta, may his name be erased; and it was not buried in Mazepevke but in Uman. Here's what happened. There once was a Jew called Anshl of Uman, simple and God-fearing. He had a scraggly mare hitched to his wagon upon which he toted goods to the courts of Polish noblemen. When Gonta set out to bury the treasure, Anshl happened to be at the edge of a nearby forest standing to recite the Eighteen Blessings beside his loaded wagon. At the words, "And our eyes will see," he caught sight of Gonta and a pack of his Cossacks digging a hole. Into it they lowered many sacks of gold and silver coins, precious stones and diamonds whose radiance almost blinded Anshl. The Cossacks dashed off in haste without noticing him. Anshl stepped out of the woods, hauled out the treasure, and hefted it onto his wagon. He dumped his own meager wares into the hole, covered them up with earth, and dashed off.

Others said:

No, that's not how it was! They claimed that the treasure was in the woman's home locked in a silver casket. It held gold coins, priceless jewelry and paper drawn on an English bank worth two hundred million rubles. It was to be guarded until the moment ordained for its distribution, the day before Shvues, 5649. Soon! This very year!

At last, here she was in Mazepevke, and all could see the treasure with their very own eyes. That raised a mighty lust in each heart. Each racing mind silently counted, "Two hundred million! Oh, my! What couldn't I do with that!?"

The woman had two aides, two treasurers, obviously fine people with honest faces. Mazepevkites crowded around them asking how to claim a share of the treasure. An aide explained, "Whoever folds one ruble into a treasurer's palm will later dip his own hand into the pile of gold, and carry off his share of one hundred rubles. Give one hundred, take ten thousand!"

A truly fine business! What mortal soul would spurn this chance to insure his future? "PAWN YOUR SHIRT AND GET RICH QUICK!"

From all over town, Mazepevkites brought money to the woman. He who had no ready cash pawned household linen, clothes and his wife's jewelry (begging her pardon). And there opened a font of measureless profit for moneylenders who were besieged with people imploring, "Here, take these clothes. Charge me plenty of interest as long as you hand over money!" The rush grew fiercer when everyone learned that the woman would stop accepting money after the 33rd day in Omer. She didn't need this business. What for? It was nothing compared to the fortune she would own!

No one doubted there was money in her treasure. First, consider that many treasures must have been buried in bygone days. And second, everybody saw the old copper pitcher near the woman brimming with rubles and other sparkling coins. How can anyone not believe? And yet the mischievous wiseacres of Mazepevke jeered and sneered at those who ran to give their money to the woman.

"See how they ask the wind to blow their money away."

"He'll see that money again when he can see his ears."

"All he'll get for his money is a fistful of rags."

But two or three days later these cynics learned their lesson and dropped their waggish ways. One by one, they, just like the others, began to sneak in the dark, out of sight, into the woman's room at the inn. They hurried to give her their last ruble because soon it would be too late to claim their share. The gates would shut, and pawning goods would help no longer. True, the woman shrank from taking money. Her aides, the treasurers, also firmly resisted, but everyone ardently begged, "Take, take! Why should it bother you to take?" The treasurers relented, and took. And they took and took from early morning to the middle of the night. The door kept swinging back and forth on its hinges, not resting a moment. As one left another entered. Men and women, old and young, boys and girls, brides and grooms shoved and bumped each other in the sides and backs, pushing to be first, as people often do.

The upright woman with the treasure wore a silken shawl across her shoulders, a clean bonnet on her head, a golden necklace studded with diamonds, topazes on her forehead, earrings, and many rings on her fingers. She lodged at the inn of our well-known innkeeper, Shabtai, and spoke hardly at all to her visitors. She relied for that on her two kinsmen, the treasurers, who bustled about the room, whispering in each other's ear. Mostly, they ignored the townspeople milling about with their little clumps of money, but now and then one caught the eye of a kind treasurer who agreed to take the money. Another claim for a share in the treasure was thus duly recorded. How sweet it was!

To Shabtai fell the task of discreet and modest spokesman. Anyone who came to see the woman had to enlist Shabtai as mouthpiece, mediator and advocate. That's how it has always been done in Mazepevke: somebody to take your side for every purpose; or, as they call him, a "side-taker". At the landlord's, a "side-taker"; when pleading with the well-to-do, or at the police station, or with the doctor, or the rabbi. Anywhere, a "side-taker". They stir neither hand nor foot without first arranging for a person to be on their side. Shabtai represented those wishing for an introduction to a treasurer. Shabtai might say, "Here is Mr. so and so, one of our good citizens, prays in the old shul." Or, "This is Mrs. so and so, a fine woman, sells milk and butter." Shabtai paved the way for a grateful Mazepevke.

For his trouble, Shabtai secured for himself a due reward. His motto was, "It pays to walk slowly behind an overloaded wagon." First, he arranged fitting dowries for his four daughters. That is, he gave the woman a hundred rubles (twenty-five for each daughter duly recorded) to stake a later claim for two thousand five hundred rubles each.

Shabtai was no fool, and pleaded his case. To the treasurers he argued that as he was the innkeeper, he was worthier than anyone off the street, and so deserved a supplement beyond those ten thousand rubles to defray those heavy wedding expenses. "Listen, gentlemen. Four weddings! That's no joke. My wife, Dvoyre (may she live and be well), will want a silk dress and a fur coat. And what about cash for the rabbi and the sexton and the cantor? And the musicians? And. . . . , and more!"

The worthy treasurers answered that if Shabtai would give them free room and board, they would later dip into the treasure and give him pearls and diamonds. Shabtai could then sell them for ready cash.

"You will *not* sell those pearls and diamonds," shrieked Dvoyre. "No! Never! Not for all the money in the world will I let you do such a thing, Shabtai, because they'll be mine! You hear?"

"Anything you like," answered Shabtai in good humor. "I won't bicker with you now. O, may Shvues come quickly."

3

As Shvues approached, the growing crowds at the inn shoved harder, until Shabtai proclaimed, "An end to this! The gates have shut. The woman can't share her treasure with just anybody."

Still, people pawned house and home, left businesses and jobs, and thrust money at the woman. She took, but not eagerly. Contracts, betrothals were canceled, and marriages were fractured, all for the sake of the treasure, the only thing on their minds. A week before the "Great Day" was to arrive, a great misfortune struck from out of the blue.

Before I tell you what happened, I must tell you this:

In these awful times, Mazepevkites do many things for a living. Among those trades is an easy one. It is dirty and disgusting: betrayal of neighbors to tsarist oppressors. A betrayer is spawned by hate and envy, and every town has its own betrayer (to our shame and pain) who has a big tongue and puts it to work. Mazepevke's honored master in this trade is "Yankl Squealer" who reminds us of "Yankl Snatcher" of old.

May these evil pursuers be expelled from God's congregation. Only then will the Jews know release from affliction. That scabby livelihood gripped us in its clutches in those dark days of choking horror and oppression.

Yankl is a distinguished family man in Mazepevke, and all show him due respect. After all, he is an informer! Every store-keeper in town (whether or not he deals in contraband), every merchant (whether he has a business permit or not), every Hebrew teacher (whether or not he has a license to teach) knows his duty: to bring a "gift" to Yankl, a few rubles. Whatever happens in town, Yankl gets his tribute (to keep the dog from barking). And this leech supports two voracious daughters with deep pockets wider than the ocean, and as insatiable as the gaping maw of hell.

Yankl's most important sense is smell. His long nose sniffs out anything, even underground! It pokes and digs. Go to Mazepevke, and the nose that gives the town its special character will be first in line to greet you.

Yankl's nose sniffed out the woman and her treasure. Shabtai the innkeeper, on advice from the aides, took Yankl aside for a chat, and slipped him a little something on the sly. But this time the yearnings of Yankl's nose were not sated. Yankl came poking and sniffing again and again, robbing Shabtai of peace. Perhaps Shabtai could have settled Yankl's nerves with a few more rubles, but Shabtai the hothead is easily vexed, and slow to beg pardon. He poured his bitter gall and boundless fury on Yankl, screaming, "Is there no limit, you leech? Will you suck your brothers' blood to the last drop? Go, go in the best of health; and keep your face hidden forever from my sight!"

Yankl turned his lengthy nose toward the door and silently departed, aflame with rage.

"Why do you argue with everybody?" asked Dvoyre, Shabtai's wife. "Don't forget. That's Yankl!"

"I'm not afraid," said Shabtai, smugly. I have enough for dowries, the weddings, your pearls and diamonds, so why should I tremble? Will he squeal on me that I run an inn? To blazes with it! After Shvues, God willing, I'll marry off my daughters, and I'll say goodbye and good riddance to the inn and the whole town. Let them burn! Nice

people like me are appalled by Mazepevke's tumult and its shady business. There's a great big world out there to see."

Soon after, on the eve of Shvues, there was a great commotion,
pandemonium, at Shabtai's inn. People came running from all over
town shouting, "POLICE! SOLDIERS WITH GUNS!"

In the confusion, the woman and her treasurers fled to parts
unknown, leaving only a pair of ripped trousers, a prayer shawl, a few
rags, and the gold key. Shabtai spent that night in jail with other honored townspeople, in a cold, cramped room (no charge for the lodging).
In the morning, they were found innocent of any crime, and released.
After much investigation, the magistrate noted in his book, that:

A) No one knew the names or occupations of the woman and
her assistants, whence they came, nor where they went.
B) The gold key was made in Mazepevke before Passover by
the red-headed locksmith, who was told it was for a holy ark in
the Land of Israel.
C) Those rascals gypped the Jews, drained their money, left
behind a town full of embittered, penniless imbeciles who
believe everything, and are held in contempt by decent types.

The magistrate wrote further: Behold this people, rascals all,
sons of scoundrels, without peers in shrewdness and cunning.

The remaining notes of the magistrate were tied with string,
and stored among the archives of Mazepevke. They now await study by
future scholars of antiquities.

A Painted Stone

BY JOHN L. STEPHENS

John Stephens (1805–1852) was a treasure-hunter in the grandest sense. He searched for cities, and he found them. With enormous persistence and almost superhuman stamina, Stephens and his artist companion Frederick Catherwood traveled hundreds of miles through the rain-forests and brushy barrens of Southern Mexico, Guatemala, and Yucatan between 1839 and 1842, looking for Mayan ruins. Most of the now famous sites, from Palenque to Copan to Chichen Itza and Uxmal are described and illustrated, often for the first time, in the volumes he published—*Incidents of Travel in Central America, Chiapas, and Yucatan* (1841) and *Incidents of Travel in Yucatan* (1843). Stephens, who trained as a lawyer before giving up the profession in favor of travel and writing, was not averse to picking up an attractive artifact along the way, as this extract demonstrates. He actually made a fairly substantial collection, much of which was lost in a fire after reaching the United States, and even went so far as to try (unsuccessfully) to purchase the entire ruined city of Copan for $50. He intended to re-erect it as a tourist attraction in Philadelphia.

★ ★ ★ ★ ★

T he next morning we resumed our journey in search of ruined cities. Our next point of destination was the rancho of Kewick, three leagues distant. Mr. Catherwood set out with the servants and luggage, Dr. Cabot and myself following in about an hour. The Indians told us there was no difficulty in finding the road, and we set out alone. About a mile from the rancho we passed a ruined building on the left, surmounted by a high wall, with oblong apertures, like that mentioned at Zayi as resembling a New-England factory. The face of the country was rolling, and more open than any we had seen. We passed through two Indian ranchos, and a league beyond came to a dividing point, where we found ourselves at a loss. Both were mere Indian footpaths, seldom or never traversed by horsemen, and, having but one chance against us, we selected that most directly in line with the one by which we had come. In about an hour the direction changed so much that we turned back, and, after a toilsome ride, reached again the dividing point, and turned into the other path. This led us into a wild savanna surrounded by hills, and very soon we found tracks leading off in different directions, among which, in a short time, we became perfectly bewildered. The whole distance to Kewick was but three leagues; we had been riding hard six hours, and began to fear that we had made a mistake in turning back, and at every step were going more astray. In the midst of our perplexities we came upon an Indian leading a wild colt, who, without asking any questions, or waiting for any from us, waved us back, and, tying his colt to a bush, led us across the plain into another path, following which some distance, he again struck across, and put us into still another, where he left us, and started to return to his colt. We were loth to lose him, and urged him to continue as our guide; but he was impenetrable until we held up a medio, when he again moved on before us. The whole region was so wild that even yet we had doubts, and hardly believed that such a path could lead to a village or rancho; but, withal, there was one interesting circumstance. In our desolate and wandering path we had seen in different places, at a distance, and inaccessible, five high mounds, holding aloft the ruins of ancient buildings; and doubtless there were more buried in the woods. At three o'clock we entered a dense forest, and came suddenly upon the casa real of Kewick, standing alone, almost buried among trees, the only habitation of any kind in sight; and, to increase the wondering interest which attended every step of our journey in that country, it stood on the platform of an ancient terrace, strewed with the relics of a ruined edifice. The steps of the terrace had fallen and been newly laid, but the walls were entire, with all the stones in place. Conspicuous in view was Mr. Catherwood with our servants and luggage, and, as we rode up, it seemed a strange confusion of things past and present, of scenes consecrated by time and those of every-day life, though Mr. Catherwood dispelled the floating visions by his first greeting, which was an assurance that the casa real was full of fleas. We tied our horses at the foot of the terrace, and ascended the steps. The casa real had mud walls and a thatched roof, and in front was an arbour. Sitting down under the arbour, with our hotel on this ancient platform, we had seldom experienced higher satisfaction on reaching a new and unknown field of ruins, though perhaps this was owing somewhat to the circumstances of finding ourselves, after a hot and perplexing ride, safely arrived at our place of destination. We had still two hours of daylight; and, anxious to have a glimpse of the ruins before night, we had some fried eggs and tortillas got ready, and while making a hasty meal, the proprietor of the rancho, attended by a party of Indians, came to pay us a visit.

This proprietor was a full-blooded Indian, the first of this ancient but degraded race whom we had seen in the position of landowner and master. He was about forty-five years old, and highly respectable in his appearance and manners. He had inherited the land from his fathers, did not know how long it had been transmitted, but believed that it had always been in his family. The Indians on the rancho were his servants, and we had not seen in any village or on any hacienda men of better appearance, or under more excellent discipline. This produced on my mind a strong impression that, indolent, ignorant, and debased as the race is under the dominion of strangers, the Indian even now is not incapable of fulfilling the obligations of a higher station than that in which his destiny has placed him. It is not true that he is fit only to labour with his hands; he has within him that which is capable of directing the labour of others; and as this Indian master sat on the terrace, with his dependants crouching round him, I could imagine him the descendant of a long line of caciques who once reigned in the city, the ruins of which were his inheritance. Involuntarily we treated him with a respect we had never shown to an Indian before; but perhaps we were not free from the influence of feelings which govern in civilized life, and our respect may have proceeded from the discovery that our new acquaintance was a man of property, possessed not merely of acres, and Indians, and unproductive real estate, but also of that great desideratum in these trying times, ready money; for we had given Albino a dollar to purchase eggs with, who objected to it as too large a coin to be available on the rancho, but on his return informed us, with an expression of surprise, that the master had changed it the moment it was offered to him.

Our hasty dinner over, we asked for Indians to guide us to the ruins, and were somewhat startled by the objections they all made on account of the garrapatas. Since we left Uxmal the greatest of our small hardships had been the annoyance of these insects; in fact, it was by no means a small hardship. Frequently we came in contact with a bush covered with them, from which thousands swarmed upon us, like moving grains of sand, and scattered till the body itself seemed crawling. Our horses suffered, perhaps, more than ourselves, and it became a habit, whenever we dismounted, to rasp their sides with a rough stick. During the dry season the little pests are killed off by the heat of the sun, and devoured by birds, but for which I verily believe they would make the country uninhabitable. All along we had been told that the dry season was at hand, and they would soon be over; but we began to despair of any dry season, and had no hopes of getting rid of them. Nevertheless, we were somewhat startled at the warning conveyed by the reluctance of the Indians; and when we insisted upon going, they gave us another alarming intimation by cutting twigs, with which, from the moment of starting, they whipped the bushes on each side, and swept the path before them.

Beyond the woods we came out into a comparatively open field, in which we saw on all sides through the trees the Xlappahk, or old walls, now grown so familiar, a collection of vast remains and of many buildings. We worked our way to all within sight. The façades were not so much ornamented as some we had seen, but the stones were more massive, and the style of architecture was simple, severe, and grand. Nearly every house had fallen, and one long ornamented front lay on the ground cracked and doubled up as if shaken off by the vibrations of an earthquake, and still struggling to retain its upright position, the whole presenting a most picturesque and imposing scene of ruins, and conveying to the mind a strong image of the besom of destruction sweeping over a city. Night came upon us while gazing at a mysterious painting, and we returned to the casa real to sleep.

Early the next morning we were again on the ground, with our Indian proprietor and a large party of his criados; and as the reader is now somewhat familiar with the general character of these ruins, I select from that great mass around only such as have some peculiarity.

The first . . . had been the principal doorway, and was all that now remained of a long line of front, which lay in ruins on the ground. It is remarkable for its simplicity, and, in that style of architecture, for its grandeur of proportions.

The apartment into which this door opened had nothing to distinguish it from hundreds of others we had seen, but in the corner one was the mysterious painting at which we were gazing the evening before, when night overtook us. The end wall had fallen inward; the others remained. The ceiling, as in all the other buildings, was formed by two sides rising to meet each other, and covered within a foot of the point of junction by a flat layer of stones. In all the other arches, without a single exception, the layer was perfectly plain: but this had a single stone distinguished by a painting, which covered the whole surface presented to view. The painting itself was curious; the colours were bright, red and green predominating; the lines clear and distinct, and the whole was more perfect than any painting we had seen. But its position surprised us more than the painting itself; it was in the most out-of-the-way spot in the whole edifice, and but for the Indians we might not have noticed it at all. Why this layer of stones was so adorned, or why this particular stone was distinguished above all others in the same layer, we were unable to discover, but we considered that it was not done capriciously nor without cause; in fact, we had long been of opinion that every stone in those ancient buildings, and every design and ornament that decorated them, had some certain though now inscrutable meaning.

This painting exhibits a rude human figure, surrounded by hieroglyphics, which doubtless contain the whole of its story. It is 30 inches long by 18 inches wide, and the prevailing colour is red. From its position in the wall, it was impossible to draw it without getting it out and lowering it to the ground, which I was anxious to accomplish, not only for the sake of the drawing, but for the purpose of carrying it away. I had apprehensions that the proprietor would make objections, for both he and the Indians had pointed it out as the most curious part of the ruins; but, fortunately, they had no feeling about it, and were all ready to assist in any way we directed. The only way of getting at it was by digging down through the roof; and, as usual, a friendly tree was at hand to assist us in the ascent. The roof was flat, made of stone and mortar cemented together, and several feet in thickness. The Indians had no crowbar, but loosening the mortar with their machetes, and prying apart the stones by means of hard wood saplings with the points sharpened, they excavated down to the layer on the top of the arch. The stone lapped over about a foot on each side, and was so heavy that it was impossible to hoist it out of the hole; our only way, therefore, was to lower it down into the apartment. The master sent some Indians to the rancho to search for ropes, and, as a measure of precaution, I had branches cut, and made a bed several feet thick under the stone. Some of the Indians still at work were preparing to let it fall, when Dr. Cabot, who was fortunately on the roof at the time, put a stop to their proceedings.

The Indians returned with the rope, and while lowering the stone one of the strands broke, and it came thundering down, but the bed of branches saved the painting from destruction.

The proprietor made no objections to my carrying it away, but it was too heavy for a mule-load, and the Indians would not undertake to carry it on their shoulders. The only way of removing it was to have it cut down to a portable size; and when we left, the proprietor accompanied me to the village to procure a stonecutter for that purpose, but there was none in the village, nor any chance of one within twenty-seven miles. Unable to do anything with the stone, I engaged the proprietor to place it in an apartment sheltered from rain; and, if I do not mistake the character of my Indian friend and inheritor of a ruined city, it now lies subject to my order; and I hereby authorize the next American traveller to bring it away at his own expense, and deposite it in the National Museum at Washington.

Solomon's Treasure Chamber

BY H. RIDER HAGGARD

For sheer schlock effect, it is hard to beat H. Rider Haggard (1856–1925), and the following chapter from *King Solomon's Mines* ought to prove it. After many adventures, the hero and his comrades have finally reached the long-sought treasure cave, and should be able guess that the extremely dubious old Gagool is up to something bad. Haggard wrote no less than thirty-four novels, most of them thrillers. Many of the best were set in Africa, where he had spent six years as a young man, among them *King Solomon's Mines* (1886) and *She* (1887). By the way, the good guys survive.

★   ★   ★   ★   ★

While we were engaged in getting over our fright, and in examining the grisly wonders of the Place of Death, Gagool had been differently occupied. Somehow or other—for she was marvellously active when she chose—she had scrambled on to the great table, and made her way to where our departed friend Twala was placed, under the drip, to see, suggested. Good, how he was "pickling," or for some dark purpose of her own. Then she hobbled back, stopping now and again to address a remark, the tenor of which I could not catch, to one or other of the shrouded forms, just as you or I might greet an old acquaintance. Having gone through this mysterious and horrible ceremony, she squatted herself down on the table immediately under the White Death, and began, so far as I could make out, to offer up prayers to it. The spectacle of this wicked old creature pouring out supplications, evil ones, no doubt, to the arch enemy of mankind, was so uncanny that it caused us to hasten our inspection.

"Now, Gagool," said I, in a low voice—somehow one did not dare to speak above a whisper in that place—"lead us to the chamber."

The old creature promptly scrambled down off the table.

"My lords are not afraid?" she said, leering up into my face.

"Lead on."

"Good, my lords;" and she hobbled round to the back of the great Death. "Here is the chamber; let my lords light the lamp, and enter," and she placed the gourd full of oil upon the floor, and leaned herself against the side of the cave. I took out a match, of which we had still a few in a box, and lit the rush wick, and then looked for the doorway, but there was nothing before us except the solid rock. Gagool grinned. "The way is there, my lords. *Ha! ha! ha!*"

"Do not jest with us," I said sternly.

"I jest not, my lords. See!" and she pointed at the rock.

As she did so, on holding up the lamp we perceived that a mass of stone was rising slowly from the floor and vanishing into the rock above, where doubtless there is a cavity prepared to receive it. The mass was of the width of a good-sized door, about ten feet high and not less than five feet thick. It must have weighed at least twenty or thirty tons, and was clearly moved upon some simple balance principle of counterweights, probably the same as that by which the opening and shutting of an ordinary modern window is arranged. How the principle was set in motion, of course none of us saw; Gagool was careful to avoid this; but I have little doubt that there was some very simple lever, which was moved ever so little by pressure on a secret spot, thereby throwing additional weight on to the hidden counterbalances, and causing the whole mass to be lifted from the ground. Very slowly and gently the great stone raised itself, till at last it had vanished altogether, and a dark hole presented itself to us in the place which the door had filled.

Our excitement was so intense, as we saw the way to Solomon's treasure chamber at last thrown open, that I for one began to tremble and shake. Would it prove a hoax after all, I wondered, or was old Da Silvestra right? and were there vast hoards of wealth stored in that dark place, hoards which would make us the richest men in the whole world? We should know in a minute or two.

"Enter, white men from the Stars," said Gagool, advancing into the doorway; "but first hear your servant, Gagaoola the old. The bright stones that ye will see were dug out of the pit over which the Silent Ones are set, and stored here, I know not by whom. But once has this place been entered since the time that those who stored the stones departed in haste, leaving them behind. The report of the treasure went down among the people who lived in the country from age to age, but none knew where the chamber was, nor the secret of the door. But it happened that a white man reached this country from over the mountains, perchance he too came 'from the Stars,' and was well received by the king of that day. He it is who sits yonder," and she pointed to the fifth king at the table of the Dead. "And it came to pass that he and a woman of the country who was with him journeyed to this place; and that by chance the woman learnt the secret of the door—a thousand years might ye search, but ye should never find it. Then the white man entered with the woman, and found the stones, and filled with stones the skin of a small goat, which the woman had with her to hold food. And as he was going from the chamber he took up one more stone, a large one, and held it in his hand." Here she paused.

"Well," I asked, breathless with interest as we all were, "what happened to Da Silvestra?"

The old hag started at the mention of the name.

"How knowest thou the dead man's name?" she asked sharply; and then, without waiting for an answer, went on—

"None know what happened; but it came about that the white man was frightened, for he flung down the goat-skin, with the stones, and fled out with only the one stone in his hand, and that the king took, and it is the stone that thou, Macumazahn, didst take from Twala's brow."

"Have none entered here since?" I asked, peering again down the dark passage.

"None, my lords. Only the secret of the door has been kept, and every king has opened it, though he has not entered. There is a saying, that those who enter there will die within a moon, even as the white man died in the cave upon the mountain, where ye found him, Macumazahn, and therefore the kings do not enter. *Ha! ha!* mine are true words."

Our eyes met as she said it, and I turned sick and cold. How did the old hag know all these things?

"Enter, my lords. If I speak truth the goat-skin with the stones will lie upon the floor; and if there is truth as to whether it is death to enter here, that will ye learn afterwards. *Ha! ha! ha!*" and she hobbled through the doorway, bearing the light with her; but I confess that once more I hesitated about following.

"Oh, confound it all!" said Good; "here goes. I am not going to be frightened by that old devil;" and followed by Foulata, who, however, evidently did not at all like the job, for she was shivering with fear, he plunged into the passage after Gagool—an example which we quickly followed.

A few yards down the passage, in the narrow way hewn out of the living rock, Gagool had paused, and was waiting for us.

"See, my lords," she said, holding the light before her, "those who stored the treasure here fled in haste, and bethought them to guard against any who should find the secret of the door, but had not the time," and she pointed to large square blocks of stone, which, to the height of two courses (about two feet three), had been placed across the passage with a view to walling it up. Along the side of the passage were similar blocks ready for use, and, most curious of all, a heap of mortar and a couple of trowels, which tools, so far as we had time to examine them, appeared to be of a similar shape and make to those used by workmen to this day.

Here Foulata, who had been in a state of great fear and agitation throughout, said that she felt faint and could go no farther, but would wait there. Accordingly we set her down on the unfinished wall, placing the basket of provisions by her side, and left her to recover.

Following the passage for about fifteen paces farther, we came suddenly to an elaborately painted wooden door. It was standing wide open. Whoever was last there had either not found the time, or had forgotten, to shut it.

Across the threshold of this door lay a skin bag, formed of a goat-skin, that appeared to be full of pebbles.

"*Hee! hee!* white men," sniggered Gagool, as the light from the lamp fell upon it. "What did I tell you, that the white man who came here fled in haste, and dropped the woman's bag—behold it!"

Good stooped down and lifted it. It was heavy and jingled.

"By Jove! I believe it's full of diamonds," he said, in an awed whisper; and, indeed, the idea of a small goat-skin full of diamonds is enough to awe anybody.

"Go on," said Sir Henry impatiently. "Here, old lady, give me the lamp," and taking it from Gagool's hand, he stepped through the doorway and held it high above his head.

We pressed in after him, forgetful for the moment of the bag of diamonds, and found ourselves in Solomon's treasure chamber.

At first, all that the somewhat faint light given by the lamp revealed was a room hewn out of the living rock, and apparently not more than ten feet square. Next there came into sight, stored one on the other to the arch of the roof, a splendid collection of elephant-tusks. How many of them there were we did not know, for of course we could not see to what depth they went back, but there could not have been less than the ends of four or five hundred tusks of the first quality visible to our eyes. There, alone, was enough ivory before us to make a man wealthy for life. Perhaps, I thought, it was from this very store that Solomon drew the raw material for his "great throne of ivory," of which there was not the like made in any kingdom.

On the opposite side of the chamber were about a score of

wooden boxes, something like Martini-Henry ammunition boxes, only rather larger, and painted red.

"There are the diamonds," cried I; "bring the light."

Sir Henry did so, holding it close to the top box, of which the lid, rendered rotten by time even in that dry place, appeared to have been smashed in, probably by Da Silvestra himself. Pushing my hand through the hole in the lid I drew it out full, not of diamonds, but of gold pieces, of a shape that none of us had seen before, and with what looked like Hebrew characters stamped upon them.

"Ah!" I said, replacing the coin, "we shan't go back empty-handed, anyhow. There must be a couple of thousand pieces in each box, and there are eighteen boxes. I suppose it was the money to pay the workmen and merchants."

"Well," put in Good, "I think that is the lot; I don't see any diamonds, unless the old Portuguee put them all into this bag."

"Let my lords look yonder where it is darkest, if they would find the stones," said Gagool, interpreting our looks. "There my lords will find a nook, and three stone chests in the nook, two sealed and one open."

Before interpreting this to Sir Henry, who carried the light, I could not resist asking how she knew these things, if no one had entered the place since the white man, generations ago.

"Ah, Macumazahn, who watchest by night," was the mocking answer, "ye who live in the Stars, do ye not know that some have eyes that can see through rock? *Ha! ha! ha!*"

"Look in that corner, Curtis," I said, indicating the spot Gagool had pointed out.

"Hullo, you fellows," he cried, "here's a recess. Great heavens! see here."

We hurried up to where he was standing in a nook, something like a small bow window. Against the wall of this recess were placed three stone chests, each about two feet square. Two were fitted with stone lids, the lid of the third rested against the side of the chest, which was open.

"*See!*" he repeated hoarsely, holding the lamp over the open chest. We looked, and for a moment could make nothing out, on account of a silvery sheen that dazzled us. When our eyes got used to it we saw that the chest was three-parts full of uncut diamonds, most of them of considerable size. Stooping, I picked some up. Yes there was no doubt of it, there was the unmistakable soapy feel about them.

I fairly gasped as I dropped them.

"We are the richest men in the whole world," I said. "Monte Christo is a fool to us."

"We shall flood the market with diamonds," said Good.

"Got to get them there first," suggested Sir Henry.

And we stood with pale faces and stared at each other, the lantern in the middle, and the glimmering gems below, as though we were conspirators about to commit a crime, instead of being, as we thought the three most fortunate men on earth.

"Hee! hee! hee!" cackled old Gagool behind us, as she flitted about like a vampire bat. "There are the bright stones that ye love, white men, as many as ye will; take them, run them through your fingers, *eat* of them, hee! hee; *drink* of them, *ha! ha!*"

There was something so ridiculous at that moment to my mind in the idea of eating and drinking diamonds, that I began to laugh outrageously, an example which the others followed, without knowing why. There we stood and shrieked with laughter over the gems that were ours, which had been found for *us* thousands of years ago by the patient delvers in the great hole yonder, and stored for *us* by Solomon's long-dead overseer, whose name, perchance, was written in the characters stamped on the faded wax that yet adhered to the lids of the chest. Solomon never got them nor David, nor Da Silvestra, nor anybody else. *We* had got them; there before us were millions of pounds' worth of diamonds, and thousands of pounds' worth of gold and ivory only waiting to be taken away.

Suddenly the fit passed off, and we stopped laughing.

"Open the other chests, white men," croaked Gagool, "there are surely more therein. Take your fill, white lords! *Ha! ha!* take your fill."

Thus adjured, we set to work to pull up the stone lids on the other two, first—not without a feeling of sacrilege—breaking the seals that fastened them.

Hoorah! they were full too, full to the brim; at least, the second one was; no wretched Da Silvestra had been filling goat-skins out of that. As for the third chest, it was only about a fourth full, but the stones were all picked ones; none less than twenty carats, and some of them as large as pigeon-eggs. A good many of these bigger ones, however, we could see by holding them up to the light, were a little yellow, "off coloured," as they call it at Kimberley.

What we did *not* see, however, was the look of fearful malevolence that old Gagool favoured us with as she crept, crept like a snake, out of the treasure chamber and down the passage towards the door of solid rock.

★　　★　　★　　★　　★

Hark! Cry upon cry comes ringing up the vaulted path. It is Foulata's voice!

"Oh, Bougwan! help! help! the stone falls!"

"Leave go, girl! Then———"

"Help! help! she has stabbed me!"

By now we are running down the passage, and this is what the light from the lamp shows us. The door of rock is closing down slowly; it is not three feet from the floor. Near it struggle Foulata and Gagool. The red blood of the former runs to her knee, but still the brave girl holds the old witch, who fights like a wild cat. Ah! she is free! Foulata falls, and Gagool throws herself on the ground, to twist like a snake through the crack of the closing stone. She is under—ah! God! too late! too late! The stone nips her, and she yells in agony. Down, down, it comes, all the thirty tons of it, slowly pressing her old body against the rock below. Shriek upon shriek, such as we never heard, then a long sickening *crunch*, and the door was shut just as, rushing down the passage, we hurled ourselves against it.

It was all done in four seconds.

Then we turned to Foulata. The poor girl was stabbed in the body, and I saw could not live long.

"Ah! Bougwan, I die!" gasped the beautiful creature. "She crept out—Gagool; I did not see her, I was faint—and the door began to fall; then she came back, and was looking up the path—and I saw her come in through the slowly falling door; and caught her and held her, and she stabbed me, and *I die*, Bougwan."

"Poor girl! poor girl!" Good cried; and then, as he could do nothing else, he fell to kissing her.

"Bougwan." she said, after a pause, "is Macumazahn there? it grows so dark, I cannot see."

"Here I am, Foulata."

"Macumazahn, be my tongue for a moment, I pray thee for Bougwan cannot understand me, and before I go into the darkness I would speak a word."

"Say on, Foulata, I will render it."

"Say to my lord, Bougwan, that—I love him, and that I am glad to die because I know that he cannot cumber his life with such as I am, for the sun may not mate with the darkness, nor the white with the black.

"Say that at times I have felt as though there were a bird in my bosom, which would one day fly hence and sing elsewhere. Even now, though I cannot lift my hand, and my brain grows cold, I do not feel as though my heart were dying; it is so full of love that could live a thousand years, and yet be young. Say that if I live again, mayhap I shall see him in the Stars, and that—I will search them all, though perchance there I should still be black and he would—still be white. Say—nay, Macumazahn, say no more, save that I love——Oh, hold me closer, Bougwan, I cannot feel thine arms—*oh! oh!*"

"She is dead—she is dead!" said Good, rising in grief, the tears running down his honest face.

"You need not let that trouble you, old fellow," said Sir Henry.

"Eh!" said Good; "what do you mean?"

"I mean that you will soon be in a position to join her. *Man, don't you see that we are buried alive?*"

Until Sir Henry uttered these words I do not think that the full horror of what had happened had come home to us, pre-occupied as we were with the sight of poor Foulata's end. But now we understood. The ponderous mass of rock had closed, probably for ever, for the only brain which knew its secret was crushed to powder beneath it. This was a door that none could hope to force with anything short of dynamite in large quantities. And we were the wrong side of it!

For a few minutes we stood horrified there over the corpse of Foulata. All the manhood seemed to have gone out of us. The first shock of this idea of the slow and miserable end that awaited us was overpowering. We saw it all now; that fiend Gagool had planned this snare for us from the first. It must have been just the jest that her evil mind would have rejoiced in, the idea of the three white men, whom, for some reason of her own, she had always hated, slowly perishing of thirst and hunger in the company of the treasure they had coveted. Now I saw the point of that sneer of hers about eating and drinking the diamonds. Perhaps somebody had tried to serve the poor old Dom in the same way, when he abandoned the skin full of jewels.

"This will never do," said Sir Henry hoarsely; "the lamp will soon go out. Let us see if we can't find the spring that works the rock."

We sprang forward with desperate energy, and, standing in a bloody ooze, began to feel up and down the door and the sides of the passage. But no knob or spring could we discover.

"Depend on it," I said, "it does not work from the inside; if it did Gagool would not have risked trying to crawl underneath the stone. It was the knowledge of this that made her try to escape at all hazards, curse her."

"At all events," said Sir Henry with a hard little laugh, "retribution was swift; hers was almost as awful an end as ours is likely to be. We can do nothing with the door; let us go back to the treasure room."

We turned and went, and as we did so I perceived by the unfinished wall across the passage the basket of food which poor Foulata had carried. I took it up, and brought it with me to the accursed treasure chamber that was to be our grave. Then we went back and reverently bore in Foulata's corpse, laying it on the floor by the boxes of coin.

Next we seated ourselves, leaning our backs against the three stone chests of priceless treasures.

"Let us divide the food," said Sir Henry, "so as to make it last as long as possible." Accordingly we did so. It would, we reckoned, make four infinitesimally small meals for each of us, enough, say, to support life for a couple of days. Besides the "biltong," or dried game-flesh, there were two gourds of water, each holding about a quart.

"Now," said Sir Henry, grimly, "let us eat and drink, for to-morrow we die."

We each ate a small portion of the "biltong," and drank a sip of water. Needless to say, we had but little appetite, though we were sadly in need of food, and felt better after swallowing it. Then we got up and made a systematic examination of the walls of our prison-house, in the faint hope of finding some means of exit, sounding them and the floor carefully.

There was none. It was not probable that there would be any to a treasure chamber.

The lamp began to burn dim. The fat was nearly exhausted.

"Quatermain," said Sir Henry, "what is the time—your watch goes?"

I drew it out, and looked at it. It was six o'clock; we had entered the cave at eleven.

"Infadoos will miss us," I suggested. "If we do not return to-night he will search for us in the morning, Curtis."

"He may search in vain. He does not know the secret of the door, nor even where it is. No living person knew it yesterday, except Gagool. To-day no one knows it. Even if he found the door he could not break it down. All the Kukuana army could not break through five feet of living rock. My friends, I see nothing for it but to bow ourselves to the will of the Almighty. The search for treasure has brought many to a bad end; we shall go to swell their number."

The lamp grew dimmer yet.

Presently it flared up and showed the whole scene in strong relief, the great mass of white tusks, the boxes of gold, the corpse of poor Foulata stretched before them, the goat-skin full of treasure, the dim glimmer of the diamonds, and the wild, wan faces of us three white men seated there awaiting death by starvation.

Suddenly the flame sank and expired.

Montezuma's Gold

BY BERNAL DIAZ DEL CASTILLO

Some of the greatest authenticated treasures the world has ever known are associated with the Spanish conquest of Mexico and Peru. Looking back at a distance of fifty years from the days when he and a handful of *conquistadors* led by Hernando Cortés brought down the entire might of the Mexican kingdom, Bernal Diaz (c. 1492–1581) was still stunned by the scale of the riches they seized. No European had ever seen anything like it before; none, thanks to the conquerors' greed, ever would again. Diaz wrote his memoirs, from which this passage is taken, in retirement in Guatemala in 1568. He was no writer, he claimed. But he had been there, in person, which was more than other historians of the Conquest could say. And in truth Diaz's unadorned and straightforward account, bloody and cruel as it sometimes is, has the cold ring of truth about it— not least the description of the squabbling over who would get the largest share of the inconceivably large prize.

★   ★   ★   ★   ★

hen Cortés and the Mercedarian friar saw that Montezuma was not willing to let us set up a cross in the *cu* of Uichilobos or build a church there, he decided to ask Montezuma's stewards for masons to build a

church in our quarters, because ever since we had entered the city of Mexico we had had to set up an altar on tables when Mass was said and then take it down afterward. . . .

When we were together in our quarters and were looking for the best place to put the altar, two of our soldiers, one of whom was a joiner named Alonzo Yáñez, noticed marks on one of the walls showing that there had been a door there and that it had been closed and carefully plastered over.

As we heard the story that Montezuma kept the treasure of his father, Axayaca, in that building, we suspected that it must be in that room which had been so recently closed and whitewashed. Yáñez spoke to Juan Velázquez de León and Francisco de Lugo, who told Cortés, and the door was secretly opened. Cortés and some of his captains went in first, and they saw so many jewels, bars and plates of gold, *chalchiuis*, and other riches that they were so excited they did not know what to say. Soon all the captains and soldiers knew about it, and we went in with great secrecy to see. When I saw it, I tell you, I was amazed, and as at that time I was young and had never in my whole life seen riches like that before, I was sure that there could not be anything like it in the whole world.

It was agreed by our captains and soldiers not to think of touching any of it, but that the stones should be put back immediately and the doorway cemented over as we had found it, and that it should not be discussed, so that Montezuma shouldn't find out about it yet.

★　★　★　★　★

Now that those little kings were prisoners and all the cities were peaceful, Cortés said to Montezuma that before we entered Mexico he had twice sent to say that he wished to pay tribute to His Majesty. Now that he understood the great power of our lord and king, to whom many lands paid tribute and many kings were subject, it would be well if Montezuma and all his vassals first gave him their fealty, as was the custom, and then gave tribute and taxes.

Montezuma said that he would bring together his vassals and talk to them about it. Within ten days almost all the chiefs of that territory assembled, but the chief who was most closely related to Montezuma did not come—the one who was said to be very brave and of very fine bearing and appearance. At that time he was in a town of his called Tula, and when he was summoned, he sent to say that he would neither come nor pay taxes, as he was not able to sustain himself now on what he received from his provinces. This reply made Montezuma angry and he sent captains to arrest him, but as he was a great lord, with many relations, he was warned of this and withdrew to his province, where they were not able to catch him.

I will leave this here and say that, except for Orteguilla the page, none of us were present at the talks Montezuma had with his chiefs. They say that he told them to recall how they had known for many years, through what their ancestors had told them, which they had noted in their books of records, that men would come from where the sun rises to rule these lands and at that time the kingdom of the Mexican would come to an end. From what his gods had told him, he believed that we were those men. The priests had questioned Uichilobos about it and made sacrifices, but he would not answer them as he usually did.

All that Uichilobos would give them to understand was that what he had told them before was still his reply, and they were not to ask him again. They took this to mean that they should give obedience to the King of Castile, whose vassals these *teules* said they were. He went on to say that at the present it didn't matter, and that as time went on they would receive a better reply from their gods. "What I order and pray of you to do with good will is to give some sign of vassalage. I will soon tell you what is most suitable. Right now I am being importuned about it by Malinche, so I hope no one will refuse. Behold that for eighteen years I have been your lord. You have always been very loyal and I have enriched you and broadened your lands. I have given you power and wealth. If at this time our gods permit that I be held here a prisoner, it would not have happened, as I have told you many times, except that my great Uichilobos so commanded me."

After they heard these arguments, all of them answered with tears and sighs that they would do as he ordered, and Montezuma was even more tearful. Then he sent a chieftain to say that the next day they would give fealty and vassalage to His Majesty.

In the presence of Cortés, Pedro Hernández, his secretary, our captains, and many of the soldiers, Montezuma and his chiefs, showing much emotion, gave fealty to His Majesty. Montezuma could not keep back his tears, and he was so dear to us and we were so much affected at seeing him cry that our own eyes were saddened. One soldier cried as much as Montezuma.

★   ★   ★   ★   ★

Between other conversations while Cortés and other captains were paying court to Montezuma, he asked through our interpreters, Doña Marina, Aguilar, and Orteguilla, where the mines were, in what rivers, and how they took the gold that they brought in grains, because he wished to send two of his soldiers, who were great miners, to see them.

Montezuma said that there were three sections, but that most of the gold came from the province of Zacatula, on the southern border, ten to twelve days distant, and that they washed away the earth in *xicales*, leaving the small grains. At the present time they were also bringing it from the province of Tustepeque, close to where we had disembarked, where they took the gold from two rivers. Near there were other good mines in a section not subject to him, but if we wished to send our soldiers there he would give us chiefs to go along.

Cortés thanked him and dispatched Gonzalo de Umbría, a pilot, with two other soldiers who were miners, to Zacatula. This Gonzalo de Umbría was the one whose feet Cortés ordered cut because he was involved in the rebellion at San Juan de Ulúa, about which I have written at length in the chapter where I was discussing it. He was given a limit of forty days to go and return.

To the north frontier he sent Captain Pizarro, a youth of

twenty-five, to see the mines there. At this time no one knew anything about Peru, and the name of Pizarro meant nothing. Four soldiers who were miners went with him, and four Mexican chiefs. They were also given forty days to go and return, for it was more than eighty leagues from Mexico.

Let us go back to say that Montezuma gave our captain a piece of woven henequen, painted and marked very naturally with all the rivers and bays of the north coast from Pánuco to Tabasco, which is more than 140 leagues. On it was shown the river Guazaqualco, and as we already knew all the ports and bays on the map except this river, which they said was very deep and strong, Cortés decided to find out what it was like and to take soundings of the port and its entrance.

One of our captains, Diego de Ordáz, who was, as I have told before, very knowing and vigorous, said that he would like to go and see this river, its lands and its people, so Cortés gave him permission to go.

Montezuma said to Ordáz that the people of Guazaqualco did not come under his rule and were very powerful. If anything were to happen, it would not be his fault, and before arriving at that province they should meet with the garrison of warriors he maintained at the border, and if he needed them he should take some of them with him. Cortés and Diego de Ordáz thanked him, and thus he left with two of our soldiers and some chiefs that Montezuma gave him.

Here is where the chronicler Francisco López de Gómara says that Juan Velázquez went with one hundred soldiers to colonize at Guazaqualco and Pedro de Ircio went to colonize at Pánuco. Because I have already had enough of observing how the chronicler strayed from what took place, I will leave it at that.

★   ★   ★   ★   ★

The first to return to the city of Mexico was Gonzalo de Umbría and his companions, who brought over three hundred pesos in gold grains, which they took from the Indians of Zacatula, where, according to Umbría, the chiefs took many Indians to the rivers, where they washed the dirt in little troughs. They brought with them two chiefs sent from that province, who brought a present of gold made into jewelry that was worth two hundred pesos. Cortés was as delighted as if the gold were worth thirty thousand pesos, for now he knew for certain that they had good mines, and he showed great affection toward the chiefs who brought the present.

Let us turn to Captain Diego de Ordáz, who returned from seeing the Guazaqualco River. He was joyfully received by Cortés and all of us, and he reported that the land was good for grazing and farming, but that it was far from Mexico City and there were large swamps.

Captain Pizarro too returned to report to Cortés, bringing over a thousand pesos of gold grains and two chiefs who came to offer themselves as vassals of His Majesty and have our friendship. They also brought a present of gold. Cortés received them well and accepted the present, but so many years have passed that I can't remember how much it was worth.

★　★　★　★　★

As Captain Diego de Ordáz and the other soldiers returned with samples of gold and related that all the land was rich, Cortés decided to demand of Montezuma that all the chiefs and towns should pay tribute to His Majesty, and that he himself, as a great lord, should also contribute from his treasury. He replied that he would send to all the towns and ask for gold, but that many of them did not have any, except for some jewelry of little value that their ancestors had left.

He immediately dispatched chiefs to the places where there were mines and ordered each town to give so many bars of fine gold of the same size and thickness as those they paid in tribute, and they took two bars as samples. He also sent to the province of the chief whose lord was that near relative of his who would not obey him, as I told about before. It was distant some twelve leagues from Mexico and the messengers brought back the reply that he would not give any gold or obey Montezuma, for he also was lord of Mexico, which belonged as much to him as to Montezuma himself.

Montezuma was enraged and immediately sent his seal and sign by some able captains to bring him as a prisoner. When this relative was brought into Montezuma's presence he spoke very disrespectfully and fearlessly. They say he had fits of madness, for he was as though thunderstruck.

Cortés came to know all of this and sent to ask Montezuma to give this man to him, as a favor, as he wished to guard him, for from what he had heard Montezuma had ordered him killed. When the chief was brought before Cortés, he spoke very affectionately and told him not to act like a madman toward his prince, and that he wished to set him free. When Montezuma heard this, he said that he should not go free, but should be attached to the great chain like the other, lesser kings.

Let us go back to say that, within twenty days all the chiefs Montezuma had dispatched to collect the tribute had returned. He sent for Cortés, our captains, and certain soldiers whom he knew, who belonged to his guard, and spoke formally to this effect: "I wish you to know, Lord Malinche, and my dear captains and soldiers, that I am indebted to your great king and bear him good will, both as a great lord and because he has sent you from such distant lands to learn about me. Furthermore, I have the thought that he must be the one who is to be lord over us, as our forefathers have told us and as our gods have given us to understand in the replies we have received from them. Take this gold that has been collected; because of the hurry more was not brought. What I have ready for the Emperor is all the treasure from my father, which is in your possession and in your quarters. I know that when you first came here you opened the treasure house and saw it all, then sealed it up again as it was before. When you send it to your emperor, say in your papers and letters, 'This is sent to you by your true vassal Montezuma.'

"I will also give you *chalchiuis* to send to him in my name, and they are not to be given to anyone else. Each stone is worth two *cargas* of gold. I also wish to send him three blow-guns with the pouches and molds for making pellets. He will be pleased to see the jewelwork on them. I also wish to give him of what I possess, although it isn't much, as I have given all my gold and jewels to you at various times."

When we heard this we were amazed at the goodness and liber-
ality of Montezuma, and with great reverence took off our helmets and
expressed our thanks. With words of the greatest affection Cortés promised that he would write to His Majesty of the magnificence and freedom with which he had given us the gold in his royal name.

After further polite conversation Montezuma sent his major-
domos to hand over all the treasure that was in the room that was plastered off. We spent three days in looking it over and taking off all the
decorations, and Montezuma's silversmiths from the town of Escapu-
zalco came to help in undoing and taking it all to pieces. I say that there
was so much that after it was taken to pieces there were three heaps of
gold that weighed more than six hundred thousand pesos, without the
silver and plates of gold, and I am not counting the grains from the
mines. We began to melt it down with the help of the Indian smiths,
making broad bars measuring three fingers of the hand across. After it
was melted into bars they brought another present and it was wonderful
to behold all the gold and the richness of the other jewelry that was
brought. Some of the *chalchiuis* were so fine that among these chiefs
they were worth a great quantity of gold. Then the three blowguns, set
with jewels and pearls and pictures in feathers of birds covered with
mother-of-pearl, all of great value.

Let us tell now how all the gold was stamped with an iron
marker that Cortés ordered made. The rich jewelry was not marked, as
it did not seem to us that it should be taken to pieces. We had neither
weights nor balances to weigh all these bars of gold and silver and the
jewelry that was left whole, so it seemed to Cortés and His Majesty's
treasury officers that it would be well to make weights of iron from one
arroba[1] to ounces. Not that they would come out very exact, but they
would be off only a half ounce or so in each lot that was weighed. After
the weight was taken, the King's officers said that there was in gold
more than six hundred thousand pesos, without the silver and other
jewelry that was left to be valued. Some soldiers said there was more.

---

[1] Twenty-five pounds.

There was now nothing more to do but to take out the royal fifth and give each captain and soldier his part, as well as the shares for those who remained at Villa Rica. It appeared that Cortés did not want to have it divided so soon, but to wait until there was more gold, good weights, and proper accounts. Most of us captains and soldiers said that it should be divided at once, for we had seen that when the pieces were taken out of Montezuma's treasury there had been much more gold in the heaps. Now a third of it was gone, taken and hidden for Cortés, the captains, and the Mercedarian father, and it kept on getting less. The next day it was to be distributed, and I will tell how it was done. Cortés and other persons kept most of it.

*   *   *   *   *

First the royal fifth was taken out. Then Cortés said that they should take another fifth because we had promised it to him on the sand dunes when we made him captain general and chief justice. After this he said that certain expenses on the island of Cuba and what he had spent on the expedition should be taken from the heap. In addition there should be set aside from the same heap the expenses of Diego Velázquez in the ships we had destroyed, to which we had all agreed, and the expenses of sending the stewards to Castile. There were the shares of those who remained in Villa Rica, of whom there were seventy, and for the horse that had died and the mare that had belonged to Juan Sedeño. Then for the Mercedarian father and for the priest Juan Díaz, for the captains, and double shares for those who had brought horses, and the same for the musketeers and crossbowmen, and other trickeries, so that there was very little left to share—so little that many soldiers did not want to take it and left it all with Cortés, for at that time we could do nothing but keep quiet, for to ask for justice was useless. Other soldiers took their shares of one hundred pesos and shouted for the rest, so Cortés secretly gave more to one and another to content them.

At that time many of our captains ordered large gold chains to be made by Montezuma's goldsmiths. Cortés also ordered much jewelry and a large table service. Some of our soldiers had their hands so full that slabs of gold, marked and unmarked, and jewelry of many kinds and workmanship were passed around publicly. There was heavy gambling with cards made by Pedro Valenciano from the skins of drumheads. They were very good and as well painted as the real ones.

This is the condition we were in, but let us leave off talking about the gold and the bad way it was divided and the worse way it was spent, and I will tell you what happened to a soldier they called Cárde-nas. He was a pilot and seaman from Triana or Condado. The poor fel-low had a woman and children in his country and had come to seek a living to take back to them. After visualizing that he would be rich in gold and being given only a hundred pesos he felt badly and very sad, and at last a friend asked why he kept sighing from time to time. Cárde-nas answered, "There is reason to feel badly, for Cortés has taken all the gold while my woman and children are dying of hunger. If Cortés gave me the share that belongs to me I could sustain them and perhaps advance them as well." We shouldn't have let Cortés take out any fifth, he said; we didn't have so many kings, only His Majesty.

When Cortés learned that many of the soldiers were discon-tented with their shares of gold and the way the heaps had been robbed, he made a speech with honeyed words and said that he did not want a fifth, but only the share that came to him as captain general, and if any-one had need of anything he would give it to him. The gold we had collected was but a bit of air; we should see the great cities there were, and the rich mines, and we would be lords of them all. He used other arguments, very well expressed. He also called Cárdenas aside and with pleasant words told him that he would be taken back to his woman and sons in Castile by the first ships to go and gave him three hundred pesos, and so left him content.

The Treasure of the Sierra Madre

BY B. TRAVEN

John Huston's great film is probably better known than B. Traven's novel, but each is in its own way a classic. Traven (? 1882–1969) was a mysterious personality, probably born in Poland, who turned up in Mexico in the 1920s and began publishing short stories and novels under a pen name. For many years he kept his real identity a secret, and it was not until after his death that he was revealed to have been one Albert Otto Max Feige. His dark, powerful, laconic fiction gained a reputation for him, and this extract from *The Treasure of the Sierra Madre* demonstrates with what skill he described the savagery a lust for treasure could breed.

★   ★   ★   ★   ★

Gold is the devil," said Howard, the old man. "It alters your character. However much you find, even if it's more than you can shift, still you think of getting more. And for the sake of getting more you forget the difference between right and wrong. When you set out you make up your mind to be content with thirty thousand dollars. When you find nothing, you put it down to twenty thousand, then to ten thousand, and lastly you declare that five thousand would be quite enough if only you could find them, no matter how you have to labor. But the moment you come on gold, you are not to be contented even with the thirty thousand you originally hoped for, your expectations mount higher and higher and you want fifty, a hundred, two hundred thousand dollars. That's how you get entangled, and driven this way and that, and lose your peace of mind for good."

"That's not my game," said one of the other two. "I can take my oath for that. Ten thousand and then I'm finished. Finished even though another million lay there to be picked up. That's the exact sum I need."

"Nobody believes it till he's been out himself," Howard replied in his leisurely way. "It's easy to get away from a gambling table, but no man has ever got away from a heap of gold which was his for the taking. I've dug for gold in Alaska and found it, I've dug in British Columbia, in Australia, in Montana, in Colorado. And made my pile, too. Well, here I am in the Oso Negro and through with it. I've lost my last fifty thousand in oil. Now I have to beg from old friends in the street. Perhaps I'll go out and have another try, old as I am. But I haven't the money. Then there's always this to consider: if you go alone it's the best, but you must be able to stand the solitude. If you go two or three together, there's always murder at your elbow. If it's a dozen of you, then each man's share is diminished, and you have quarrelling and murdering without any disguise. As long as you find nothing, you're all brothers. But as soon as the little heaps of dust get bigger and bigger, the brothers turn cut-throats."

In this way the old man got going on those tales about gold which are listened to more eagerly by those who drift in and out of such places as the Oso Negro than the most bawdy love stories. When an old gold-digger like this began on his stories he might keep it up all night. Not a man would sleep a wink and not a man call out: "Give us a chance to get to sleep." In any case, whether the tales were of gold or robbery or love, such a request would be in vain. A man might express his desire to sleep. But if he expressed it too often or too emphatically there was trouble, because the story-tellers maintained they had as good a right to be there as those who were there to sleep. A man has the right to spend the night telling stories if he chooses. If you don't like it you have the right to go and find a quieter place. No one should travel at all or put up in hotels who can't sleep in peace amid the thunder of guns, the rattle of wheels, the chumping of motor engines, and the coming and going and laughing and singing and chaffing and quarrelling of his fellow men.

"Have you ever heard the story of the Green Water Mine in New Mexico?" asked Howard. "You can't have. But I knew Harry Tilton who was there, and I had it from him. A band of fifteen men went off to find gold. They didn't go quite in the dark. There was an old tradition that in a certain valley there was a prolific gold-mine which the Mexicans had found and worked and which later on the Spaniards took from them after the Indians had been forced by merciless tortures—tongues pulled out, skulls gimleted and other such Christian attentions—to betray its whereabouts.

"Close to the mine in a hollow among the mountains there was a small lake, and the waters of it were as green as an emerald. That's why the mine was called the Green Water Mine. La Mina del Agua Verde. It was an uncommonly rich mine. The gold was in thick veins, you had nothing to do but extract it.

"The Indians, however, had laid a curse on the mine, so the Spaniards said, because every Spaniard who had anything to do with it came to grief. Some by snake-bite, others by fever, others again through terrible skin diseases and other diseases of which the cause could never be discovered. And one day the mine was lost. Not a man could be found who had ever been there.

"When the consignments of gold ceased and no report either came through, the Spaniards sent an expedition. The position of the mine was accurately marked on maps and the way to it was easy to follow, and yet the mine was not to be found. And there was no difficulty in locating it. There were three sharp rocky peaks, and when you had them in a line with each other you were on the right track, and when a fourth peak, of a shape you couldn't mistake, came into view and stood at a particular angle to the line of march, then you were so close to the mine that you could not miss it. But though the search went on for months, neither the mine nor the mountain tarn was ever found. That was in 1762.

"This prolific mine has never been forgotten by anyone interested in gold-mining.

"When New Mexico was annexed by the Americans, there was a new rush to find it. Many never returned. And those who did were half crazed by the vain search and the delusions that came on them while they hunted around among the rocks in that valley.

"It was in the 'eighties, 1886, I believe, when some more went to look—these same fifteen men I am speaking about. They had transcripts from the old reports and copies of the old Spanish maps. There was no trouble with the four hill-tops. But however they took their bearings by them, there was nothing to be seen of the mine. They dug and blasted here and there and not a trace could they find. They worked in gangs, three men to each, so as to quarter the whole territory. Their victuals began to run short, but they would not give up.

"One evening one of the parties of three was preparing a meal. The fire burned up, but the coffee didn't boil, because the wind was strong and cooled the can. So one of them started to scoop a deeper hollow for the fire. And as he dug and got down a foot or a foot and a half he came on a bone. He threw it aside without looking at it and then pushed the fire down into the hole after he had made flues to give it air.

"While they sat eating their food, one of them took up the bone without thinking and drew a figure with it in the earth. The man nearest him said: 'Let me have a look at that bone.' After a look he said: "It's the bone of a man's arm. How did it get here?'

"The one who had dug the hole now said that he had come on it while digging and thrown it out.

" 'Then there must be a whole skeleton here. Why should there be just an arm bone?' the other said.

"It was now dark and they wrapped themselves in their blankets and lay down to sleep.

"Next morning, the man who had found the arm bone, whom I'll call Bill, because I don't know his name, Bill, then, said:

" 'Where that arm bone came from there must be a skeleton. Now I had an idea in the night. I asked myself, how came this skeleton to be here?'

" 'That's easy,' said one of the other two. 'Someone killed or died of hunger.'

" 'That's possible, of course,' Bill said. 'There have been plenty of guys about here. But I don't believe they were killed or died of hunger just here. It's occurred to me that the mine was buried by a sandstorm or an earthquake or a landslip or something of the kind, and that explains why not a Spaniard ever came back. They were all buried close to the mine. It's true this bone may just as well belong to someone who was searching before us and lost his life here, but it's just as likely it belongs to one of the buried Spaniards. And if his arm is here so is his skeleton. And if we dig down to the skeleton we'll perhaps come on the mine. What I say is, let's dig a bit here where the fire was.'

They dug and, sure enough, they found the skeleton, bone by bone. They dug in a circle round about and found another, and further on a third. And so they got the direction which the landslide or the earthquake had taken. They followed it and came on tools and at last on nuggets of gold which had clearly been scattered abroad.

" 'We've got the mine all right. And what now?' asked Bill.

" 'Let's call the others,' said one.

" 'I never credited you with a lot of sense,' said the third, 'but I didn't know you were quite such a dam' fool. We'll hold our tongues and go back with the rest in a few days. Then in a few weeks we'll come back, us three by ourselves, and open the mine up.'

"They all three agreed to this. They collected the few nuggets and pocketed them. With the proceeds they would be able to fit themselves out well for the job. Then they shoveled all the earth carefully back. But before they had done, one of the other gangs came up. They looked suspiciously at the signs of digging and then one of them said: 'Hey, you guys, what's the game here? You want to keep us out of it, do you?'

"The first three stoutly denied having found anything and having meant to play a dirty trick. There was a quarrel, and as though the very air had betrayed them, two of the other gangs came up in the midst of the argument. They were just in time, for the first two gangs were on the point of coming to terms and agreeing to shut out the other three.

"Now, of course, the second gang drew back and accused the first of its treachery. A man was sent to summon the remaining one and when it arrived council was held. It was resolved to hang the three members of the first gang for having intended to conceal their find.

"The three were hanged. There was none to dissent from the verdict, for now there were their three shares to divide among the remaining twelve.

"Then they set to work and the mine was opened up, and sure enough it was almost inexhaustible. But very soon provisions ran so short that five men were sent off to replenish them.

"Harry Tilton, who told me the story himself, decided that as he was satisfied with his share up to date, he would not go with these five men. So he took his share and went. A bank paid him twenty-eight thousand dollars for his gold, and he bought himself a farm and settled down.

"The five men bought pack-horses, good tools and a plentiful supply of provisions and had the claim registered. Then they returned to the mine.

"But when they got there they found the camp burned to the ground and all the men who had stayed behind murdered, or, rather, killed by the Indians. There were signs of a terrible fight having taken place while they had been absent. They buried the bodies of their dead comrades and started working the mine again.

"They had not been at it more than three or four days when the Indians came back. They were more than sixty strong. They attacked at once and killed them all. One of them, however, was not killed outright but severely wounded and left for dead. When he recovered consciousness he set off to crawl away—for days or weeks—he didn't know. At last he was found by a farmer who took him to his house. He told his experiences, but he died of his wounds before he had been able to give an exact account of the place where it had all happened. The farmer set off to find the mine. He searched for weeks, but he never found it. Harry Tilton, who was in one of the northern states, heard nothing of all this. He was content to live on his farm and bothered no more about it; he imagined that all his comrades on the expedition were wealthy or prosperous men, who after they had got all the gold they wanted had gone east. He himself was a silent man. He had spoken of having made his money gold-mining. But there was nothing uncommon in that. And as he made little of his gold-digging days, the existence of this rich mine was again forgotten.

"But as time went on, the rumor grew that Tilton had made his money in a very few days. He did not deny it. And so it was plain that the place where he had dug must have been very rich in gold. He was pestered more and more by gold-diggers to work out a map that would make it possible to find the mine again. This at last he did. But more than thirty years had passed. His memory was no longer fresh. I set out with one of the parties which went by his map.

"We found all the places which Tilton had described. But the mine itself we never found. Perhaps it had been buried again by a land-slip or earthquake, or else the Indians had obliterated all trace of it, and done it so well that nothing was to be seen. They did not want anyone in their territory; for a mine like that would have drawn men in hundreds to the spot, and thrown the whole neighborhood into such a tumult that nothing would have been left of the life they were accustomed to.

"Yes, if one could find a mine like that," Howard ended, "one would be a made man. But you might search for it for a lifetime and find nothing. It is the same in any other line of business. If a man hits on the right business and has luck, there's his gold-mine. Anyway, old as I am, if anyone's after gold, I'm his man. But you need capital first, just as for all else."

The story Howard told had nothing in it to act either as an inducement or a deterrent. It was the usual gold-digger's story; true, no doubt, and yet sounding like a fairy story. But all stories which tell of great winnings sound like fairy stories. If you want to win a fortune, you must take a risk. If you want gold, you must go and look for it. And Dobbs determined that night to go and look for gold, even though he were armed only with a pocket-knife.

There was only one perplexity. Was he to go alone, with Curtin, with old Howard, or with them both?

★ ★ ★ ★ ★

Next morning Dobbs told Curtin the story he had heard from Howard. Curtin listened attentively and then said: "I dare say it's true."

"Of course it's true. Why should he have been telling lies?"

Dobbs was surprised that any should doubt the truth of the story. But the doubt which Curtin implied made an effect upon him. Its truth had seemed to him to follow as obviously as night after day. There was nothing in the story which need have been invented. Yet the doubt which lay behind Curtin's words turned it into an adventure story. And though so far Dobbs had looked upon the search for gold as no more than the search for a pair of boots in the various stores of a town, or as the search for work, he now suddenly realized that looking for gold must necessarily have something mysterious about it. He had never before had this queer feeling of something uncanny, mysterious and strange when the talk fell on gold-diggers. When Howard told the story in his matter-of-fact way, he had not felt that there was any difference between gold and coal. They were both in the ground, and coal could make a man just as rich as gold.

"Lies," said Curtin. "I didn't say that. The story itself is no lie. There are hundreds such stories. I've read them by the yard in the newspapers that print such yarns. But, whatever else in this story may seem improbable, I'm certain that bit of it's true where those three fellows try to get away with it and put the rest of them off the scent."

"You're right." Dobbs nodded. "That's the curse that hangs over gold."

The Lost Magato Trail, the Skeleton, and the Diamond Bags

BY HEDLEY A. CHILVERS

This is the true story—though fictionalized in the telling—of a murder that took place in 1903 in South Africa, just at the end of the Boer War. Treasure played a part in it, though only as what Alfred Hitchcock used to call the McGuffin—the motivating force that made the whole plot work. Hedley Chilvers, who was born in 1879, was the author of several books on South African history and native affairs. The tale of "The Lost Magato Trail" is taken from a volume of South African treasure-hunting stories called *The Seven Lost Trails of Africa.*

★   ★   ★   ★   ★

1

Those who traverse the gorges and dry river-beds of the country north of the Crocodile River in the eastern Transvaal, camping perchance under a multitude of stars, will be adventuring through a region little changed in a hundred thousand years. It is alive with game and infested with lions, as it was in the comparatively recent days when the dark, bearded gold-seekers of Babylon came down in their long coats and caps—you may see them still on the ancient friezes—and slept in terror, surrounded by deadwood fires.

The drowsing of bees, wasps, hornets, and of strange insects with multi-coloured wings, the glow of veld flowers, the war of the Wild, and anon the peace of God, all these have part in their own hour and time in the life of these places. And in the night—in the silence—these regions remain as of old, savagely asleep, or coy and virginal, but ever rich and mysterious, the untended gardens of the forgotten gods.

Now it so happened that these wilds became, fittingly enough, the setting of a sombre drama shortly after the Anglo-Boer War: the drama, it might be called, of the lost Magato trail. The romantic character of this affair took powerful hold of Africa, indeed inspired a thousand pens to attempt to place it in all its dark significance before the world. It fascinated intensely the late H. B. Irving, who visited the Dominion in 1912. Sir James Rose-Innes, too, the one-time Chief Justice of the Transvaal, who tried the charge of murder which arose out of it, said: "It is the most incredible, the most romantic, affair that has ever come before me."

And it originated, as most of the great crimes of the world have originated, in the love of a man, primitive and coarse-fibred, for a woman who would have none of him.

2

This man, Philip Swartz, burgher of the Transvaal Republic, a short, thick-set, stop-at-nothing sort of fellow, with a pair of mighty arms, and a good man in the bush withal, was encamped one evening towards the end of the Anglo-Boer War in this wild country near the Transvaal-Mozambique border. His camp was a little to the north of the Crocodile River. His life, begun in evil, had had its share of luck; for the Republican authorities had been desirous aforetime of examining him concerning a farmer who had vanished—together with a span of sixteen oxen—in circumstances which suggested foul play; but before they could put their suspicions to the proof the Anglo-Boer War had intervened, Swartz had joined the Boer forces, and the matter had lapsed.

At this moment, prompted as it would seem by the declining

sun, he was looking somewhat anxiously at the heap of dried wood which he and his companion Pretorius had collected.

"I hope there's enough of it," he growled, "to burn through the night. Otherwise, the lions. . . ."

"There's enough," the other said.

"A fool's game this," Swartz went on; "this wandering about! If we cross the mountains into Mozambique we'll be arrested, and if we stay here we'll be killed by lions. There's only one thing to be done—to rejoin the commando."

"The only thing," the other assented.

Night fell. They piled the brushwood high and lit it: the light glared fitfully on looming cliff and escarpment; the veld was eloquent with savage sound; they heard the mocking laughter of the hyena; and, as ever, divided the night into watches—one remaining awake to tend the fires, the other taking his rest.

They were fugitives belonging to General Ben Viljoen's commando which was then being harried by the British about the Leydsdorp-Komati Poort territory. The commando itself had become dispirited. It had learned that even in the mountains, whole battalions of British infantry might lie in wait for them; they felt that all life had become uneasy and uncertain; so that footsore, hungry and thirsty, many of them had fallen into the mood for desertion—and Swartz and Pretorius were among them. But deserters who had preceded these two across the border into Mozambique had been captured by the Portuguese, and news of these captures had reached other Boer fugitives following the trails towards the border, causing them to turn back. Among those who were thus turning back were Swartz and Pretorius; and at the moment this narrative begins they were resolved to pick up the trail of Viljoen's commandos, and to rejoin the comrades they had so recently forsaken.

Next day they continued their trek. The heat became greater as the day advanced, and the afternoon sun beat upon them fiercely; and, as often as not, they would talk of the deaths of travellers in the bush—travellers who had come upon the water-places when they were dried up, and had finally perished. And now as they trekked on they suddenly beheld a strange and terrible spectacle. They found themselves before a skeleton, the white bones of which had been stripped by the vultures. But close to the skeleton were three bags of diamonds and five bars of gold.

"We're rich men," cried Swartz.

"They're no good to us," replied Pretorius.

"We're rich men, I tell you," Swartz said, running his fingers through the gems.

"We can do nothing with them. If we carry them back to the commando they'll be stolen. If we don't reach the commando we'll end like the skeleton there. They're no good to us, I tell you."

"You miserable fool," the other said. "We can at least carry them to some spot we can recognize afterwards—some place near a river-bed where, say, there are Cream of Tartar trees. We can always recognize Cream of Tartar trees. And we can bury them there and come back for them after the war."

They shared the spoils; and tramped on for some hours until, reaching the banks of the Brak River, they found certain Cream of Tartar trees, and at a measured distance from these trees they buried the treasure, resolving to return for it when the war was over.

3

Long after, when Swartz was in the condemned cell at Pretoria and about to expiate the last and worst of his crimes, he offered a map of the position of the *cache* to more than one visitor. He adhered to his story—his strange and fantastic story of the skeleton and the diamonds—and there are many highly-placed police and treasury officials to-day who are convinced of its truth; who maintain that Swartz and Pretorius did find a great treasure somewhere in the Transvaal between Magato's country and Delagoa Bay. Nor is the belief unreasonable. It is based upon the fact that for years previously the fiery old native chief Magato had been sending native emissaries on lone trails across country laden with diamonds from the Kimberley mines. Many of his boys had worked in the mines and had stolen these diamonds, which they had presented to their chief. The chief proposed to exchange them for guns—for Magato had long resolved on the arming of his tribesmen so that they might be ade-quately equipped for any military occasion against the redoubtable whites.

There is evidence that transactions associated with these war-like ambitions had actually taken place. The late Howard Chadwick (who had been brought to the Rand from Kimberley as chief of the Johannesburg C.I.D. towards the end of the Boer War by Sir Richard Solomon, then Attorney-General of the Transvaal) used to recall an eccentric Englishman in Kimberley in the 'nineties who had boasted that he intended to nego-tiate "guns-for-diamonds" deals for Magato if he could secure a wealthy intermediary. He let it be known that the Chief wanted two good pieces of artillery and intended to get them. The wealthy intermediary, it is said, was forthcoming, and the two men were seen constantly together in Kim-berley. Gradually came rumours of intensified gun-running from the coast to Magato's country, and the story of the exchange of stolen gems for guns was frequently discussed in the diamond town. Magato died in 1897. The story of the native runner—dead in the lonely bush with his gold and diamonds still about him—was not, therefore, an extravagance; nor is it remarkable that a widespread belief persists to-day in the existence of this great treasure, hidden by Swartz and Pretorius, and never retrieved.

4

Swartz and his companion eventually struck the trail of the commando, but the unit was dispersed shortly afterwards by the British. Swartz was wounded in the thigh and captured; Pretorius was killed. Later on, and before he could unearth his treasure, Swartz was sent to Ceylon as a prisoner of war. He remained there until 1903, and often wrote optimistically to certain of his women friends in Johannesburg.

"When I return," he hinted in one of his letters, "my days of poverty will be ended."

Now Swartz was in love with one of two pretty sisters living under the roof of his foster-mother in Johannesburg, and while in Ceylon he certainly hoped one day to marry her. But, on his return from Ceylon, he found that the woman had married an ex-member of the Republican police, one Van Dyk, and that her sister had espoused a cab-proprietor, Van Niekerk. His return was thus in many ways disappointing; and though inclined to brood over his ill-luck—indeed he must have brooded over it more deeply than was generally supposed—he seems to have focused his hopes eventually on Mrs. Van Niekerk and to have restored his peace of mind somewhat by plotting the death of her husband. The Magato treasure had to be retrieved; Van Niekerk had to be removed. And, with his thoughts pointed in this direction, he determined to propose an expedition to the Blyde River to find this treasure, and, incidentally, to persuade Van Niekerk to accompany the expedition. Would it not, he asked himself, be comparatively easy then to shoot his rival and, when far away from civilization in one of the loneliest corners of Africa, to conceal his body beyond all chance of detection?

These ideas undoubtedly occurred to him and he acted readily upon them. His attitude towards the treasure has never been clearly disclosed; but his determination to remove Van Niekerk has never been in doubt. It became for him henceforth an all-absorbing motive. Meanwhile he frequently indulged in eccentric talk, much of which was afterwards remembered.

"You will be a widow before long," he told the astonished woman, to whom he pretended a gift of prophecy.

"How so?" she asked.

"The lions will get your husband."

Meanwhile Swartz proceeded with sinister intent to recount in likely quarters his experience of the skeleton and the bags of diamonds. Among the first to warm to the project was a certain James Colville of Johannesburg.

5

Now Colville was an original character with something of a reputation for astuteness. He was sufficiently astute indeed to score off most of his associates (in a perfectly legal way of course), and he was also well known in the racing world.

Colville was told by Swartz's brother-in-law, Van Dyk, of the circumstances in which Swartz had come upon the skeleton and the bags of diamonds, and he was impressed. At any rate he agreed to pay the cost of railing a properly-equipped Cape-cart to Pietersburg—then the rail-head—and of the four mules required to pull it from Pietersburg to Leydsdorp and on to the Blyde River. The details of the personnel and equipment of the expedition were afterwards discussed. Swartz recommended as members of it both Van Niekerk—the man whom he was secretly resolved to kill—and Van Dyk, his brother-in-law. These, he urged, should travel with them. It was also suggested that a certain Donovan should be invited in this treasure-hunting expedition.

"He can get weapons and ammunition for us," Van Dyk explained, "and we can then easily shoot all the game we shall need."

Donovan was, in some ways, the most remarkable man of the party. Unknown to Swartz he was a member of the Transvaal detective force who had made himself prominent in the Australian police force in 1897 by his single-handed capture of P——, the notorious outlaw, at Cabramatta in New South Wales. He chased him for three miles on foot through the Australian bush, and then bailed him up with a revolver. He had indeed an intimate knowledge of the bush, which in Australia and South Africa are not dissimilar. But at first he was not told by Swartz, Van Dyk, or Van Niekerk of the story of the treasure. Indeed, it was only while travelling in the train to Pietersburg that he learned the real aims of the party. Thus the curious position arose that the chief characters in the drama were all somewhat at cross-purposes. Briefly, Swartz intended to kill Van Niekerk near the Blyde River and to keep any treasure for himself, even if this involved the murder of the whole of the party, this last desperate resolve being indicated by an incident that occurred later and which will be duly related. Colville, believing the story of the buried diamonds, was of course anxious to get them, but was ignorant (it is hardly necessary to state) of the sinister intentions of

Swartz. Donovan, for his part, at first thought he was on an ordinary shooting trip.

6

The final preparations were made. It was decided to truck the Cape-cart at Johannesburg. The whole party entrained on May 4, 1903, for Pietersburg.

"Be careful of Philip," was the last anxious injunction of the wife as she bade Van Niekerk farewell. Man and wife never met again.

The members of the expedition detrained uneventfully at Pietersburg on May 5. The cart was fitted up for the long journey into the wilds, and there was plenty of rough joviality as the final preparations were made. They set out. The region to be traversed was, as already related, infested with lions; its roads were mere tracks. But Colville proved most companionable, his stories of travel through the Australian Bush, his quaint confessions, and his sense of humour only being rivalled by the experiences of Donovan, whose life had been spent in still more adventurous contacts in the Antipodes. On the other hand, Van Niekerk proved so lethargic that, as his companions afterwards said, he would not even trouble to dodge the branches of the overhanging trees as the Cape-cart jaunted through the bush; with the result that on several occasions he was nearly swept off. Moreover, he was generally the last to alight when the mules were battling up some hot sunny slope. Once he punctured the water-bottle.

"You are a careless fool," growled Swartz as he inspected the hole. "But, no matter, we're getting near the treasure now," he added, as if communing with himself.

Daylight was fading when the party halted on the edge of the Blyde River. Although tired and hungry all had been greatly heartened by Swartz's constant declaration that they were nearing the *cache*; and so with light hearts they collected wood to make fires. At dawn next day they again struck camp, leaving the cart behind them at the river, and they rode or led the mules into still rougher country, until they reached a tributary of the Brak, twenty miles beyond the Blyde. They got to this deserted spot at five o'clock on the evening of May 17, and at once set about the business of forming their camp. As darkness was imminent, each member went off on some task. Donovan departed to get wood, leaving his coat on the ground. Van Dyk and Colville set off on the same errand. The stage was thus set for the terrible drama.

Swartz and Van Niekerk were alone.

"Now, let's be off," Swartz remarked gruffly.

And so the two departed, each with a gun, and as all thought, purposing to shoot game for the evening meal. They disappeared presently into the thicket surrounding the sloping banks of the almost dry river, and none of the party ever again saw Van Niekerk alive.

7

Only a faint glimmer remained in the sky when the foragers returned to camp and lit their fires. Swartz and Van Niekerk were still absent. But presently two shots were heard from the south-west.

"They've got a buck," exclaimed Donovan.

Two more shots echoed from a point further east. Then silence. A lengthy interval elapsed. Three big fires were heaped up, for the lions were heard roaring in the distance. The flames flickered reassuringly against the yellow ledges overhanging the river.

"Where can they be?" inquired Donovan, who sat facing one of the fires.

"Perhaps treed by lions," suggested someone.

Long afterwards Donovan explained that just at that moment as he sat staring into the fire over which some guinea-fowl were grilling, puzzled and uneasy at the disappearance of Van Niekerk and Swartz who alone knew the location of the treasure, he felt instinctively that he was being stalked. And looking around suddenly he saw a man's legs touched by the flicker of the campfires coming stealthily towards them. The head was hidden by the trees.

"Who's that?" he shouted, clutching his revolver.

For answer, Swartz promptly announced himself and came trudging boldly into the firelight with his carbine.

"Where's Phanie?" (Van Niekerk) was the general query.

"I don't know," replied Swartz, placing the rifle casually on the ground. "I wounded a koodoo which ran past him. I told him to shoot it, but he didn't. So I chased it myself, and that's the last I saw of him. Up a tree, I suppose."

"We heard other shots to the south-east," somebody remarked.

"I fired one," replied Swartz. And that seemed to explain it. Van Niekerk had fired the other shot and had then lost himself after shooting vainly at the koodoo. He was now probably up a tree. But Donovan was left with the indefinable feeling that something was wrong. He was not sure of Swartz. And that night he caught himself speculating as to whether, when he saw the legs of Swartz in the firelight, and challenged him, that challenge had not saved their lives; indeed, whether Swartz's arrival in camp after dark had not been timed to facilitate the murder of the other members of the expedition.

"I believe," the old detective always said, afterwards, "that when Swartz was stalking the camp we were so placed with regard to the fires that he could have shot us all. And he knew it. So that had I not challenged him when I did he would probably have killed us."

That night, nevertheless, the belief prevailed generally that Van Niekerk was up a tree hiding from the lions; and Donovan fired many rounds from his revolver in order to draw the attention of the missing man to the position of the camp. He fired at intervals during the night. Without avail, however. Van Niekerk did not return; and the impression gradually deepened that he had despaired of finding them, and had gone back to the cart at the Blyde River. His curiously lethargic character, somewhat half-hearted attachment to the expedition, and lack of sense of direction in the bush, all strengthened this presumption, so that no very protracted search was made for him. Swartz now professed anxiety to avoid delay. He urged them to push on to where, he said, the treasure was hidden. They therefore set out once again. Donovan left two notes—one in English and the other in Dutch—attached to the trees, notifying the absent man of the direction they had taken, and of the probable time of their return. And now, after a long and wearisome journey, the treasure-hunters approached a ridge, from the top of which Swartz intently scanned a distant kopje with a pair of field-glasses.

"If you wait here," he said, "I will go and search for some marks which I made when I buried the treasure."

So the party waited. They heard Swartz call, they heard him direct them towards a hill, they caught the distant report of a Browning pistol, fired apparently to attract their attention: but they failed to reach him, and he vanished.

"We can do nothing now," said Donovan at long last. "Swartz was our guide, and he alone knew where the stuff is hidden. He's gone. So we'd better go back to our last camp, and then to the cart at the Blyde River."

The remaining members of the party were now thoroughly angry with Swartz and disheartened. They halted some 300 yards from their last camp, in a site among rocks and trees, and again fired off various rounds—which echoed eerily about the rugged country; but there came no answering reports, and so they lay about their fires through the night, each man adding more wood as he awakened. Donovan once created a blaze thirty feet high by igniting a dead and hollow tree, and the glare lit up the gloomy hills for miles around. The signals drew no response however. Then they trekked back to the cart which they had left on the Blyde River. Here they made a remarkable discovery. They found a note purporting to be signed by Van Niekerk pressed between the spokes of one of the wheels near the axle which read: "Tired of the job. This day I have gone to Johannesburg and I may go on to Bulawayo."

Donovan took possession of the letter. He felt that it might yet throw light on the dark places of this mysterious expedition; for he now, more than ever, suspected that something sinister lay behind the disappearance of the two men; and although he could not quite understand the absence of Van Niekerk's nail-screw tracks on the ground, he at that time still thought it possible that Van Niekerk might have been to the cart and have gone ahead. An examination of the vehicle showed that it had been robbed: that ammunition, blankets, rugs, brandy, and even cuff-links had been stolen; and Van Niekerk, upon whom fell the blame, was freely reviled for having thus deceived the rest of the party.

8

The remains of a fire, however, suggested that one of the missing men was not far ahead, and the whole party determined to go on in resolute pursuit. They left provisions in the fork of a tree for the benefit of whoever might be left behind. Donovan was the only skilled bushman left with the pursuers. He took charge, and made up his mind to follow the shortest possible cut to Leydsdorp and, if possible, to get there either before or on the heels of Swartz or Van Niekerk. And so they trekked on with their cart until they reached first the Oliphants and then the Selati rivers, where they met a native, virtually the only human being they had encountered in that land of lions and wild game. The native told them that a white man was a short distance ahead making for Leydsdorp. Almost simultaneously they heard a shot.

"That," exclaimed Donovan, "is my revolver. It is the only one of its kind in the country."

They hurried on. Presently they came upon Swartz himself, dangling his feet in the river. He looked famished and woebegone. He had no shirt.

"Where have you been?" he was asked.

"I told you to follow me," he retorted, "and you didn't. I couldn't find you. So I went off to where the diamonds were hidden, got them, tied them up in my shirt, and hid them again in the banks of the river."

"Why didn't you return to the cart at the river?"

"Because," he replied, "I took the shortest way back to Leyds-dorp."

Argument and recrimination ensued. Someone proposed that the party should return to the Blyde River to get the diamonds which

Swartz claimed to have found, and at the same time to hunt for Van Niekerk, but Swartz demurred. He declared that the expedition was exhausted and that the animals were in no condition to do the journey.

9

Swartz now began to shun his comrades. He seemed to realize that his conduct must seem curious, and he noted the growth of a new suspicion in their eyes. He would go away and sit alone some distance from the camp. At last, on May 22, they reached Leydsdorp. Donovan proceeded at once to the office of the South African Constabulary there.

"I want to report the disappearance of a member of our party," said he, and related the circumstances of the case.

"The lions must have got him," commented the officer in charge; "one even came in here and took a donkey away the other day."

So nothing was done at the moment; and the party travelled on to Pietersburg—a distance of ninety-three miles—inquiring, as they went, for Van Niekerk.

Pietersburg was, as already mentioned, the railhead. The party prepared to truck their belongings from there back to Johannesburg; and Swartz, who made various excursions into town, was seen to change two sovereigns, a circumstance which seemed curious, for on the forward journey all knew that he had no money, whereas Van Niekerk had had two sovereigns which, as he told everyone, he intended to send to his wife at the first opportunity.

Donovan became still more suspicious. And Swartz was aware of the fact. On the train journey to Johannesburg he hid himself in his bunk. He evidently felt that the net was fast closing round him and did not wish to incriminate himself further.

"Can you?" Donovan whispered to Van Dyk at a wayside halt, "manage to get Philip on to the platform?"

By some little subterfuge, Van Dyk got him there; whereupon Donovan slipped into his compartment, seized the suspect's note-book, and in a few brief seconds compared the handwriting on the note left at the cart (and purporting to have been written by Van Niekerk) with Swartz's own scribblings on letters and chits in his note-book. The comparison proved exact. The letter left at the cart had not been written by Van Niekerk but by Swartz. The circumstances all pointed more strongly than ever to foul play. The implication was that Van Niekerk had been inveigled away at the forward camp and probably murdered by Swartz. On their return to Johannesburg, Donovan's first act was to report all the facts to Howard Chadwick, the chief of police.

It is not necessary to conclude the story in detail. Swartz bluffed his way about Johannesburg for some weeks. Then an official expedition was dispatched to search for Van Niekerk; and presently came the startling news that his remains had been found near a large waterhole, remains which had been attacked by vultures. These remains supplied the additional evidence needed to bring the crime home to Swartz; for it was proved from them that the unfortunate man had been shot and robbed. Swartz was tried, condemned, and executed on February 15, 1904, after one of the most sensational trials in South African history.

The Salvage of the
Laurentic Treasure

BY PIERRE DE LOTIL AND JEAN RIVOIRE

Unsuccessful treasure hunts are far more common than successful ones. Things usually go wrong—the treasure isn't where it is supposed to be, it can't be found, it can't be reached, somebody else beat you to it. "The Salvage of the *Laurentic* Treasure," which is taken from *Sunken Treasure* by two French writers, describes a happy exception. In this case, divers working in icy waters off the coast of Ireland more than eighty years ago managed to recover almost every bit of a lost treasure. But the account of their feat makes chillingly clear just how difficult and perilous even—or especially—success can be. It should be noted, moreover, where the recovered treasure went: straight back into His Majesty's Treasury.

★　★　★　★　★

In the year 1917 the fishermen and sailors of County Donegal were astonished to see, from the rocky coast of Horn Head, a Royal Navy tug steaming up and down on the horizon in the area where the *Laurentic* had been wrecked.

The *Laurentic*, a former White Star transatlantic liner, had been transformed into an auxiliary cruiser during the war and had been torpedoed in January 1917 off the coast of Ireland.

245

Some men, who had approached the tug, said that there were divers on board and that they were continually making descents. How could they dive in the open sea, and what were they looking for in the wreck? The *Laurentic* had made many crossings to the United States, and each time she had brought back a cargo of arms and munitions. But when the German torpedo had sent her to the bottom with some two hundred men of her crew, the *Laurentic* had just left England. What could she have been taking to the United States from a country which had been at war for thirty months and was short of everything?

Towards the end of 1917 the divers left as discreetly as they had come.

The armistice of 1918 had hardly been signed when, from the rocks of Horn Head, the silhouette of the little tug was once more seen on the horizon. Sometimes steamers and even destroyers came to visit her.

These manoeuvres went on for several months. The diving had been resumed. Such divers as could be approached were as close as oysters. It was not until August 1923, when everything was finished, that the Admiralty raised the veil on the secret. Before the *Laurentic* was torpedoed her holds had been loaded with gold and silver ingots to a total of forty tons, being sent by the Treasury to hundreds of American industrialists. These citizens of a neutral country wished to be paid in hard cash.

It was Captain G. C. C. Damant, a specialist in submarine work, who in 1917 had been put in charge of the job. Finding the wreck was not difficult. Shore stations had taken wireless bearings of the S.O.S. when she was torpedoed, and the sinking ship had been observed by lookouts on land. And it did not take much dragging of the sea bed to find the ship lying in twenty-two fathoms of water and heeling over sixty degrees to port. The depth presented no difficulty, and ordinary conventional diving suits could be used. No, the real source of difficulty was that the wreck was exposed to the Atlantic swell, and on her superstructure the divers had to spend most of their time clinging to the ship's rail. When the *Laurentic*'s crew had taken to the boats the tackles had been left hanging, and now the sea was making them lash to and fro like gigantic whips, and one diver was alarmed to see the heavy block at the end flying past the glass window in front of his nose.

The divers' task was to find the entry-port on the starboard side of the second-class baggage room and blow it open with guncotton. Despite the difficulty of working in these conditions, the divers soon found the port, blew it open, and removed the heavy iron doors which had fallen inside the ship. Various cases had to be moved out of the way, and then Diver Miller opened the steel door of the bullion room with a hammer and chisel and slid down onto the boxes of gold. These boxes were only about a foot square by six inches deep, but they weighed 140 lbs. and were worth about £8,000 each. It was an awkward job for one man to carry them up the steep, slippery deck to the entry-port, where he could be given help from above. Nevertheless Miller got one box out that night and three next morning.

The job looked as if it would be easy. But they were working in mid-winter and were harried by gales and snowstorms. A violent northerly gale blew for a week. The coast was scattered with wreckage from the *Laurentic*, much of it identifiable as gear that had come from below decks. Obviously she was beginning to break up.

When the diving-ship returned to her moorings—which had suffered badly in the storm—the divers were surprised to find that the entry-port was forty feet deeper than it had been before and that they could only crawl a few feet along the passage inside, for the wreck had collapsed so much that the ceiling was only eighteen inches from the deck. They therefore set about lifting the ceiling with explosives and shoring it up so that the divers could again reach the bullion room. They succeeded, only to find that its floor had collapsed and the gold had slid away downwards and to port. They soon realized that the route through the entry-port was not only difficult but extremely dangerous, with tons and tons of more or less unsupported wreckage lying above the divers, and the whole wreck moving and making the most ominous noises as it went on collapsing. They therefore decided to blast a way vertically downwards through the wreckage. Explosives have little effect on a structure that has collapsed and is no longer rigid; to break the steel plates it was necessary to haul them up taut with wire cables and then fire the charge when they were under stress.

One day Diver Blachford was working in this way, lying under a metal plate and forcing in the guncotton charge, while the men on the salvage ship's deck were keeping the plate hoisted up with a wire cable and listening to his telephoned instructions, when suddenly the taut cable flew up into the air and lay slack. A faulty shackle had broken and Blachford was lying under the steel plate. There was a long pause and then the diver's voice was heard again on the telephone.

"Give me all the air you can, sir."

They opened the valve wider.

"That's right, give me more yet, and get another diver down here as quick as possible."

Diver Clear was standing by on deck. His helmet was quickly screwed on and a new cable and shackle prepared. But they were hesitant about giving Blachford more air. The pressure was already very high—almost high enough to burst his suit. But the suit might already be torn and flooded and he needed the air to keep the water away from his face. Meanwhile the roar of the extra air pouring into his helmet made it impossible for them to hear his voice. When they eased off the supply so that he was audible they heard him saying slowly and clearly "Give me more air!" But considering the risk they did not dare to do so.

Diver Clear soon followed Blachford's air-pipe down to the wreck, and the plate was hoisted up again and the luckless diver freed after being trapped for less than ten minutes. He was none the worse, but he had felt as if the plate would break his back, and the extra air inflating the suit had eased the strain. It had not occurred to him that the suit might have burst and drowned him.

Then danger threatened from another quarter. German submarines were laying mines in the area and British minesweepers sometimes exploded them with their sweeps. When a mine blew up only two miles from the wreck it gave the diver a severe and dangerous shock. So diving had to be halted whenever the minesweepers were within five miles. Nevertheless another diver was given a bad shock by a mine exploding six miles away. It was not until the divers had spent two months clearing away broken plates of steel and basketfuls of lumber and smashed furniture that they reached the gold again. Miller found ten bars lying loose. By September some £800,000 worth of gold had been returned to the Treasury, and wintry weather was setting in. The divers had other more urgent work elsewhere, and during the summer of 1918 what Captain Damant calls "even more exciting work" kept them busy. So that they did not return until eighteen months had passed.

They were surprised to find that the wreck had altered little in their absence and it was not long before they began finding more bars of gold. But this little treasure trove was soon exhausted, for apparently the gold had become separated into two parts as the wreck collapsed and many tons of debris had to be removed before they reached the rest. In their demolitions the divers had already cut through a good deal of the wreck, and high superstructures were overhanging the place where the divers were working. Captain Damant grew anxious about it but he writes:

> So long as gold was coming to hand I was very reluc-
> tant, however, to break off the work for the purpose of
> dealing with these superstructures, which certainly con-
> tained none of the bullion. The decision was fortunate,
> for on resuming work in the spring of 1920 we found
> that the winter gales had done all that was necessary and
> a bit more.

Both superstructures had collapsed. The hole where the divers had been working was entirely filled with steel plates and planked deck-ing, and their familiar landmarks had moved so much that it was difficult for them to know where to start digging. Moreover, the excavation was now no longer protected by the superstructure from the waves and tides. There was a huge supply of debris and inexhaustible supplies of sand and stones. In fine weather the divers would begin to clear away the sand and rubbish, then a storm would come and fill in the hole again. They tried using large pumps and dredger grabs, but for various reasons these devices failed. So the divers worked by hand, and Captain Damant has given us a detailed account of the way in which they worked:[1]

> The implements were simply sacks, into the mouths of which had been tied steel scoops resembling the front part of a coal-scuttle, a fire hose carrying a high pressure of water, and the bare hands. Let us follow the actions of one of the divers. He has been dressed and put into the water some minutes beforehand and is waiting just below the surface for the word to go down. Four minutes before it is time for his predecessor to leave the wreck the order is given and he slides rapidly down the thin wire "shot rope" which is put on afresh daily and leads directly to the spot where the work is being done. To slide down the 126 feet takes a minute or slightly less: the increase in atmospheric pressure of 55 lbs. per square inch produces no physiological effect, though, of course the descending diver has frequently to force open his Eustachian tubes. On first reaching the wreck he hauls down 30 feet or so of his own air-pipe, ties it with a lanyard to some convenient part of the wreck, and gives the order by telephone, "Haul taut air-pipe." Those above pull it up into as nearly a straight line as the tide will allow, so that there is no curving bight of pipe flowing out and liable to catch in distant parts of the wreck. The lanyard of course prevents any of the strain from coming on to the diver, whom it would pull off the bottom. The diver can generally see 20 feet or so, beyond which distance all is vague mist. He has landed in the bottom of a sort of crater, the sides of which are formed by jagged

---

[1] Quoted by Sir Robert H. Davis in *Deep Diving* (London).

shelves of plate, each one piled high with toppling masses of broken wood and indescribable junk.

Near the bottom of the shot rope stands a large hopper or bucket, painted white so as to be conspicuous in the general gloom, and into this a diver is struggling to lift a bulging sack. It is to help him that our friend has gone down early: he stumbles across, gives a heave to the sack, and seeing it flop into the bucket with the raising of a cloud of black mud, turns his back and makes for a canvas hose close at hand. This hose terminates in a specially strong conical metal pipe about 2 feet long. The diver gets down flat on the sandy floor of the crater, grips the metal pipe in his right hand, and asks for the water to be turned on from above. With a powerful jet issuing, the nozzle can be thrust deep into the caked silt and the diver's left hand follows it up, exploring this way and that among the pebbles, chunks of iron, and other hard objects buried in the sand. It is now absolutely pitchdark on account of the cloud of mud and dirt raised by the hose; and if a bar comes to hand, the diver lays it behind in contact with his leg.

Twelve minutes after leaving the surface he gets the order to start bagging sand and the water is stopped. With one of the bags already described he gets to work on the loosened dirt, scraping it in with his bare hands or a bit of wood. Perhaps during the hosing period he has located bars without being able to work them out, and he will now direct his digging towards them, bringing a knife or a crowbar to bear and working against time; for after 13 minutes on the bag the order to "Come up" is given from above. He has five minutes now in which to put his bars, if any, into the bucket, lift in his heavy sack of sand, and gather up into coils the slack pipe between himself and the lanyard. Giving the order, "Up pipe," he casts off the lanyard, watches his pipe go up all clear, and then throttles the air-escape valve on his helmet so that in a moment he is sliding rapidly up the shot rope again. Thirty feet below the surface (the exact spot being indicated to him from above) he checks his ascent, and, letting go the wire shot rope, swings through the water to a short hanging rope steadied by a weight at the end.

There he passes through the decompression period.

Although there was no individual reward for finding gold, a bonus of about one-eighth of one per cent of its value was divided between the entire ship's company. "Nevertheless," Captain Damant remarks, "the competition was as keen as possible, each diver's score was reckoned from day to day, and the lucky fellow who sent up £45,000 worth on one dive received a prize of a tin of cigarettes." He also has some shrewd remarks about human nature and the problems of the man in command of a team of treasure seekers:

> There was a tendency for some men to spend their whole half-hour in poking about for odd bars and getting the derrick wires down to turn over likely plates, leaving the dull sand-shifting to the next fellow. It was odd to find oneself cursing X for bringing up untold gold and blessing Y for producing a sack of dirty sand and stones; but there was no doubt that the gold would give itself up in greater bulk than ever if only the sand could be got rid of.

To encourage the Y's Captain Damant had the bright idea of measuring the quantity of sand each man sent up and thus instituting a new competition. This worked wonders until the rest of the divers realized that Balson was the strongest of them all and that there was no point in trying to beat him.

And so the slow and tedious work went on through the summers of 1920 and 1921, during which only fifty bars of gold were salvaged. But more and more of the wreckage was being cleared out of the way, and when they returned in 1922, the divers were delighted to see a number of bars sticking up from the sand, and they collected nineteen bars on the first day. Gradually the excavation got down to the metal of the wreckage, which lay in folds and corrugations under which the gold sometimes lay. This meant that the divers would have to work head downwards, a dangerous position for a man in conventional gear, for the legs of his suit are liable to fill with air, and up he goes like a balloon.

> Taking the smallest possible air supply, [writes Damant] and often getting that stopped for a minute at a time, they would dig away with their hands till the accumulation of air began to lift them, when they would crawl out backwards and raise their heads so as to let it escape, then back again to the job like a terrier at a rabbit hole.

A diver named Light was working in this way, when he felt a bar of gold with the tops of his fingers, and in his excitement stayed upside down for a minute too long. His weighted boots were lifted off the sand and his legs floated up to the plates above. He asked for his air supply to be stopped, but it was too late, he was forced to let go with his hands, and he floated up until he was stopped with a jerk some forty feet from the bottom because his pipe and cable had been made fast, as usual, to the wreck. His suit was blown up so tight that he could hardly move and there was nothing upon which he could get a purchase to turn himself over. There he swung like a mine in mid-water. He reported that there was water in his helmet, but "only a little." A quart or so, in this position, would have drowned him. Luckily another diver, Blachford, was already in the water, and he was lowered down Light's pipe to the point where it was fastened to the wreck. He could then probably have climbed up Light's pipe and turned him over. "But," as Damant modestly admits, "by an error for which I was responsible" he was told to get astride Light's pipe, cut the lanyard and then ease the hapless diver up to the surface. But Damant had underestimated the human balloon's buoyancy and both divers shot to the surface in a flash, fortunately arriving on the right side of the ship without hitting her hull. Light was quickly brought aboard, where he was found to be quite unhurt, and put into a compression chamber to decompress slowly, while Blachford went down again to decompress in the usual way.

During 1922 £1,500,000 worth of gold was salvaged, the best day's haul being £150,000 worth of ingots still lying in the remains of their boxes. As a rule all trace of the boxes had vanished and the bars themselves had often been bent double or "squeezed out like so much putty" or had pebbles or rivet-heads embedded in their soft metal. It was a good year. The divers had learned to keep pace with the silting, and Captain Damant had established that the remaining bars were almost certainly lying on the flattened-out bottom of the ship and could sink no further into the sand.

In 1923 they did even better and salvaged nearly two million pounds' worth of gold, leaving 154 bars, worth about £240,000, still to be accounted for. When they returned in 1924 the great sheet of plating was almost completely cleared. But there were holes and rents in the metal through which some of the bars might have made their way. So the divers set to work under this carpet of metal and began finding bars not only under the holes but often at some distance from them. These straying bars had not moved, but the whole sheet of steel had gradually worked over the sea bed for several yards. In the end the work under the metal became too difficult and dangerous, and the whole layer of steel was cut into pieces and removed. In this way 129 of the outstanding 154 bars were salvaged by the end of the year. The divers were well satisfied with their work and thought it would be fruitless to continue. They had saved 99 per cent of the sunken gold at a cost of between two and three per cent of its value, and they had done so without any serious accidents.

No treasure hunt had ever before been so fruitful, and none has been so since.

The Treasure of "El Chato" Nevárez

BY ARTHUR L. CAMPA

Arthur Campa (1905–1978) wrote about lost mines in the Southwest; he also spent time looking for them. Like J. Frank Dobie he was a scholar and a college professor, an expert on the folkways of Spanish America and a man with an exceptional understanding of the historical context from which so many stories of treasure sprang. The following tale is open-ended—the treasure, Campa suggests, may still be there in Soledad Canyon. *Treasure of the Sangre de Cristos* (1963), the book from which this chapter is taken, is a rich collection of treasure-hunting stories. When it was first published, a reviewer remarked that it would make any reader want to try his luck. Fair enough—but don't give up the day job.

★ ★ ★ ★ ★

L ate in the fall of 1913 Ben Brown left his prospector's camp one afternoon to look for a deer along the foothills below the Organ Mountains. Toward the end of the day he came upon a good-sized mule deer buck as he reached the top of a ravine, but before he could get him in the sights of his Winchester the deer bounded gracefully and disappeared in the arroyo below him. The buck was not entirely unharmed because Ben Brown's quick shot from the hip had caught him in the shanks, as the trail of blood indicated. Confident that the wound would slow the critter down, Ben followed the trail over the scrub-covered arroyos and through the thick chamiso expecting to find him lying somewhere along the trail. Apparently the deer was not badly wounded; he outdistanced the young prospector by keeping constantly under cover and always out of range until he disappeared. Tired and disappointed by his long and unsuccessful hunt, Ben Brown threw himself down at the foot of a gnarled juniper standing on the brow of the first hill he came to.

As he sat listening to his own breathing, Ben's eyes glanced over the landscape hoping to see something move, anything that would make a meal for a hungry mining man. Gradually his gaze shifted to the ground where he was sitting, and before long his prospecting eye caught a peculiarity about the hillside, which at first glance had not been apparent. He got to his feet and began a closer inspection of the terrain; something about it intrigued him. In a few minutes it became quite clear that the place where he had been sitting was a fill-in of some sort. The question that arose in his mind was why anyone would bother to fill a depression of a hill so far away from nowhere, but if it was a fill-in, what was it hiding?

Still on his feet he began to scan the horizon to get his bearings, and when he turned his face eastward he paused to take a second and more careful look; he had made a startling discovery. Three conical peaks leading toward the mountain range behind them stood out in perfect array. He leaned his gun against the juniper and started walking toward the rising sun—"One, two, three . . ." and on, until he reached two hundred fifty. He stopped, looked back, and put together a pile of rocks, then turned north and began counting the same number of paces. He had reached the top of another rise from which he could see straight ahead into the Jornada del Muerto.[1] He went back to the tree and

[1]Arduous though travel was through the Jornada del Muerto, so named because of the number of people who perished while crossing it, it was regularly used because it was a convenient short-cut. The Spanish Trail, which followed the Rio Grande north most of the way, left it at Robledo just north of the modern city of Las Cruces and did not rejoin it until about ninety miles north at Fray Cristobal. The Rio Grande swings on an arc to the west

walked down the arroyo counting one hundred paces. There was no spring visible, but when he scraped the surface with his toe he noticed that the sand was moist.

Ben Brown felt sure that he had accidentally stumbled upon the location of a treasure he had learned about from a convict, a member of a gang working under him during the building of the road between Hot Springs and Socorro. He had never thought of searching for it, but the depression of that hill, the three conical peaks, and the faint trace of water from what may have been the "dripping spring" the convict gave as the third landmark, was enough to persuade him that he had run into the hiding place of "El Chato's Treasure."

El Chato was a renegade who held out in the mountains from Tortugas Peak north to the Caballo Range, harrying the traffic of the Camino Real and assaulting the pack trains loaded with cargo coming up from Chihuahua. His specialty was the *conductas*[2] with little or no military escort, and any time valuables were being transported El Chato could be expected to attack from his hideout in the mountains east of the Río Grande in southern New Mexico. He had earned the name of "El Chato," meaning "Pug-nose," in an encounter with a Spanish cavalryman who had come close to ending his career with a sabre blow. Between 1639 and 1649,[3] he terrorized the countryside along the Mesilla Valley, and with his band of cutthroats defied the scant protection which the Spanish government sent beyond El Paso del Norte. According to tradition, his hideout was in Soledad Canyon in the rugged Organ Mountains, but no one had dared to follow him to his lair.

---

and the Jornada is a straight line. Oñate, the first colonizer of New Mexico, used it when he brought his settlers in 1598.

[2] *See* Cleve Hallenbeck, *Land of the Conquistadores*, 303. This author states that the trading caravans from New Mexico converged from places as far north as Taos at an established location and then proceeded on their way to the Chihuahua Fair. He gives the following statistics: "*Conductas* left in November, rendevouzed in Sevillita of La Jolla, arrived in Chihuahua in January. There were as many as 300 wagons, 600 mules, 400 horses. Women and children. They used the boleta in trade."

[3] The dates given in the El Chato story do not accord with the historical conditions at that time. There was, for example, no presidio at El Paso until after 1680. The discrepancy is typical of the manner in which traditions develop.

The best haul on record made by El Chato came toward the end of his depredations, and probably was the last one he ever made. He chose for his victims a band of missionaries coming up the Spanish Trail with an *atajo* of pack mules loaded with church property and other valuables they were bringing from Mexico City. They had begun their journey in Acólmán,[4] a monastery thirty-nine miles northeast of Mexico City founded by Fray Andres de Olmos in 1524 and later modified and enlarged by the Augustinian monks. El Chato learned through his grapevine that these monks were not bringing an ordinary cargo of church supplies, but that they had with them an assortment of golden chandeliers, baptismal urns, chalices, and no small amount of coined silver.

Toward the close of the day, in the spring of 1649, the caravan of pack mules and robed friars reached the foothills below the Organ Mountains and expected to make Robledo before nightfall, the place where travelers rested their animals and prepared for the ordeal of the grueling Jornada del Muerto. Suddenly, from the recesses of the mountains emerged a band of ruffians riding at full gallop into the group of startled and tired monks. The pack mules, excited by the sudden apparition, scattered over the hillsides, but the men drove them with their latigos back towards the mountains away from the trail and their rightful owners. Some of the churchmen tried to hold to the halters of their pack animals, but the relentless outlaws whacked the *reatas* with their knives and drove the entire *atajo* out of sight into the mountain fastness.

It was indeed a sad group of missionaries who walked back to the presidio[5] of El Paso del Norte three days later to report the daring

---

[4]The publication of José Montes de Oca, *San Agustín de Acólmán*, gives an up-to-date account of the old monastery from its founding to the present time. On the reproduction of the monastery's north facade there is this interesting legend: "Acabose esta obra año de 1560 reinando el Rey Don Felipe nuestro Señor, Hijo del Emperador Carlos V, y gobernando esta Nueva España su II virrey, don Luis Velasco con cuyo favor se edificó."

[5]There were three designations used in colonial days for settlements of various sizes. The large cities usually had an "*ayuntamiento*" and the smaller towns, a *cabildo*; but out on the frontier of the empire there were garrisons with nothing more than soldiers and sometimes a missionary or two. These were called *presidios*, and El Paso as one of the northernmost frontier governments went by that name for a long time. There are still towns in both California and Texas that have retained the name "presidio."

daylight attack of El Chato. The small garrison had to wait until rein-
forcements were sent for to Durango, and as soon as the troops arrived
they were augmented by volunteers who had personal accounts to settle
with the infamous cutthroat. These soldiers were disguised as travelers.
El Chato and his men, lured from their hideout by this device, attacked
them, and in the battle that followed, every member of his band was
either killed, fatally wounded, or captured. El Chato himself, whose real
name was Pedro Nevárez, was taken prisoner and sent under guard to
Mexico City where he was tried and hanged. Some accounts say that
before he died he tried to make amends for his sins by giving a map of
his cache in the Organ Mountains, while other versions say that he was
tight-lipped to the end.

Probably nothing would ever have been known about the treasure of the famous outlaw had the Apache Chief Victorio[6] not attacked
the mission church in Doña Ana. After tearing down and burning all
they could find, the Indians scattered papers, books, and correspondence
over the mesa on the way out of the village. Some of the church records
made interesting reading, but nothing caused so much comment as a
copy of a letter some priest had written to the monastery of Acólmán
back in the seventeenth century. According to this letter, one of El
Chato's badly wounded men had dragged himself to the priest's quarters
somewhere in the valley the night after the attack and before dying gave
a complete description of his accomplices as well as the location of the
hoard in the nearby mountains. The priest conveyed this information by
letter to the church authorities in Mexico City but kept a copy for his
own records. The part of the document, which has appeared in many
versions is the following:

> In Soledad Canyon there is a natural cave on the brow
> of a hill opening toward the south. There is a cross cut
> into the rock above the entrance of the cave and directly

---

[6]Chief Victorio was a Chiricahua Apache, who left the reservation in 1877, and went on the
warpath with his two principal lieutenants, Loco and Nana. He spread terror throughout
southern New Mexico and Arizona until 1881, when he was attacked and killed by Mexican
troops in Chihuahua. He was succeeded as a raider by the well-known Geronimo.

in front of a young juniper tree. For better directions, (*para mejores señas*) there are three medium sized peaks toward the rising sun whose shadows converge in the morning 250 paces east of the cave's entrance and a little to the south. Two hundred and fifty paces from this point directly north you will come to a promontory, a *loma*, from where by looking straight ahead you can see the Jornada del Muerto, as far as the eye can see. The distance from this point back to the cave should be exactly the same as the distance to the place where the shadows converge. One hundred paces from the entrance of the cave down to the nearby arroyo, and in line with the point of convergence, you will find a dripping spring.

The entrance to the cave has been covered to a depth of a man's height, (*un estado*) and ten *varas* beyond the entrance of it there is an adobe wall which must be taken down. At the bottom of a long tunnel, the cave separates into two parts: the left cave contains coined silver, more than two *atajos* can carry, the right cave contains golden chandeliers, urns, crucifixes, gold images and monstrances of beaten gold.

Eventually the story of the dying outlaw's confession reached the ears of treasure-hunters as far east as New York. They arrived in Las Cruces, New Mexico, seeking guides to take them into the mountains. The local residents too were not idle; some set off small dynamite charges in the belief that the detonation would echo wherever there was a cave or would cause a landslide that would lay bare the opening to the treasure. Many attempts ended in disappointment and even discomfort to the treasure hunters. Will Douthitt and his partner Lewis from Estancia, New Mexico, claimed to have found a document in a church in Mexico City in the early twenties with which they located a cave certain to be that of El Chato. They reported to the sheriff of Torrance

County that when they were returning from the cave with two gold bars taken from a "cord" stacked inside, they were waylaid by a band of masked men who, tortured them with hot wires and forced them to give up the gold they were carrying. Back in Estancia they tried to get Governor Dillon to send a detachment of the National Guard stationed in the village at that time to protect them, but when he refused they went back alone and were once more intercepted by the band of masked men and robbed.

Ben Brown, the prospector working a claim near the Organ Mountains, never reported anything so simple as walking into a cave and coming out loaded with gold bars. The version he had learned from the convict on the chain gang got considerable support when Prof. George Sánchez of the University of Texas was shown a manuscript at a convention in Tempe, Arizona, by one of the professors attending the meeting. This man, whose name I was never able to run down after a year of correspondence, had a brother in El Paso who worked in a shop where they repaired ancient and outmoded strong boxes. One day while removing the worn interior wall of a Spanish safe, they came across a manuscript that someone had placed between the inner lining and the steel wall. According to the repairman in El Paso, the strongbox had originally come from the Acólmán monastery, and had been brought to the shop for repair.

I tried to follow up the trail of this letter, but by the time I got to it Pearl Harbor was attacked and the investigation was suspended while I spent the next three years in the Air Corps. At the close of the war, I took up the trail again but by that time no one remembered the name of the informant and many of those who had attended the meeting in Tempe were dead.

The interesting point about the letter taken from the strongbox was that it complemented the version of the dying outlaw's confession that Ben Brown knew and was guided by when he made his original discovery. This was based on the tradition that El Chato had decided when he felt the noose tightening around his neck to expiate his sins and tell where he had buried his ill-gotten treasure. Several copies of this confession have appeared in various places at different times, and this proliferation has led to the conjecture that the sacristan of the priest in Mexico who officiated at the hanging of El Chato made copies for his friends, and may have even profited by selling them. One of these documents is filed in the library of the New Mexico Museum in Santa Fe with the date of February 10, 1650. Another version was published by Otto Goetz in the March, 1940, issue of the *New Mexico Magazine*. All of these confessions are supposedly written in Acólmán's Convento de San Agustín. In some of the versions the sacristan signs himself "Vicente Vasques," but in the one given below, the copyist adds the following statement:

> This is a copy taken from the original by the Sacristan of the Convent of San Agustín of the City of Mexico, Bicente Basones, 10th of January, 1861.

This *derrotero* was not the one that Ben Brown used as a guide, but the confession made by El Chato before his execution.

> City of Mexico. Convent of San Agustín. April 5, 1650. Guide which Pedro Nevárez, alias 'El Chato' left on his death.
>
> Ask at El Paso del Norte for the Organ Mountains which are along the river to the right. It's about two days on horseback at a good rate, and the sierra is somewhat scattered, topped with some crested peaks. You will find two Passes, Tortugas and Soledad, covered with numerous junipers. Before reaching the first Pass, go halfway up the mountain until you come to a thick cedar. Measure 100 *varas* straight down to a blue flagstone marked with a large cross. Remove this rock and dig to a depth of an *estado* and there you will find six *atajos* of silver bars.
>
> Return to Soledad Pass and follow the trail to

the spring which runs toward the meadow. It is over-grown with cattails. Continue along the slope of the mountain and look for three large cedars standing wide apart. Directly in front of these are three flat rocks and between them and the cedars is covered the mine of the Spaniard Jorge Colon. The flat rocks can he distin-guished by a large cross cut with a crowbar.

The opening to the mine, which is so rich that you can cut the solid silver from the vein, is covered with heavy timbers and a red rock moved on top of it by 25 men using levers. You may be able to see part of the opening by removing the dirt and the gravel on top. You can also notice the marks on the rock made by the crowbars.

As you enter the mine you will find a large number of beaten gold images, chandeliers, crosses, vases, platters, monstrances, crucifixes and many things of gold and silver. After removing all this, go down the ladder where you will find large stacks of silver bars and mining implements. As a further sign, as you walk toward the first mountain Pass of which I speak, you will notice a draw or deep hollow. The treasures are located on either side, one toward the rising sun and the other toward the setting sun.

Although Ben Brown knew nothing of this map, his informa-tion and the written account had a number of points in common: the spring, the cross cut on the rock, and *Soledad* applying to either peak or canyon. Either story mentioned enough buried treasure to entice the most cynical treasure-hunter, and for a man like Ben Brown who had dug himself into mountains with much less to go on, the spot by the juniper tree in the barren hills of southern New Mexico was good enough for a try.

Early in the morning after his initial discovery, Ben Brown

arrived with a pick and shovel, eager to begin digging as soon as the converging shadows of the three peaks verified the location. He did not have long to wait; as the sun rose higher the gaps between the shadows cast by the *picachos* began to close until they formed a single unmistakable shadow on the hillside. In his excitement, Ben wanted to clear out the entire depression, but when he realized the size of the project he did some close figuring and decided to cut a shaft straight down against the hillside where the opening of the cave should be. By midmorning he had dug his own height into a square hole wide enough to give him elbow room, and was about to sit down to catch his breath when his shovel bit into solid rock. Ben Brown forgot how tired he was; he cleared away the loose filling around a flat, smooth rock running perpendicularly into the shaft he was digging, and uncovered the most important clue: a roughly hewn cross, cut deeply into the face of the rock. It was no freak of nature; the chisel marks were clearly visible when he rubbed off the soil that stuck to the grooves.

A very tired, but very excited prospector sat down at the bottom of the pit to roll a cigarette and turn over in his mind the first day's findings. The more he thought it over the more convinced he became that he was on the right trail. When would he find the cave? That would have to wait until the following day. Just now he had other things to attend to. He covered the face of the rock, climbed out, and headed back to his mining claim in the nearby Organ Mountains.

Ben Brown was up early the next morning; it was moving day for him. The tent, bed-roll, and tools were loaded into an ancient automobile to which he affectionately referred years later as his "wobble-knee" when the knee-action type of wheel suspension was put on the market. He drove to Las Cruces and stopped at a grocery store and also at the country clerk's office to register a new claim. His next problem was to find a trail for his car back to the new campsite through the dry arroyo beds and the chamiso-covered mesas. The old "wobble-knee" chugged, strained, and steamed over the rough terrain and broke a new path over the crust of dry sand until it reached the dead end of an arroyo just below the hill where he had been digging the night before.

He carried his gear and supplies to the foot of his now familiar juniper tree, and as soon as his tent was up he proceeded to set up the monuments for his new claim. In one of these he concealed an empty tobacco can with an official sheet of paper stating that Ben Brown of Doña Ana County was now working this "mining claim."

The cross on the rock marked the mouth of a cave, but not an open cave. Before Ben could enter he had to clear away the muck and topsoil with which it had been sealed for centuries. There were tons of loose earth to move out and the treasure-hunter began to wonder why El Chato and his brigands had taken so much trouble to conceal their loot. Each shovelful had to be relayed from the cave to the shaft and then to the surface. While moving the fill to the surface Ben found a copper coin, a Spanish *cuarto*, with the date 1635 on one side and a sovereign's profile on the other. It was clear to him that someone had been there long before him. Days later he came to the adobe wall the directions told about. It too came down with a crowbar. Beyond it on a shelf was the dry skeleton of a lizard, which disintegrated at the touch of his hand, but the most encouraging sign was a small tool about a foot long with a pick on one side and a hatchet blade on the other, a miner's tool made of Spanish hand-forged steel.[7]

A short distance beyond the adobe wall, the cave dropped down to a forty-five degree angle and narrowed to the point where the earth had to be taken out a bucketful at a time. Ben would go down, drag himself back on his belly where he could stand upright, and empty each bucket on the surface. It was tedious and slow, but he kept it up the first year until bad weather and an empty larder forced him to leave.

Another grubstake was not easy to lay aside for a man with two little girls to support, and so Ben Brown found a place up in the Magdalena Mountains at the ranger station in Water Canyon. He panned enough gold in the creek back of the cabin to keep him and his girls going. During weekends he played the fiddle at country dances, and the

---

[7]When Prospector Ben Brown found the mining tool in the cave, he sent it to the Field Museum in Chicago for identification. He was told that it was hand-forged Spanish steel.

hunting season provided him with a little cash from hunters who could profit by his knowledge of the outdoors. For several years he alternated all these varied activities, going down to the Organ Mountains whenever he got a little ahead, to clear out more muck and get closer to the treasure.

In the fall of 1934 while hunting in the Magdalena Mountains, I came across Ben Brown, now a middle-aged man with a greying stubble of beard and a mischievous squint to his blue eyes. We hunted together for three days, got our deer, and went down to his cabin to try some of the venison chili con carne he had been telling me about. We spent most of the night swapping tales about the country and getting better acquainted. Ben asked me if I could get him a copy of J. Frank Dobie's *Coronado's Children;* he had heard it contained some awfully good yarns. The next time I was in Austin I told Frank about Ben Brown and together we inscribed a copy of his book "To Ben Brown, the prospector of Water Canyon."

The following season I went directly to Ben's cabin. Early the morning after I arrived we walked up Seven Mile Canyon to the top of Old Baldy, where we sat down to eat lunch and swap a few more tales about the country. Ben had enjoyed Dobie's book immensely, but there was one story he had not found in it.

"Have you ever heard about El Chato's treasure down by Las Cruces?" he asked.

I told him the version of the story I knew, and he listened attentively to the end.

"That's the story all right, but you've got the location wrong. Most people do; they think that Soledad Canyon is in the Organ Mountains and that ain't right. The name of the canyon is the same, but it's in another range of mountains. That's the reason nobody has even come close to the treasure."

It was my turn to listen. He told me the story I have just related, and at the end surprised me by asking if I wanted to take a look at the cave.

"Come some weekend and we'll drive down and see what it's like. Don't mention it to anybody; you come down by yourself."

The following spring we drove down to Las Cruces, where I spent the most sleepless night of my life at a hotel, and early the next morning we back-tracked to the village of Doña Ana. From the highway we turned east, drove under a railroad trestle through an arroyo and followed the winding bed toward the foothills over a blurred trail until we came to the end at the foot of a steep hill.

"We'll have to walk the rest of the way. It ain't far," said Ben.

When we had gone up the hill a way, he stopped and pointed to what looked like the tailings of a mine shaft. I asked him about the juniper that was supposed to be at the entrance of the cave.

"I cut it down the second day. People might use it for a landmark and come snooping around."

The shaft had been enlarged in order to accommodate a hand winch Ben was using to lift the fill-in to the surface. We went down a ladder to the entrance of the cave; it was the size of a small room.

"Well, this is it. Shall we go in and look around?"

We did. The tunnel against the hillside had the appearance of a natural cave, very similar to the subterranean formations extending east to the well-known Carlsbad Caverns, except that there was no moisture and the floor was covered with topsoil. For a short distance we walked upright; then we stooped, and finally began crawling on all fours. About two hundred feet down into the earth we came to a point where the cave split into a Y going in two directions. I took one side and Ben followed along the other. This was as far as he had cleared. The fill-in made it difficult to move, even though I was now dragging myself on my belly. Finally I reached a place where the rocks on the cave floor would permit no further progress. By the beam of a five-cell flashlight I could see that the opening continued indefinitely, and by bathing the walls and ceiling ahead with light I was able to take a few time exposures with my camera.

Satisfied that I had gone as far as I could, I started to back out and found myself tightly wedged in the narrow opening. My efforts to dislodge myself uphill raised so much dust that I found it difficult to breathe, and so I lay still until the dust settled down and I gathered myself together. I knew Ben was on the other spur of the cave but there was so much earth between us that my cries for him could not be heard. After a very long wait during which I had an opportunity to review most of my past life, it was reassuring to feel Ben's hands gripping my ankles. The opening was large enough for him but not for a person fifty pounds heavier.

When we got back to the surface and had cleared our lungs of the dry dust of the cave, Ben pointed out the landmarks of the three peaks, showed me the dreaded Jornada, and led me down to another hole he had cleared out down the arroyo. At the bottom was a cement drinking trough filled with water seeping from the wet sand around it. According to Ben, the travelers on the old Spanish Trail watered their stock at this point just before starting the dry trek across the desert.

On the way back to Magdalena, Ben was trying to formulate a plan whereby he could get power machinery to finish cleaning out the cave. The only solution was to find someone in Albuquerque interested in such an enterprise on a share basis.

There was an elderly lawyer by the name of John Baron Burg, who had married into the well-known Spanish family of Otero, and who still had some of the pioneer spirit of adventure. He agreed to finance the whole operation on condition that he retain possession of the dig to exploit as a tourist attraction in case nothing was found. Ben was willing to go along with this stipulation; and so the three of us drove down to the cave again. Just about the time we were to begin the formal deal, the Taylor Act was passed by Congress, and under this legislation the lawyer said he could not acquire possession of the property. Thus the arrangement fell through.

Except for an occasional trip to keep his claim active, Ben made very little progress during the depression years; but he continued to nurse the hope that when one of his other claims in Water Canyon came through he would have enough funds to dig the treasure he was sure lay at the bottom of the cave.

"I ain't given up yit! Look at this mining tool and at this coin. How did they get there into that hole? Someone was down there before me and for a very good reason. Some day I'll find out."

He had not found out by the time World War II broke out, but he found out that a tungsten claim he had in the canyon and another small mine he called "The Little Pittsburg" was salable. This left him free to roam around the mountains and continue his prospecting. On his way to Socorro he stopped a few miles below the entrance to Water Canyon and spent the afternoon walking over the hills south of the highway. Among the specimens he brought back to the car was a rock with traces of perlite. He had heard that there was a market for this mineral, and so he sent some samples to be tested in Denver. When he got his report he staked out the whole hillside where he had picked up the specimen and began a new type of mining.

Upon my return from Europe at the end of World War II, I drove down to Water Canyon to look up my old friend, and to my great surprise found him living in a cabin with a brand new roof and with a shiny automobile parked in his front yard under the pine trees. As I drove up to the front door, a bald-headed man, hardy and spry from outdoor living, walked out out of the cabin.

"Do you know if an old gopher by the name of Ben Brown is still roaming around these hills?" I asked.

With his accustomed grin and squint he answered, "He is, so fur as I know. The sheriff ain't caught up with him yit."

We went into the cabin where Ben poured the usual cup of coffee for me and one for himself out of a shiny percolator! Around the room I noticed running water, a sink, a new stove, and an electric refrigerator.

"Well, Ben, it looks as though you finally dug up El Chato!"

"No, not yit. I found another one right in my back yard. Did you notice that big plant down the road a ways?"

It was the property of the Great Lakes Carbon Corporation, a processing plant working a claim that Ben had sold to that company during the war. The income tax he had paid after the sale was greater than his earnings during all the years he had been prospecting.

Eventually we got around to the cave in Doña Ana County when I spied the Spanish forged steel tool lying on a shelf.

"It's still there, but I've got something better cooking. Come over during the hunting season and we'll talk about it. We can drive down there any time you're free. I'll drive my car this time."

Ben Brown is no longer worried about funds. He started chasing a wounded deer one afternoon, ran into a treasure site, and later struck a fortune in his back yard. He is still waiting for another pot of gold at the end of an arroyo in southern New Mexico. The last letter I received from Ben added an interesting note:

> I could tell you a lot more if I could talk to you,
> but I can hardly write so you can read it. My spelling is
> very bad but maybe you can figure it out some way. Best
> of luck to you. As ever, your friend,
>
> BEN BROWN.

The Secret of the Ebony Cabinet

BY RICHARD D. ALTICK

The hundred-year search for the papers of James Boswell, biographer of Samuel Johnson, shows vividly how treasures need not be gold or silver or precious stones. Rare books and manuscripts may be just as valuable and elusive, and many men—and women—have devoted their lives to hunting for them. Nor do you have to be a literary buff or a historian to sense the excitement involved. Take, for example, the ongoing search for Dead Sea Scrolls. Or the long struggle to find James Boswell's mysteriously missing literary remains, as described here by Richard Altick (b. 1915) in his wonderful compilation of true literary detective stories, *The Scholar Adventurers* (1960). Today, more than fifty years since the publication of Boswell's papers by Yale University began, new discoveries in them are still emerging. It does make you wonder whether a good look though those old papers in the attic might be worthwhile.

★　★　★　★　★

1

What James Boswell, Esq., of Auchinleck, Scotland, wanted most in life—apart from such immediate consolations as wine and complaisant ladies, both of which were always plentiful in his life—was fame. Probably his lifelong hunger for public notice was the result of a gnawing conviction of personal inadequacy and, as time went on, of failure. In any event, it led him (to mention only the most famous instances) to compete with Shakespeare for public attention during the Stratford Shakespeare jubilee of 1769, by parading the streets with a placard in his hat reading "Corsica Boswell"; to edify the audience at Drury Lane Theatre one night by giving spirited imitations of a cow's moo, followed by somewhat less successful imitations of other animals; to appear at a public execution atop a hearse; and to indulge a peculiar whim by returning to London, after a walk in the suburbs, perched conspicuously on a dung cart.

Such exhibitions as these earned Boswell, if not fame, at least notoriety; and notoriety, after all, was something; for the moment, at least, he was in the public eye. But Boswell still had his heart set on being remembered by uncounted ages to come. And that is one reason why he so industriously cultivated the company of Dr. Samuel Johnson. If Boswell were not to be remembered as a lawyer (he was an undistinguished one), or as an essayist and occasional poet (roles in which he displayed only the most mediocre gifts), perhaps he could cheat oblivion as the friend, and eventually the biographer, of Dr. Johnson.

And he did. His *Life of Johnson*, from the day it appeared, assured that the name of James Boswell would never be forgotten. But one can cheat oblivion in a number of ways, and the way in which Boswell did it was not the one that most of us would prefer. How much it cost him was summed up neatly, far too neatly, as we now realize, in Macaulay's famous paradox about the greatest English biographer being the greatest fool in history.

To any reader of the *Life of Johnson*, however, it is clear that Boswell yearned for a purer fame, a fame that comes not from making oneself appear a vain, stupid ass in order that the subject of one's biography should seem all the more imposing a figure, but from the sheer interest of one's own character. Boswell, above all, wanted to be remembered as James Boswell, Esq., a man worthy of permanent fame—not notoriety—for his own sake; who, even if every copy of the

Life of Johnson were somehow wiped out, would still have an unchallenged place in the annals of eighteenth-century England.

Macaulay showed the world exactly how to view Boswell, and for nearly a century few readers doubted the justice of his estimate. But we can imagine the biographer shouting from his assigned seat in purgatory (where his sins of the flesh undoubtedly sent him), "The ebony cabinet! Look in the ebony cabinet!" For it was there that the real James Boswell, the Boswell who would count for something if anybody ever troubled to look him up, resided; at least, he had been placed there, lovingly and carefully, by the mortal James Boswell before he died.

In Boswell's will, when he died in 1795, was found a provision relating to a certain "ebony cabinet," a family heirloom which had come down to him from his great-grandmother, and which still remained in the ancestral home at Auchinleck, near Edinburgh. In his concern that the cabinet never leave the family, he provided in his will that any heir who "alienated" it was to forfeit a thousand pounds.

Why this anxiety for a piece of furniture? Partly, of course, because it *was* an heirloom, and the Boswells were very proud of their ancient line. But more importantly, because it contained the most valuable of James Boswell's papers: the papers which, if the world ever saw them, would amply justify his faith that he would not be forgotten. For years Boswell had preserved the written records of his daily life with the assiduity of a Scottish magpie. The precise extent and nature of these records were known to no one but himself, but in the *Life of Johnson* he dropped teasing references to his "archives," which sounded pretentious enough. It was plain, at any rate, that those "archives" at Auchinleck contained many letters to and from Dr. Johnson, because they were often quoted in the *Life*; and was it not probable that they included also the great mass of notes from which Boswell had reconstructed the details of the Johnson story, of those wonderful days and nights of talk at Bolt Court and Streatham, and on the windswept highlands of Scotland?

His canny eye still fixed on posterity, Boswell in his will gave specific directions for the use to which the accumulated papers in the ebony cabinet were to be put. He directed that three of his friends—the Reverend William Johnson Temple, Sir William Forbes, and Edmond Malone—in their capacity as literary executors, should go through the archives and publish all such parts of it as they saw fit. What more could a man do to insure that he would be remembered after death?

But the public desire to read Boswell's personal papers, a desire which in any case Boswell certainly overestimated in respect to his own generation, was not gratified. As we now know, the appointed literary executors did go through the contents of the ebony cabinet very carefully; but then one of them died, and the two remaining executors decided to delay any further action in the matter until Boswell's second son, one of the younger children who Boswell had directed should share the proceeds of publication, was of age. No further attempt was made to edit or print the archives, and the only three men who knew what they contained died without revealing the secret.

And, as things were going, it was a secret which no one especially cared to disturb. For who, after all, was this strange being Boswell, who had written so inexhaustibly fascinating a book? Mr. Macaulay told the readers of the *Edinburgh Review*, and his words echoed down through the century: "He was . . . a man of the meanest and feeblest intellect . . . servile and impertinent, shallow and pedantic, a bigot and a sot, bloated with family pride, and eternally blustering about the dignity of a born gentleman, yet stooping to be a tale-bearer, an eaves-dropper, a common butt in the taverns of London." Thus, while the subjects of Queen Victoria were endlessly grateful to Boswell for having managed somehow, despite his intellectual vacuity and disgusting personality, to write a great book, they were not sorry to be deprived of any further knowledge of the author.

Only a few persistently curious bookmen, members of the clan who must know as much as can be found out about any literary figure, regardless of his manners or his morals, were bothered about Boswell. Agreed that he was all that he portrayed himself to be, with incredible ingenuousness, in the *Life of Johnson*—an impertinent, petty, vain, weak-willed, toadying, hypochondriac, superstitious, officious, inquisitive, shameless creature—was he nothing more? Did these self-revelations, seemingly so comprehensive, actually give us a complete picture of the man? Or might there not be another side to Boswell, a side which was revealed only in the private papers he had locked up for posterity in the ebony cabinet?

At the same time, of course, the riddle of the ebony cabinet was also on the minds of those who, much more in the tendency of their age, wished to know more about Dr. Johnson. But to all men, the cabinet at Auchinleck was adamantly denied by the Boswell family, which now consisted of ladies in the sternest Victorian mold who knew that the whole world shared Macaulay's opinion of their embarrassing ancestor. James Boswell, Esq., was a closed chapter in the family history, Dr. Johnson or no Dr. Johnson. And anyway, the cabinet was empty— for the Boswell ladies never contradicted the rumors which had spread through the literary world, early in the century, that Boswell's papers had been burned.

Apparently, then, Boswell's papers, whatever they contained, were gone. James Boswell would have to be content with being remembered as a conceited devotee of the fleshpots who had somehow blundered into writing a great book; the increasing fold of Johnsonians would have to remain deprived of the important knowledge of their idol which was contained in his biographer's files but not used in the *Life*; and the few Boswellians, a strange sect who could not help entertaining an inexplicable love for the man who could on occasion be so candid about his weaknesses, would know nothing more of him. And that was the situation in the middle of the nineteenth century.

But if ever coming events cast their shadows before, they did on a certain day in 1850 in the French town of Boulogne-sur-Mer, when one Major Stone of the East India Company, a gentleman otherwise unknown to history, happened into a little shop to make some casual purchases. When, upon his return to his lodgings, he unwrapped his parcel, he discovered that the wrapping paper was a fragment of an old letter—written in English. With idle curiosity he looked at the signature on the letter, and identified it immediately as that of a man known to every Englishman with a smattering of literary culture. It was "James Boswell"!

To the everlasting credit of the major, he immediately traced the source of the wrapping paper: an itinerant vender who was in the habit of passing through Boulogne once or twice a year, supplying the shops with their needs. And by good luck, the Boulogne shopkeeper had not yet used that portion of his newly purchased stock which contained the major's quarry. Money changed hands, and Major Stone found himself the owner of a large number of letters which Boswell had written to his most intimate friend, the Reverend William Johnson Temple.

How the Boswell-Temple letters got to the counter of a small shop in Boulogne can easily be explained. Temple's daughter Anne had married Charles Powlett, a clergyman who for some reason had moved from England, about 1825, to a little town only a few miles from Boulogne. So much is certain; for the rest, one need only postulate the death of the surviving member of the couple, or simply a general house-cleaning, the two circumstances under which most masses of privately held documentary material emerge from hiding. The peddler happened by, bought masses of scrap paper, and began to resell it not long afterward in Boulogne.

The Boswell-Temple letters, published late in 1856, were the first important addition to public knowledge of Boswell since his death. Naturally there was some skepticism; forgers were at large in England, and only four years earlier there had been the notorious case of twenty-five forged Shelley letters, for a proposed edition of which Browning had written an introduction. But all doubts of the authenticity of these Boswell letters were answered by their unquestionably genuine Boswellian flavor and the agreement of much internal evidence with the already established facts of his life. The contents of many of the letters, however, were not such as to invite public laments that the rest of his papers had perished. Even though they were severely expurgated before printing, they proved beyond question that Macaulay had been largely right in his condemnation of Boswell. In particular, Boswell's frequent confessions to Temple revealed him to be a rake of unusual persistence and not too fastidious tastes. He was not quite the man whom the Victorians wished to admit to their parlors. And so, after this brief flourish of interest, Boswell's fame remained just about what it had been before: highly dubious. The chief effect of the publication of the Temple letters was the still more resolute strengthening of the bars at Auchinleck against any impertinent inquirer. When, some twenty years later, George Birkbeck Hill, the editor of the great critical edition of the *Life of Johnson*, went in person to the Boswell seat, the door was virtually slammed in his face.

2

In 1905 few people heard the news, and fewer gave any thought to it, that the last member of the family at Auchinleck had died, and that her estate had passed to the only remaining male descendant of James Boswell: his great-great-grandson, Lord Talbot de Malahide. In due time the Boswell heirlooms were transferred to the new owner's home at Malahide Castle, near Dublin. Presumably the ebony cabinet was among them. But it was a transaction of which the world of bookmen was told nothing.

Seventeen years later, an American scholar made the first great step toward rehabilitating Boswell as a man deserving of independent literary—and psychological—study. In his book *Young Boswell*, Professor Chauncey Brewster Tinker of Yale University, arguing that Macaulay's influential verdict on Boswell's character was not necessarily the right one, approached Boswell with sympathy instead of disgust. And by concentrating attention on the younger Boswell, before his momentous friendship with Johnson really developed, Tinker demonstrated that Boswell was worth attention for reasons apart from his relationship with the more famous man.

The demonstration was continued, with greatly broadened scope, when, in 1924, Professor Tinker brought out his two-volume collection, the first ever made, of Boswell's private letters. Perhaps the most sensational aspect of this edition was the publication for the first time of those sections of Boswell's letters to Temple which had justly been thought unfit for Victorian eyes. But the Boswell letters had a deeper significance. It was not only that they displayed in more detail the impressive scale of Boswell's physical excesses. More relevantly, by the publication of a mass of Boswell's private letters to his friends, they threw light on facets of his personality which, for obvious reasons, are not prominent in the *Life of Johnson:* the often torturous self-reproaches and religious doubts, the frequent attacks of "the spleen," the honest resolves and high-minded aspirations which made Boswell's life a moral chiaroscuro. Now at long last it was plain that Boswell was infinitely more than Johnson's zany: he was a man who took himself with passionate seriousness, a man of almost pathologically introspective nature.

The evidence which Professor Tinker was able to set forth in the form of the then available letters of Boswell was sufficient to place the man in an entirely new light. But the real drama of Boswell and modern literary scholarship was only beginning. If so much of a hitherto unsuspected Boswell had been revealed by the careful collection and study of the letters known to be available, how much more could be learned if his extensive private archives were still in existence! If Boswell had displayed so much of himself in his private letters, what might he not have confessed in other, perhaps even more confidential, letters, or (was it not easily conceivable?) in diaries! The tradition persisted, of course, that the contents of the ebony cabinet had been destroyed. But while Professor Tinker was working in the manuscript collection of the Pierpont Morgan Library in New York, he came across a letter from Malone, one of Boswell's literary executors, to a daughter of Boswell, telling of the presence at Auchinleck *at that time* of a great mass of Boswell papers which he had gone through before the decision was reached to postpone the fulfilment of Boswell's will. This letter was dated 1809—and the rumor of the destruction of the papers had been abroad, and in print, at least two years earlier!

This at least was a clue: certainly not conclusive, but suggestive. At least, it proved that the now hoary rumor had not been correct during the first years of its circulation. But there was still the chance, a strong chance considering the way in which the Boswell descendants regarded their indiscreet forebear, that the papers had been destroyed at some subsequent time during the long century—perhaps after Macaulay's devastating attack, or after the publication of the letters to Temple. Anything to preserve what was left of the ancient Boswell family pride! In any event, there was the tradition—and nothing more. Could not the question whether the contents of the ebony cabinet still existed be settled, once for all?

By an incident proper to detective fiction, it was. During his systematic search for Boswell letters, Professor Tinker had advertised in Irish newspapers. Among the replies he had received had been a mysterious, unsigned note advising him to consider Malahide Castle. Tinker of course knew that the Boswell possessions had been transferred there in 1905; and so he wrote a letter of inquiry—a masterpiece of diplomacy, it must have been—to the present Lord Talbot. Lord Talbot replied in a brief and ambiguous note. And that was the end of that approach.

But for some time certain literary circles in England had been whispering that somebody—somebody—had actually gone to Malahide Castle and *seen* the precious contents of the ebony cabinet! One of these rumors eventually reached the ears of Wilmarth S. Lewis, now the editor of the great Yale edition of Horace Walpole's letters, who had been a student of Tinker's. Lewis passed the word to Tinker, and the latter decided that the only thing to do was to make a trip to Ireland.

In the summer of 1925, therefore, he presented himself at Malahide Castle, one of the most ancient buildings in the British Isles still inhabited—a perfect setting for the romantic drama soon to be enacted there. He was admitted to the sacred precincts, and Lord Talbot readily admitted his possession of large quantities of Boswelliana. In fact, he showed Tinker the famed ebony cabinet itself, still full of papers. When Tinker asked about particular manuscripts which he knew had been in the Boswell archives, Talbot obligingly drew them forth and let him examine them.

Tinker, then, had discovered that the story of the destruction of

Boswell's papers was false, that those papers were in existence, in obviously greater quantity than anyone had suspected. He suggested to Lord Talbot that some arrangement should be made for the scholarly study and arrangement of the hoard, but Talbot demurred. Tinker therefore returned to America for the academic year of 1925–26. He had had a dazzling glimpse of unimaginable riches, but his hands were empty.

And then, into the impasse, came a new figure, Lieutenant-Colonel Ralph Heyward Isham, a New York financier whose heart was firmly set in Johnsonian locales. Colonel Isham heard Tinker's story and made up his mind to lay siege to Malahide Castle. He had a powerful ally in the economic situation of the middle 1920's: the ancient British families were generally in a bad way because of the stiff income-tax rates, and at the same moment there were flush times in Wall Street. Doubly armed with Boswellian fervor and excellent financial credentials, he visited Malahide in July, 1926, and left bearing in his hand as a souvenir an important letter from Goldsmith to Boswell and in his head the knowledge that Lord Talbot was open to persuasion. The persuasion occupied a year and a half, at the end of which Colonel Isham returned to Malahide and brought away with him the greater part of the Boswell papers; the rest followed him to New York within the next eight months.

Colonel Isham had succeeded in buying from Lord Talbot over one million words of completely unexplored Boswelliana. Although, as I have said, Boswell had prided himself upon being an archivist, no one had ever suspected just how diligent a preserver of papers he really was. He had faithfully kept copies of a great many of his own letters. He had kept the letters sent him by the many notable figures of the time whom he "collected" in his own long career of tuft-hunting, as well as those he met in the Johnson circle. But most startling of all, it was now revealed that he had kept an intimate personal journal over a period of thirty-three years, a daily record filled not only with his reports of meetings with Johnson and other members of the famous company, but with ruthlessly frank accounts of his own complicated inner existence. Here was James Boswell, Esq., at length and in three dimensions.

But ironically enough, the opening of the cabinet, far from ending the long mystery, had simply substituted one riddle for another. The cabinet had proved to contain much that, in the light of previous knowledge of Boswell's archive-keeping habits, it had been expected to contain—and much, much more besides, such as the journal, an undreamed-of windfall. On the other hand, it did *not* contain a great mass of other material which should have been there. There were, for example, no letters from Dr. Johnson himself, and none from Wilkes or Garrick, two of the most important figures in the *Life of Johnson.* Why had they disappeared—and where were they now, if indeed they still existed?

And another precious relic of the Johnson-Boswell friendship was missing, although the reason for its absence seemed, unhappily, all too clear. One box, when it was opened, proved to contain little more than dust. The fragments of sixteen leaves, which were all that survived of the contents of the box, were identified as pages of the manuscript of the *Life of Johnson.* Evidently the large bundle of manuscript which had been shipped in this box from Auchinleck to Malahide had lain exposed to the damp for many decades and thus had become extremely fragile. At some point between Auchinleck to Malahide the box had received a jolt, and the paper had simply disintegrated into dust. If the surviving scraps were a sure indication of what the whole bundle had been composed of (and there was no reason to doubt it), the manuscript of the *Life of Johnson* was gone forever.

Severe though this loss was, the richness of Isham's treasure-trove made it seem, in comparison, almost trifling. He immediately arranged to have his acquisitions scrupulously edited and printed. They appeared in a sumptuous eighteen-volume limited edition, printed on antique paper with eighteenth-century type at the press of William Edwin Rudge in Mount Vernon, New York. In their bright red bindings, replete with inserted facsimiles of many of the most significant documents, they are an inexhaustible joy to the reader who has access to one of the 570 sets that were printed. One of the most interesting passages in the whole great work is a comment by Geoffrey Scott, the British scholar who saw the initial volumes through the press. Having enumerated the principal classes of missing documents, he wrote: "That the missing elements now exist is improbable . . . Further discoveries . . . even in this realm of miracles, can hardly be looked for."

The words, written in 1928, represented the considered judgment of a hard-headed scholar not given to day-dreaming. What he failed to recognize was that this was no ordinary realm of miracles. For before the last volume of the edition came from the press in 1934, two more unanticipated events had occurred, each in its own way as dramatic as the revelation to the outside world of the contents of the ebony cabinet.

In April, 1930, members of the Talbot household happened to open a long disused croquet box stowed away in a closet. Instead of wickets and mallets, it proved to contain a whole new cache of Boswell papers, including the original manuscript of Boswell's second most famous work, the *Journal of a Tour to the Hebrides with Samuel Johnson, LL.D.!*

For the common reader the *Tour* is in many respects a better introduction than the *Life* to Johnson and Boswell. It is livelier, more continuously anecdotal; and it contains in essence all the qualities which make the *Life* so eminently readable, without the many slack passages of that work. The discovery of the manuscript of this book was a substantial consolation for the loss of the manuscript of the *Life*.

For the *Tour*, as published in 1785, was a decidedly indiscreet book. Boswell's "naïveté" never was more conspicuous than in his forth-right comments on the decidedly rudimentary hospitality shown to Dr. Johnson and himself during their sightseeing jaunt in the Highlands in 1773. He was so forthright, indeed, that one offended Scottish laird challenged him to a duel, which was only narrowly averted. But the original manuscript from the croquet box proved to be infinitely more indiscreet than the published version. Boswell, under advice, had gone through it and done a wholesale job of cutting, paraphrasing, and otherwise censoring his own remarks. Some of his alterations were due to the presence in the England of his time of the first faint blushes of prudery; others obviously sprang from his anticipation, however incomplete, of the personal offense which many living persons would take, with justice, from his mention of them.

Colonel Isham acquired the contents of the croquet box, and the new purchase joined the other materials being edited by Professor Frederick A. Pottle of Yale as successor to Geoffrey Scott, who had died in 1929. Pottle and his assistants discovered that Boswell had been so eager to cancel certain passages in the manuscript that he had inked them out seemingly beyond possibility of recovery. Boswell, however, had not foreseen the tenacious devotion of twentieth-century scholars, who patiently read the deleted sentences, letter by letter, through the ink. The deletions were, one might add, well worth restoring, for they reveal Boswell at his most uninhibited and most entertaining.

3

And so the neglected croquet box had provided a totally unsuspected treasure. What more was to be found? The longer Pottle and his associates worked among the papers from Malahide Castle, the more profoundly they realized their possession of a mass of manuscripts absolutely unique in its revelation of the life of a man. Yet they could not forget that the ebony cabinet had not yielded up all that had been expected, and Pottle wrote in the Preface to his catalogue of Isham's collection:

> The Malahide Papers contain no letters of Johnson, no letters of Wilkes, no letters of Garrick. Documents which Boswell refers to in the *Life*, and copies which we know from the Journal he made of his own letters, are as often missing as not. The letters from more or less obscure correspondents, though large in number, can by no means include the entire contents of Boswell's files.★

★From Frederick A. and Marion S. Pottle, *The Private Papers of James Boswell from Malahide Castle* . . . New York: Oxford University Press, 1931.

The only portion of Boswell's papers in the Malahide purchases which Pottle regarded as virtually complete was the journals. Of these, only one section was missing; but it was one of the most serious gaps of all, because it covered the period of Boswell's first acquaintance with Johnson and thus probably contained his detailed account of his initial impressions of his idol.

Pottle wrote the passage I have quoted in 1930. So far as he knew, the materials whose absence he regretted were lost forever; in fact, he offered the theory that Boswell's younger son, James, might have removed from the cabinet "various dossiers of correspondence in which he was particularly interested," and that in the confusion following his death and that of Alexander, the eldest son, they might have been lost.

But here is the most astounding irony of all. Almost at the very moment when Professor Pottle was writing, a scholar three thousand miles away was bringing to light many of the very items which had disappeared "forever"!

In 1930, Claude Colleer Abbott, a lecturer in English literature at the University of Aberdeen who was conducting research on the eighteenth-century Scottish philosopher James Beattie, was led to papers accumulated by Beattie's friend and executor, Sir William Forbes, writer of the "official" life in 1806. Sir William had also been a friend and one of the literary executors of Boswell, but Abbott seems never to have toyed with the idea that he might find himself stalking bigger game than James Beattie.

Forbes's papers were at Fettercairn House, the Scottish country place of Lord Clinton. With the permission of the owner, Abbott began to make a systematic search of the vast, rambling mansion. Evidently Sir William and his son had been as conscientious archivists as Boswell himself. Abbott found himself waist-deep in eighteenth-century documents; there were papers everywhere—crammed into large wooden and metal boxes, piled on tables and floors. There was ample material on Beattie, and on Forbes's other acquaintances, many of them of some note in the latter part of the eighteenth century. But almost immediately Abbott realized that in this house of unsuspected treasures Beattie and Forbes were minor quarry indeed. At the bottom of one of the first piles he explored, he came upon a stout bundle of old manuscript which turned out to be, of all things, the missing section of Boswell's journal— the one for the first months of his acquaintance with Johnson! "At the moment," he writes, "my chief thought was: 'If this is here, well, anything not in the Ebony Cabinet may be here, too.' "

Perhaps it is just as well that few scholars ever find themselves in the situation in which Abbott was placed: the strain upon one's mind and will is so severe as to be almost unbearable. Surrounded by huge masses of entirely unsorted papers, knowing that at the top of the old mansion was a great attic crammed with the debris of generations, convinced now that unsuspected treasures lay everywhere around him— how was he to proceed? His own narrative of his successive short stays at Fettercairn House in the fall and winter of 1930–31 offers a vivid instance of how, on occasion, a researcher must draw upon every ounce of will-power in his constitution to keep from dashing off in all directions at once. He forced himself to proceed systematically, taking each bundle and box as it presented itself, moving from cupboard to cupboard—and trying not to think about the still unexplored attic. This stern self-control had its rewards; the discoveries were more evenly distributed through the whole term of his search.

In the bottom of a great wooden chest, mercifully in a corner which had not been attacked by the damp that had eaten away some of the other contents, Abbott discovered the letters written by Boswell to Forbes: a series as revealing in its own manner as that series to Temple which had been discovered so many years before in the little shop at Boulogne. And near by, wrapped in a tattered page of the London *Times* for 1874, were wads of letters, over a hundred in all, from Dr. Johnson to various correspondents who appear prominently in the *Life*. Valuable though these were in themselves, they gave promise of still more precious revelations. Was it not within the realm of possibility that somewhere in this bewildering storehouse Abbott might find the lost letters of Johnson to Boswell himself?

Such ever present possibilities sustained Abbott's spirit as he worked through almost literally tons of material, much of it dealing with routine estate and business matters of the Forbes family, but inter-larded time and again by papers directly concerned with Boswell and his circle: letters from Forbes to Boswell; a draft of a "Criminal Opera" by Boswell; miscellany relating to the *Life of Johnson*. And still the attic was to come!

At last, having surveyed the contents of every parcel and chest downstairs (more careful examination had, of course, to be postponed), Abbott was ready to invade the attic. That dark continent, as if to wel-come him, yielded up one of its treasures almost immediately; for among the broken chairs, discarded ornaments, baskets, and other debris of an old family he found a large collection of letters to Boswell from other correspondents. Then his luck departed, and several days passed in hacking his way through the jungle, with dust in the lungs and aching muscles as his only tangible rewards. Large wooden boxes, pried with difficulty from the surrounding lumber, proved to hold only yellowed rolls of wallpaper. But, he writes,

> when I removed the next up-sided table I saw, wedged in between other furniture, a small sack, rather like a small mail-bag, with rents here and there from which letters were ready to drop. Quickly I dragged it out. A loose letter fell. It was written to Boswell. Down the winding stairs I hurried the sack, wondering whether all the contents could possibly concern Boswell. Before emptying the papers I drew out another loose letter. The omen was favourable. Soon I knew the truth. The sack was stuffed tight with Boswell's papers, most of them arranged in stout wads, torn here and there, and dirty, but for the most part in excellent order. Neither damp nor worm nor mouse had gnawed at them. My luck held.★

★From Claude C. Abbott, *A Catalogue of Papers Relating to Boswell, Johnson, and Sir William Forbes Found at Fettercairn House, 1930–31*. Oxford: Clarendon Press, 1936. Quoted by per-mission of the publishers.

It was probably the richest find of all; for the bag, measuring twenty-five inches by nineteen and once used for seed beans, was crammed with such long-lost treasures as the correspondence between Boswell and the Corsican patriot General Paoli, letters from Wilkes and Burke to Boswell, and the letters of William Johnson Temple to Boswell which provided the other side of the correspondence found in Boulogne.

Abbott had not been disappointed, then: by a sure instinct, he had saved the icing of the cake until the last.

The discoveries at Fettercairn House accounted for much of the Boswell material which had been missing from Malahide Castle—except for items like the supremely desirable Johnson-Boswell correspondence, which Abbott was forced to report he could not find, and whose whereabouts remains a mystery today. How all these Boswelliana had found their way to Fettercairn was easily explained. Sir William Forbes, as one of Boswell's literary executors, had received the mass of documents for examination and ultimate editing and publication; but the death of Temple, another of the executors, had interrupted the project, as we have seen. Forbes never returned his share of the papers to the Boswell family; and upon his death, in 1806, all his effects, including the Boswell hoard, had been transferred to Fettercairn House, the seat of his son, who had married the only daughter of Fettercairn's owner, Sir John Stuart. And here they had remained, untouched except by damp and mice, until Professor Abbott, seeking information on James Beattie, had stumbled upon them.

After the drama of Fettercairn House had been announced to the world, a nice question of ownership was raised and had to be settled before the papers themselves could be made available for scholarly research. Obviously the papers legally were the property of Boswell's heirs; but Colonel Isham had purchased from Lord Talbot the copyright of all of the Boswell papers in his possession. And was it not true that the newly found papers, though not physically in Talbot's possession, belonged to him—since he was the heir to the Auchinleck estate? Eventually litigation was instituted in the Scottish courts; and the resultant decision in 1939 involved as fine a Gordian knot as a Scottish judge ever contrived to tie. Lord Talbot, it was decreed, was entitled to a half-interest in the new treasure—which meant, actually, that Colonel Isham was entitled to it, as Talbot's assignee; but the other half-interest resided with the Cumberland Infirmary, the residuary legatee under the will of the last of the Auchinleck Boswells, who had died in 1905. Neither party, however, was prepared to buy out the other. And so matters stood when the war began. The Fettercairn papers were kept under lock and key, and the only information on their nature was that to be found in Abbott's printed catalogue, which listed over sixteen hundred items of choice Boswelliana in such economical terms as merely to intensify the impatience of scholars to see the documents themselves.

But even during the Second World War, indeed because of the war, the romance of Boswellian discovery went on. The scarcity of space for storing grain made it necessary that every disused building in Ireland be utilized for the purpose; and in 1940 the authorities requisitioned a ramshackle old cow barn on the estate at Malahide. Considering the record of that incredible estate, it would have been surprising indeed if something dramatic had not happened when the barn was examined. The barn was faithful to the tradition of its environment. In its loft was found one more cache of eighteenth-century papers—including some of the most valuable Boswell-Johnson treasures yet unearthed.

Lady Talbot notified Colonel Isham of the discovery, and after long negotiations Isham bought these newly found documents, which arrived in New York in the fall of 1946. Meanwhile he had also been negotiating for the purchase of the Fettercairn House papers, and at last these too fell into his possession. Thus he had made a clean sweep of the field. The original treasure from Malahide Castle, the windfall from the croquet box, the papers from Fettercairn House, the cache from the cow barn—all finally were brought together, after a century and a half of separation.

In November, 1948, Colonel Isham exhibited the newly arrived materials to some of America's leading eighteenth-century scholars. Despite the tense international situation, the aftermath of a memorable national election, and the supposed lack of popular interest in literary matters, Isham's formal unveiling of his treasures occasioned an extraordinary burst of journalistic discussion. The *New York Times* devoted the better part of a page in its regular news section to excited articles on the dramatic episodes by which the papers had been discovered and on the superlative literary and biographical importance of the material. Newspapers all over America carried long press dispatches on their front pages, and popular columnists, in a totally unprecedented display of literary erudition, wrote dissertations on Boswell and Johnson.

Colonel Isham revealed that he was in possession of three times as many letters to and from Boswell as he had received in his original purchase: 2,200 letters to Boswell from such men as Edmond Malone, Sir Joshua Reynolds, and David Garrick, and 600 letters from him. There were 100 hitherto unknown letters from Dr. Johnson to correspondents other than Boswell; some equally unknown juvenile poems by Johnson, and copies of books by him of which no other copies are known to exist. There were important manuscripts by Reynolds, including a twenty-eight-page character sketch of Oliver Goldsmith whose existence had been unsuspected. And—possibly the most gratifying of all revelations—it was shown that the regret over the supposed disintegration of the manuscript of the *Life of Johnson* was premature. The manuscript had not, after all, been in the box which had proved to contain a heap of dust. Instead, here it was in Isham's possession: 1,300 pages of it, mainly pages torn from Boswell's ordinary journal, heavily edited by Boswell and then sent as copy to the printer.

Permission Acknowledgments

The editor and publisher gratefully acknowledge permision for use of the following material:

Excerpt from Howard Carter. "The Tomb of Tut-Ankh-Amen" from *Tutankhamun: Anatomy of an Excavation.* http://www.ashmol.ox.ac.uk/gri/4sea1not.html. Used by permission of the Griffith Institute, Oxford, England.

Excerpt from Richard D. Altick. "The Secret of the Ebony Cabinet" from *The Scholar Adventurers.* Columbus: Ohio State University Press, 1987. Used by permission of Ohio State University Press.

Extract from *Exploration Fawcett* by Brian Fawcett published by Hutchinson/Pimlico. Used by permission of The Random House Group Limited.

Excerpt from Sholem Aleichem. "The Treasure," 1889. Translated from the Yiddish by Louis Fridhandler. *Mendele Review* 04.011 (30 July 2000). http://shakti.trincoll.edu/~mendele/tmr/tmr04011.htm. Used by permission of Louis Fridhandler.

From *The Bernal Diaz Chronicles*, translated by Albert Idell, copyright © 1956 by Albert Idell. Used by permission of Doubleday, a division of Random House, Inc.

Chapter 2 from *The Treasure of the Sierra Madre* by B. Traven. Copyright © 1963 by B. Traven. Reprinted by permission of Hill and Wang, a division of Farrar, Straus and Giroux, LLC.